I Don't Care if We Never Get Back

I Don't Care if We Never Get Back

30 Games in 30 Days on the Best Worst Baseball Road Trip Ever

Ben Blatt and Eric Brewster

Grove Press
New York

Published simultaneously in Canada
Printed in the United States of America

FIRST EDITION

ISBN: 978-0-8021-2274-2
eISBN: 978-0-8021-9216-5

Grove Press
an imprint of Grove/Atlantic, Inc.
154 West 14th Street
New York, NY 10011

Distributed by Publishers Group West

www.groveatlantic.com

14 15 16 17   10 9 8 7 6 5 4 3 2 1

Contents

For Walter Solomon, Stephen Blatt,
and our friends at 44 Bow Street

Preface

With one out in the fifth inning on June 15, 2013, Tampa Bay Rays pitcher Alex Cobb threw a cutting fastball to Kansas City Royals first baseman E. J. Hosmer. It was the 4,123rd time in 15 days we'd seen a 108-stitch leather ball hurled 60 feet 6 inches from the pitcher's mound to the batter's box. In the span of those 4,123 pitches, we'd seen the ball hit the catcher's mitt, the ump's mask, the backstop's net, the dirt's chalk and, among other parts of the batter, his bat. From there the ball ricocheted off fielders' gloves, outfield walls, fair play barriers, grandstands, foul poles, dugouts, adverts, vendors, coaches, fans. Some were never heard of again, smuggled away to the bedrooms of children to be placed on the altars of youth. Others, hit too hard and by enemy bats, were sent back to the field. A few retreated to the protective pockets of umpires. And the rest, all finite victims of infinite paths, were returned to the pitcher.

The 4,123rd pitch took a shortcut.

Eric remembers the pitch with perfect clarity because Eric was angry. After 15 consecutive days of slimed and sugared ballpark food, he had finally found a barbeque stand hiding in the corner of Tropicana Field. Despite no particular love for barbeque, the stand promised him what seemed nothing less than revolutionary within stalking distance of home plate: food that wasn't fried. Reassuringly overpriced to the tune of $12, the BBQ grilled chicken called to him like poultry with a phone. So when the park employee broke his twenty and handed him a cardboard plate with two thin strips of maybe-chicken and enough fries to rebuild a potato, Eric saw nothing but lost calories heaped upon a lost dream.

According to the calendar, it should have been the halfway point of our road trip, Game 15 of 30 in as many days. But it wasn't, of course. Like any good schedule, it had blown up long ago. And this had been more than just a good schedule. It was the best schedule — at least according to Eric's best friend, Ben.

Ben's 22 years on earth had been spent obsessing over baseball and math. He used his lifetime of focused quantitative education to calculate what he claimed was the "optimal" way to visit all 30 ballparks in 30 days, and had somehow convinced Eric to help him make it happen. Wandering around the other side of Tropicana Field in search of a hot dog and beer — which he considered the "optimal" baseball foods — Ben struggled to come to terms with the imperfections in the diamond of his algorithm. Eric saw nothing but 90-foot diamonds of dirt.

The trip had sickened Eric to the point of a refined psychosis, a looming sense that each and every ballpark was out to spite him, masterfully constructed to shorten his fuse till there'd be nothing left to light. The drunks got drunker, the fatty food fattier, the innings stretched on and on. Soon he discovered within him the power to change the course of the games themselves. If he hadn't slept in a day, he could make a game meander into extra innings. If he fell asleep in the stands, he could make the game end on the spot. The little things built up and towered higher than the sickly yellow foul poles, obscuring his view no matter where he sat.

So when he paid $12 for a $3 meal, he was angry, because those $9 were going to a gargantuan professional sports conglomerate he'd conditioned himself to despise. And when he was angry, he was always on the lookout for other things to be angry about, because it was a tragedy to let such passionate anger die.

Consequently, in a rare moment of in-game awareness, Eric happened to actually be paying attention when Cobb threw what happened to be the 4,123rd pitch of our trip. In 141 hours of driving during the prior 14 days, we'd covered 9,032 miles and endured 131 innings lasting 2,625 minutes alongside 449,465 other spectators. Five days earlier and 1,250 miles away, we'd already seen Hosmer hit and score a run.

But this time around, the ball cracked off the barrel of Hosmer's bat and traveled two-fifths of a second at the speed of 102 miles per hour straight to Cobb's head. The impact could be heard from the second tier in the grandstands, the sum total of the play a swift *crack-crack*, as though a 38-inch wooden stick had blasted the ball not once but twice. Except that the second *crack* belonged to a human head. Cobb's hands shot up. He collapsed to the ground.

A few things happened then. The ball, still playing baseball, rolled back toward home plate. Rays catcher José Lobatón scooped it up and threw it to first to record the inning's second out. The umps called time as medics rushed to the mound, followed by the infielders, then the outfielders and coaches and then Hosmer too. The players knelt around the mound like protectors of the realm, soldiers in a daily battle waiting for a knighting that might never come. A few prayed. Most just stared. Those off the field clung to the dugout railing, holding their own heads in half-conscious awe, perhaps wondering how they got off so lucky. Cobb, for his part, was alive and kicking, his dirt-stained legs shooting through the indoor air as blood dripped out from his right eardrum.

And in the stands, 18,593 fans stood and collectively made not a single perceivable noise. Fathers hung their heads and sons stood on their tiptoes. A preemptive moment of silence, just in case, just in case. It was a throbbing mass manufactured to throb. Now it could not so much as move, staring unified toward center stage, looking away only to look at each other, to raise one eyebrow and purse two lips and ask without speaking if we'd just witnessed a man get killed. Eric had in his mouth one half of one strip of chicken, and eventually he remembered it and swallowed.

After ten or so minutes, the medics raised Cobb onto a stretcher and wheeled him off the field. He lay prostrate and never raised a reassuring hand. We applauded anyway.

No one was quite certain of the correct course of action. Normally the Jumbotron told us what to do.

Ben returned to our seats with a hot dog and beer and asked what happened. Baseball was the answer.

Baseball would be the answer every day on this trip, to every question. It was that rarest of endeavors that was a suitable response to all that could go right and wrong. From heroic miracles to mundane pleasures to national tragedies, the sport was always at the ready to put America at ease. Need a metaphor for struggle? Step into the batter's box. The quest for perfection? That'll be 27 up, 27 down. Triumph and heartbreak? Welcome to the bottom of the ninth. Throw in a few cheating scandals, congressional privilege and a playoff series that declared the best team in America the best in the world and you had yourself a national pastime.

Our road trip was devised to touch every base of that 30-ring circus. It was our suspicion that if we saw it all—the good, the bad, the ugly and the Miami Marlins—we'd have no choice but to have learned something by the journey's end. We grew up with baseball in our hearts and TV sets, on the splotchy grass of our backyards and the pages of the morning paper. We were two young white males living in a country that had spent more than a century championing young white males who pranced around ballparks in back alleys and on the greatest of stages. But the days of Cracker Jack boxes containing real prizes were long past. This was the 21st century, and America's darling was a globalized game struggling to find its footing in a world that was always getting bigger, faster, grander. As all evolved around it, baseball remained baseball, for better or worse—and it was often a little of both. It broke a barrier here and changed labor laws there, but it never stopped being one bat, one ball and nine men on the field. The stresses of stasis were readily apparent, splashed across headlines in the form of doping charges and fractured notions of idyllic charm.

All those apt and endearing metaphors went both ways. Had baseball lost its soul? And what did that say for the nation that held it so dear? This is a book about two guys who watched a lot of buddy cop movies growing up and decided to visit the scene of the crime. Or more accurately, all 30 crime scenes, and in 30 days. We made it our official mission to miss not a single moment. We had one rule that would guide us in our trip spanning 37 U.S. states: we would not miss a single pitch over the course of the entire trip. And we would strive to do it in 30 days, because baseball was an emotional saga carved from the harsh simplicity of a numbers game. We figured the rest would take care of itself.

And it did. By trip's end, we'd seen it all—walk-off glories, dipping attendances, pastoral gallantries, front-office farces, rookie sensations, careers at their curtain call, little kids in big jerseys, big adults in little jerseys, hot dogs and beer, wine and caviar, winners and losers. And long and bumpy stretches of America everywhere between.

This is the story of how the ultimate trip through America's pastime nearly killed us, baseball and everything we thought we knew about swinging for the fences.

With Alex Cobb tucked into an ambulance on its way to an emergency room, the game resumed and baseball returned to doing what it did best. It played ball.

Ben downed the last of his frothing beer. Eric did not finish his chicken.

Three innings later, in the top of the eighth, Rays reliever Joel Peralta threw a strike against Royals third baseman Mike Moustakas. The crowd cheered like it was a crowd, the first time in an hour. Peralta delivered a second strike. The entire audience rose from its seats, the energy suddenly swelling. Peralta stretched into his windup and delivered one more blazer. Moustakas swung and missed. The crowd erupted. Voices cracked vocal cords as towels were launched triumphantly into the air. Children danced in the aisles and bearded men high-fived. A giant "K" manifested itself in the outfield—the tenth strikeout of the game. For the uninitiated, the Jumbotron flashed a joyous explanation: "Rays Strike Out Ten Players, Fans Get FREE Papa John's Pizza."

Everything was going to be okay.

Part I

Are We There Yet? No.

Game One:
New York Yankees

There was a $13 charge to cross the George Washington Bridge. Washington himself had only been charged with treason when he crossed a river, and even accounting for inflation that seemed like a decent deal.

Ben had "run the numbers" months ago. The trip, in total, was projected to tally up over $3,200 in gas charges, $1,800 in food, $2,500 in motels, $1,200 in tickets and another $1,000 in incidentals. Eric wasn't sure where those figures were coming from, but he felt like we were getting a solid break on incidentals.

Ben, as it happened, liked to run the numbers. Running the numbers was a solution to everything. Could we afford this trip? Just barely, according to the numbers. Was it possible to successfully complete? It was certainly possible, the numbers declared. How many miles would we travel? How many gas stations would we grace with our 14-gallon

Toyota RAV-4 tank? How many roads must we drive down before we could call ourselves men?

"I'll run the numbers," Ben said.

A few of the numbers were simple enough for Eric to calculate on his own: 29 Major League Baseball teams littered across America, and one deposited in Canada for good measure. In total, 30 teams, 30 stadiums. To see them all, 30 games. To do it poetically, 30 days.

Ben did not like poetry, but he ran the numbers and the numbers seemed to back up the poetry. He was an applied math major in college, his specialty statistics. And so, with a degree in doing math and then applying it, he set out to conquer his one true love. Baseball had always been the woman of his dreams, smart, strategic, athletic, all-American, passionate, pacing, occasionally climactic. He'd grown up inside the batter's box, swinging and missing his way through little league like half the ten-year-old boys in America. A New Hampshire native, he'd latched onto his home team, the Red Sox, like any upstanding New England citizen. When they won, life was good. When they lost, life was not worth living. They rarely won.

Until they did, in 2004, in one of the most chaotic victory marches in modern baseball history. Down 3–0 in the American League Championship Series against the Yankees, they salvaged a win, and then another, and because they could, a third and a fourth. No one had ever done that before. It was Ben's team who did it first. The Sox then plowed through the World Series to claim their first title in an excruciatingly well-documented 86 years. Ben watched each game on his living room TV like a disciple who had the convenience of belonging to the cult of a television evangelist. He was in the eighth grade at the time, a five-foot-tall white male in a small-town middle school. To not be able to recite every moment of every game was worthy of ostracization, and with good reason. Baseball was existence, a daily war, a summer slog; if you were lucky, it was a fall classic. Everyone played and everyone watched, and everyone did it together.

And everyone had their favorites. The huggable Big Papi, the slick Johnny Damon, the bloodied Curt Schilling. They had lost for so long that when they spontaneously won, it triggered a widespread state of jubilant confusion. Glory, sweet glory, but why now all of a sudden? For no clear reason, they had finally broken the Curse of the Bambino, the Sox's fabled punishment for trading away the greatest player of all time to the Yankees in exchange for a theatrical production. But baseball was always theater, an off-Broadway show that ran 162 times a year in nine-act increments. The parts were recast every season, the plot tinkered with each twist and turn, but the drama was always the same. The Sox, instant champions, had proven with aplomb that they had never lost their theatrical flair. No one could say just how the curse was broken, and that was fine, as long as the curse was no more.

Except for Ben. He knew exactly why the curse was broken. He knew that someone had run the numbers.

In Ben's high school yearbook, he listed three people he considered role models: Albert Einstein, Larry David and Theo Epstein. A Yale grad who at the age of 28 found himself general manager of the Boston Red Sox, Epstein ran the numbers.

Sabermetrics is the analysis of baseball through objective evidence and statistics. Its name stems from SABR, the Society for American Baseball Research. Its fundamental tenet is straightforward: the numbers don't lie. In a sport grounded in over a century of managerial hunches and gut feelings, running the numbers triggered nothing short of a revolution in the game. While its public coronation may have come with the Michael Lewis bestseller *Moneyball*, the movement had been quietly building for decades. When Epstein strolled into Fenway Park, crafted a roster based on numerical analysis, and proceeded to shatter an 86-year losing streak, Ben knew he would never come closer to liking poetry. Which was why, if you'd traveled to New Hampshire and asked a certain 13-year-old boy to name his favorite player on the Red Sox, you would have been given the name of a man who suited up for games by putting on a collared shirt and tie.

So it was only natural that ten years later, Ben's idea of fun consisted of writing an algorithm to determine the fastest possible road trip to watch a game at every Major League Baseball stadium. It was a silly exercise, a happy combination of his three great passions—numbers, baseball and calculated recklessness. He had no intention of actually going on the trip. He merely wanted to see if it was possible.

It was. At least, according to his algorithm's parameters. With 30 teams there were 265,252,859,812,191,058,636, 308,480,000,000 possible trips that would take you to all 30 parks. It was a few too many, even for a modern computer to go through one by one. Using a method known as linear optimization, Ben had structured a program to algorithmically slice and dice through the combinations, ruling out trips for being physically impossible or just too slow, until only a smaller subset of schedules remained. Most of those trips, thanks to the delicate scheduling act of home and away games and afternoon and night games, would take months to complete. But with teams playing a game an average of eight out of every nine days over the course of six months, Ben was confident a few of those trips would be enticingly swift. With two teams in cities like New York, Chicago and Los Angeles, it could be possible to hit two stadiums in a single day.

Of course, the mode of transportation would affect potential outcomes profoundly. While a plane ride from coast to coast was a mere six hours, a drive straight across the country took nearly two days.

Ben was a baseball purist. Amidst the slog of data, one equation came first:

$$Baseball = America$$

The property stood firmly at the heart of Ben's existence. And there was a second equation he knew to be true:

$$Road\ Trip = Quintessential\ American\ Experience$$

And then, allowing the following equality, which seemed reasonable enough:

$$America = Quintessential\ American\ Experience$$

You could deduce one final equation by the transitive property:

Baseball = Road Trip

It was a little rough around the edges, and Eric was highly doubtful of Ben's powers of deduction, but the result was simple enough. The trip would have to be done by car. Every single mile of it.

For the sake of convenience and maybe even the prevention of a grisly death, Ben mandated a handful of other parameters. For every twelve hours on the road, the trip must provide eight hours of sleep. To avoid a gratuitous cross-country haul, the trip must finish within a few hundred miles of where it began. Accounting for agonizingly slow parking lot escapes and the average game time of two hours and fifty-eight minutes, a four-hour cushion was given for each game to occur. Drive time estimates from one stadium to every other stadium were determined by Google Maps.

And it had to be fun. It *had* to be. It was baseball. How could it not be fun?

Ben plugged each team's schedule into his algorithm and 40 hours later, he had himself a 34-day whirlwind tour of America that started and ended in Kansas City. It was June of 2011. He put the study up on his college stat club's website.

Then the *Wall Street Journal* came calling. And when CNN requested he stop in at an affiliate station for an interview on his way from Kansas City to St. Louis, he had to explain he wasn't actually driving to St. Louis at the moment. He was sitting in his dorm room reading a math textbook and eating cereal. He explained that while the trip was theoretically doable, he was fairly certain it was idiotic.

Ben was accustomed to a life spent slouching over a computer with a bundle of scratch paper always within arm's reach. He was a certifiable bookworm, even if he might have been a worm who only liked books written with numbers. He had grown up a math prodigy. It was a blessing in theory, though he knew as well as anyone that theories could only be so reliable.

But the idea for the fastest possible baseball road trip was different. You didn't have to be a genius to see its simple charms. The website with the results of his algorithm started getting some hits, and then suddenly a few hundred thousand more. Ben had never seen so many hits without someone scoring a run.

Soon it was all he could think about. *Was* it possible? Or more important, was it possible in a way that didn't end in sleep-deprived misery or road kill? And why did so many people care?

He was a sophomore in college at the time. He pushed the trip to the back of his mind. A year passed, then another. And that easily, he was a senior, about to graduate, about to be coronated a real person with responsibilities and necessities and blah, blah, blah. He'd get a job, and it'd turn into a career, and 50 years later he would retire.

He reconfigured the algorithm. His car, a silver 2006 Toyota RAV-4 with 119,000 miles under its belt, sat in a garage in New Hampshire. He could drive it down to New York in an afternoon. Graduating on the second-to-last day of May, his calendar was empty for the month of June, safe from the threat of gainful employment. June had 30 days. Two years ago, the trip would have taken 34 days to complete. But with every season came a new set of schedules and a corresponding set of permutations.

He ran the numbers with the new parameters: 30 games at four hours a game, with a minimum hour of rest for every four on the road. It was to begin June 1, 2013, in New York City and end June 30 back where he started in the City of Dreams.

The algorithm yielded one result.

June 1: New York Yankees, 7:15 PM
June 2: Pittsburgh Pirates, 1:35 PM
June 3: Philadelphia Phillies, 7:05 PM
June 4: Boston Red Sox, 7:10 PM
June 5: Washington Nationals, 7:05 PM
June 6: Detroit Tigers, 1:08 PM
June 7: Milwaukee Brewers, 8:10 PM
June 8: Colorado Rockies, 7:15 PM
June 9: Arizona Diamondbacks, 4:10 PM
June 10: Kansas City Royals, 8:10 PM
June 11: Minneapolis Twins, 8:10 PM
June 12: Chicago Cubs, 2:20 PM
            Chicago White Sox, 8:10 PM
June 13: Baltimore Orioles, 7:05 PM
June 14: Miami Marlins, 7:10 PM
June 15: Tampa Bay Rays, 4:10 PM
June 16: Cincinnati Reds, 1:10 PM
June 17: Cleveland Indians, 7:05 PM
June 18: Toronto Blue Jays, 7:07 PM
June 19: St. Louis Cardinals, 8:15 PM
June 20: Texas Rangers, 2:05 PM

June 21: Los Angeles Angels, 10:05 PM

June 22: San Francisco Giants, 4:05 PM

June 23: Seattle Mariners, 4:10 PM

June 24: Los Angeles Dodgers, 10:10 PM

June 25: Oakland Athletics, 10:05 PM

June 26: San Diego Padres, 10:10 PM

June 28: Houston Astros, 8:10 PM

June 29: Atlanta Braves, 4:05 PM

June 30: New York Mets, 1:10 PM

Or, if you're a visual learner, as Eric was diagnosed in fifth grade:

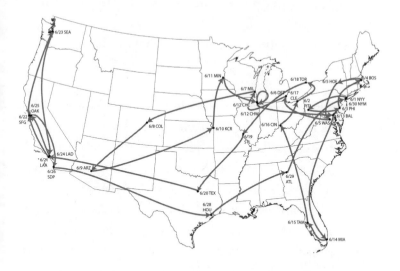

June 12 was a doubleheader in Chicago. June 27 was an off day, providing 42 hours to make the 21-hour drive from San Diego to Houston. Milwaukee to Colorado was 15 hours of driving in a 19-hour stretch. Arizona to Kansas

City was 19 in 26, Seattle to Los Angeles 20 in 26. Chicago to Baltimore was 13 in 17, Tampa to Cincinnati the same. Factoring in stops for gas, food and sleep, a single ill-timed traffic jam would destroy the entire trip.

To get 30 in 30, everything had to go right.

As Eric liked to put it, nothing could go wrong.

Ben handed the tollbooth worker $13 in exact change and headed across the Hudson.

"Which way to Yankee Stadium?"

"Just get to New York first," Eric promised. It had been 20 minutes and his GPS app was already malfunctioning.

Ben merged under the sign for New York City. "If you're this bad at navigating the whole way, we'll never get anywhere."

He had graduated exactly two days ago.

The Yankees were the pinnacle of baseball the way that no sports team was the pinnacle of anything else. Baseball without them would have been an action series with 29 heroes and no villain. It was our first of 30 games, and we were beginning with the baseballest of them all.

We'd heard great things about Yankee Stadium. "The Yankees play there," people would say. "The Yankees play there," would note others. Gone, as of four years ago, was the original Yankee Stadium, a ballpark so emblematic of what a baseball stadium was supposed to be that it was often referred to as "The Stadium." And others still called it the "Cathedral of Baseball." It's a strange religion that will bulldoze its hallowed place of worship. Unless we're talking money.

The new incarnation was a concrete juggernaut, dropped from the Heavens squarely into the Bronx. It felt like a fresh-faced Yankees rookie: new and terribly burdened by the fact that this was the Yankees. When a club won a World Series it was not just the players who slid on over-sized, diamond-encrusted rings. The fans were champions, the peanuts were champions, the weather on the day of victory was championship-caliber weather. The floorboards were champions, one necessary piece in the overwhelmingly complex structure a professional sports team encompassed.

The floorboards of the old Yankee Stadium had won 26 championships. The concrete slabs at new Yankee Stadium could claim one.

We huddled with the masses and swarmed our way through the turnstiles, entering the premises a half hour before the opening pitch. Some fans showed up hours in advance to watch batting practice or experience a 50,000-person stadium 49,000 people below capacity. With 30 games ahead of us, we knew there'd be no need to get ahead of ourselves.

Ben had imposed a simple rule for how the trip would operate: for a game to count, we must be inside the stadium for every single out, from first pitch to last. If we were not present for the entirety of the game, the game would not count. This fundamentally elongated the trip length, and not only because it meant more time spent at each ballpark. It prevented us from quick getaways that, to more lenient goers, would technically constitute witnessing a game at each ballpark. If you could arrive late or leave early, other-wise impossible game combinations suddenly became very doable. You could watch the first pitch in an afternoon game in Detroit and catch the last out of a Chicago night game without breaking a sweat.

Ben considered this cheating. In fact, Ben considered many things cheating. While researching the trip, we had discovered a few people had embarked on similar 30-day trips before, albeit with less stringent standards. Some would leave games early to catch another being played simultaneously. Others simply boarded a plane every night to their next destination. One group of four men had completed a 30-day, 30-game trip completely by car, but had finished 3,000 miles away from where they started. Considering it would have taken them 42 hours to drive back across the country, if they so elected, this would have counted as a 32-day trip in Ben's mind. Ben still respected their trip—they just didn't have the benefit of an algorithm designed to drop them off in the same city where they started.

But most important to Ben was the need to truly attend every game. According to Ben's definition, that meant attending each game in its entirety. If a game went 17 innings and cost us three hours we needed on the road, preventing us from getting to the first pitch of the next game, that was just how the ball bounced. If we missed a single pitch over the course of 30 days, we would fail.

Eric quickly noted that according to Ben's definition, attending the game was different from watching it. You could hypothetically attend an entire game without actually *watching* any of the game itself. It was a necessary distinction. In practice, it would be almost inconceivable to physically witness every single pitch of every single game. In the

three-to-four-hour stretches during which we would be underslept, underfed and overstimulated, we would inevitably
need to purchase food or run to the bathroom. This did not
trouble Ben because it was not in opposition to a fan's natural
ballpark experience. Almost no one at a ballgame witnessed
every single pitch. You walked around the stadium, you visited
the team store, you ate the local specialty, you drank the local
beer, you visited the outfield, you visited the infield, you took
your picture with the giant statue of the player from 40 years
ago whom you pretended to know. You went to the bathroom.

But Ben was nervous about Eric's excitement over
this semantic disparity. Ben could see him taking it to the
extreme, entering a ballpark's gates, finding a bench and
passing out on the spot, determined to wake up three hours
later without having even witnessed the field of play.

"That beats the purpose of it," Ben argued.

As he would come to do with increasing regularity,
Eric sighed. "That beats *your* purpose."

Eric, for lack of a better way to phrase it, didn't like
baseball. Some saw this as a problem for a guy about to go
on the most exhaustive American baseball road trip possible.
Eric saw this too.

There were two kinds of people just about everywhere
you looked, and the same went for baseball. From what Eric
could discern, there were those who could stay awake during a baseball game, and those who fell asleep. He'd have
had a better idea of which population was larger had he not
been so often asleep.

But it was more than a matter of per-minute excitement.
He considered himself an avid sports fan. When he was 14

and got his first email account, his address was the nickname
and number of his favorite Los Angeles Clippers player. This
was at a time when the Clippers had posted losing seasons
for over a decade. Despite relentless ribbing from friends,
he defiantly uses the same address to this day. Not only did
he know how to root for a team, he knew how to root for
one of the worst franchises in sports history. Passion was
not a problem. And in high school, he'd wandered onto the
golf team, competing in a district where some of the schools
and players could not even afford clubs. Playing on public
courses in matches where a good score was considered one
where you didn't cheat, he'd always been destined for the
sort of subpar performance that entailed a scorecard full of
bogeys. Yet even though he wasn't much good at golf and
the game could give baseball a run for its money on the
boredom spectrum, he could nonetheless enjoy it. It was a
game where you got to be your own enemy, a psychological farce to the bitter end, and at its worst was still a stroll
through a lush though flag-laden park.

Eric perused football and hockey, could hold his own
in soccer and watched every single hour of Olympics coverage network broadcasts offered up. He could name all ten
decathlon events without having ever competed in a single
one of them.

Liking sports was not the issue. Baseball was special.

It was slow, unnecessarily slow. And it was long. And
the food was overpriced, and the stands were littered with
spit and sunflower seeds, and the managers bickered over
calls that would never be changed, and the players jogged
to first like a $6 million salary wasn't enough to make them

run, and there were steroids pumping through their blood and the record books, and it was slow, and it was long. Eric had a long list of grievances he was happy to relay, but he also understood that no sport was perfect. They all had their troubles, from the court to the pitch to the field, and right on into the front offices and press boxes and across the stands.

But it was only baseball that was the American pastime. Hockey had Canada, soccer had the rest of the world, football had our wallets. Only baseball stood on the hallowed ground of the American conscience itself. Basketball was engaging, golf was trying. Baseball was a long-running metaphor to every triumph and tragedy and truism our nation faced. And surely some of it held merit. There was beauty in walk-off home runs and perfect games and flatly winning that even Eric could plainly see. Yet it was still just a game played on dirt and grass with a stick, a ball and enough rules to fill an encyclopedia. It had British roots and was played around the world. It seemed no more American than anything else. Even so, it was The One True American Sport. Eric resented it less for what it was than for what it was supposed to be.

But here he was, along for the ride, at Ben's side, attending game one of 30. He had no desire to go on an American baseball road trip. Born and raised in Southern California south of LA, he went to college in Massachusetts because it was on the other side of the country. He hadn't applied to a single school in monolithic California. "I want to try seasons, or something," he explained.

He'd hopped up and down the coasts a few times but had never seen the in-between. The longest he'd ever spent in a car was a seven-hour haul from home one winter in search of snow.

So when Ben offered him a seat in a supposedly sturdy vehicle that would traverse the nation six different ways, touch ground in 37 states and pass through nearly every major American city, Eric was too enamored to remember his distaste for baseball. All he could think of was small-town diners and towering monuments and a lot of people from a lot of places who knew a lot of things he didn't.

Or at least that's how he was justifying it to himself in his own mind.

Even as he listened to Ben babble on about the Red Sox-Yankee rivalry on the drive toward the Bronx—before the actual 30 consecutive days of baseball had even commenced—he was already growing bored. He wished he could be given one last chance to reconsider the trip. He wished he could be given one last chance to reconsider the friendship.

But Eric's first encounter with Ben, a chance run-in during his first week of college as he strolled through campus in an LA Dodgers hat looking for his next class, could not be undone. It was fate.

"You're a Dodgers fan?" Ben asked, striking up a conversation.

"No, but the sun's out," Eric said, ending the conversation.

We did not talk to each other again for a year. That was fate too.

It was not until we both became writers for the same campus humor magazine that we became true friends. It was a community of students who devoted equal effort to carefully crafting witty prose and poorly executing drunken toasts. We made each other laugh, half the time at our own expense, and the other half at the other's. Ben was willing to be teased for being a stat-nerd, baseball-nerd, nerd-nerd in exchange for teasing Eric about being so sarcastic and cynical that the thought of him loving or obsessing enough over any topic to be deemed a nerd in its field was unthinkable. In truth, we were both more complex than this, or at least so we told ourselves alone at night in front of mirrors. And so was our friendship, though we did not desire it to be. Being young men, it was often easier to bond over stereotypes we had willingly morphed into than express what was truly going on inside our heads during a Saturday night out in college.

As the years passed we became more and more insepa-rable, or so we thought ourselves to be. We hadn't shared a confined six-by-eight-foot space, as we would in the car for the next month, but we ate together, took classes to-gether and pretended not to know each other when talking to girls. We were as inseparable as college friends could be.

Cut to a Tuesday during Ben's senior year. It was lunch-time, and we were both in the dining hall we had agreed was the best place to eat lunch together on a Tuesday. Every day had its own lunch spot. Like most of our lunches, this one consisted of Ben reminiscing about his life's greatest achievements and Eric pretending to listen. As Ben waxed poetic about his baseball computer program and the math-ematical complexities, Eric nodded and grunted throughout with appropriate rhythm, ensuring his friend that he was not actually paying attention but still loved their eternal friend-ship enough to keep up the charade that he was.

"So are you going on the trip this summer?" Eric asked, proving he was not listening to Ben's many descriptions of this trip as a "theoretical exercise."

"It would be too hard. Eighteen thousand miles of driving and a new city every night. I don't think I could find a single person who would want to do this."

"Then why are you telling me about it for the fourth time?"

There it was.

Ben had been fantasizing about the trip for years now. He'd spent the summer devising a plan to turn it into a reality. He just needed to find someone who was equally nuts to devote a month of their lives to nothing but driving and sitting in the grandstands.

"You and me," said Ben. "Our last hurrah. After I graduate, we'll be on opposite ends of the country and too poor to visit each other on anything other than Skype. We'll see each other at reunions in five-year increments where we'll have nothing to talk about but my progressively receding hairline. This is our last chance to do something neither of us will ever forget that does not involve getting matching tattoos."

Eric sighed. "Did you plan that rousing speech?"

Ben shrugged. "Maybe. Will you do it?"

"No."

"Please?"

"Yes."

"*Please*," Ben said again, then realized Eric had said yes. And then Eric realized he'd said yes.

He hadn't yet processed the scale of what he had committed to. He did not comprehend that spending a whole month visiting baseball parks with just one of his buddies in a cramped car might not be a 30-day joyride.

He didn't care about the number of miles we'd travel or how many innings we'd see. Unlike Ben, he hadn't spent his life memorizing the indexes of math textbooks. At school he studied filmmaking and economics, the two most romantic pursuits of knowledge the world had ever known. He'd seen enough road trip films to know that we would get into a heated argument somewhere on the side of the road in Minnesota, and he had enough common sense to know that Ben forgot to factor in highway tolls and parking passes on his proposed budget sheet.

But he justified the trip to himself as the perfect way to see the country. He knew that a lot of baseball would be happening too, of course, but a daily four-hour pit stop seemed bearable in exchange for a ticket headed almost everywhere he'd always wanted to go. For someone who had never been on a road trip, it seemed to be the most thorough road trip possible. Ben was driving to see baseball, Eric was driving to see America. We just happened to be in the same car.

Eric had disclosed to Ben this reason, seeing America the Beautiful, as the true and sole reason he was willing to go through with the trip. Naturally, this did not sit well with Ben, who vowed the trip would convert Eric into a lifelong fan who understood what the game was truly about.

"What is the game truly about then?" Eric asked.

"You just couldn't understand," Ben eloquently explained.

But Eric was happy to take the challenge in stride. By the end of the month, one way or another, he'd understand what baseball was about. Thirty games were all but certain to accomplish that much.

And maybe he'd finally understand what America saw in the sport—or at the least, what Americans claimed they saw in the sport that they saw in America. He was more than willing to be proven wrong. He was just fairly confident he'd be proven right. He predicted that by month's end, not even Ben would be able to stomach another pitch, that baseball's greatest fan would be unceremoniously felled.

"Not a chance," Ben said.

Eric shrugged. "Strong words coming from an odds maker."

Sixty years ago, a Yankees ticket went for $1.60, which was a significant amount of bubblegum. Another 40 years prior, every ticket was a flat 50 cents.

Today a spot in the bleachers went for $15. For $300, you could land a Field MVP seat, which put you so close to the action you had a legitimate chance of being named the player of the game.

The history of ticket prices has been an exercise in horizontal as well as vertical growth. As prices predictably rose almost every single year, the gap in same-stadium seat pricing escalated with equal tenacity. The average ticket price in 2013 clocked in at $27.73. Including parking, food and precious incidentals, a trip to the park for a family of four was estimated to set the college fund back $208. The right seats at the right game on the right day could rocket face values toward four digits, providing peanuts and Cracker Jack at only a tenth of the average American household's annual income.

The ballpark was not always a case study in price gouging and profit maximization, though it's hard to imagine a universe in which it did not become one. The result was a strange class war played out in the stands. Premier seats were cushioned and offered enough legroom to partake in the seventh-inning stretch without standing up. The nosebleeds were hard and stacked, built on inclines threatening to tumble one narrow row into the next. Premier seats came with a waitstaff, menus and unpronounceable cocktails. For $9, the nosebleeds came with $9 beer. The premier seats were fitted with ballpark hosts, rally girls and security guards. For one reason or another, the nosebleeds might lead to bloody noses.

There was nothing particularly illogical about it. The fans sitting in premier seats paid thirty times as much as nosebleeders for their in-game experience. Outside the roped-off areas that required special bracelets and invisible stamps on your right hand only please, the fans were for the most part indistinguishable. But when the game began, so did capitalism. Every stadium came equipped with a promotion wherein two fans were blessed with a Seat Upgrade, usually sponsored by the ticketing service StubHub. Plucked from the oblivion of the world-away bleachers, these fans were for one day given the glamorous opportunity to live like the other half. Their smiling faces broadcast on the Jumbotron, it was clear what we were all here to achieve.

Thanks to a friend of a friend who had season tickets, we entered Yankee Stadium as first-class fans. For almost every other ballpark, we would have the cheapest seats in the house — even 30 days of nosebleed tickets added up with impressive speed. But because we'd lucked out and magically landed two tickets through a good friend for free, we had the best seats in the house. The beauty of a ticket was that it was a tangible commodity, far more wondrous than actual money. You could hand anyone a ticket, anyone in the world, and all the glamour and comforts were instantly theirs. In the warped land of fandom, a $100 ticket was worth far more than a $100 bill. The bill was nothing more than money. The ticket was an *experience*.

So when the field attendant led us down the first base line and seated us in the row directly behind the entry to the Yankees dugout, we looked at each other like a glorious mistake had just been made and did a very bad job of acting like we belonged there.

A safe six feet away from the likes of Mark Teixeira and Robinson Canó, we shut ourselves up and eavesdropped on the players talking about baseball like only professional All-Stars possibly could.

"I'm hungry," said Canó.

"Yeah," said Teixeira.

It was unbelievable.

Ben, however, was somewhat uncomfortable. Fidgeting in his cushioned seat and gripping an armrest, he turned his hat backwards, hiding the bill. He crossed his arms over his chest, concealing the logo on his shirt.

On June 1, 2013, the Yankees happened to be playing the Red Sox, and Ben happened to be covered head to toe in Red Sox gear.

"I didn't know we'd be so close to them," Ben whispered so the Yankees couldn't hear.

Eric glanced around the stadium, scouting out any allies Ben might have. "Isn't this supposed to be biggest rivalry in sports?"

"*Supposed* to be?"

"Then don't hide. Heckle."

"What would I say?"

"All the things everyone always shouts way up there," Eric said.

Ben could not believe how little he understood. "They'd be able to hear me."

"Isn't that the point?"

Ben pretended to occupy himself with the game's program.

"Are you honestly telling me that you only shout at them when they can't hear you, and then as soon as you're within earshot, you respectfully sit in silence and say nothing at all?"

"It's complicated."

"You're a terrible fan."

"You're a terrible road trip buddy."

It had been an hour.

The Red Sox, despite fighting on enemy turf, got off to an overpowering start. A five-run third inning capped by a Daniel Nava grand slam left pinstripe fans with little to cheer about. Ben, still rigidly quiet, only revealed a half grin from the safety of his seat.

With the game suddenly looking like a blowout, a far fiercer competition emerged. As our seats were pressing up against the dugout, we sat in prime ball-catching territory.

Though unlikely to nab a live ball hit straight off a player's bat at such a close angle, anything that was sent backwards against the backstop was then scooped up by the Yankees ball boy, who occasionally flipped the prized possession into the stands. Then we could all descend like vultures. A second opportunity presented itself if the top of the inning ended on a strikeout. Yankees catcher Chris Stewart would then jog the ball back to the dugout, where it had nowhere to go but up.

But their tosses were rarely without aim, usually directed at a fan who caught their eye. Almost without exception, this fan was a six-year-old girl sitting with her father at the end of our row. In the first inning, the ball boy snatched the first foul ball and tossed it her way. Then, all of five minutes later, Stewart jogged back to the dugout and tossed her his ball too.

She stored the balls in her cup holder. Depending on who was running back to the dugout, she either kept on her Yankees hat or removed it to reveal two ponytails. This strategy of pretending to be a different six-year-old girl earned her another foul ball in the third and yet another strikeout ball in the fourth. The balls flooded out of her cup holder, forcing her to commandeer the confines of the holder in the next seat over. She was a consummate professional, a natural, the greatest ball-grabber we had ever seen. Ben's jumping and waving and beckoning didn't stand a chance against her seemingly innocent smile. Suspecting his Red Sox attire was responsible for his empty hands, he removed his hat entirely and put his shirt on backwards to conceal the dangling laminated socks. It was no use. The balls gravitated to the young maestro without end.

With five balls in as many innings, she gathered up her loot and followed her satisfied father up toward the exit. They'd gotten what they'd come for. Ben, having never caught a foul ball his entire life, had never hated a pigtailed six-year-old girl with such unforgiving passion.

"You'd be a great father," Eric lied.

"I'm too young to think about that."

"Too young to have children, too old to catch a ball. You're trapped in the worst kind of baseball purgatory there is."

Ben put on his hat. "I'm trying to watch the game."

Watching the game was one sensory option. For those looking for a more intimate experience, there was always the option of purchasing New York Yankees perfume, a thing that apparently actually existed according to an advertisement over in left field. In all, Ben counted 46 different advertisements displayed around the stadium, a tally conducted for no identifiable reason Eric could discern. Ben's best guess about himself was when he was upset, he counted things. Advertisements, Red Sox fans, even-numbered players — anything he could set his eyes on. And five balls in two cup holders. He could not help but glance at the oversized blue holders even after the young girl had left.

He wanted a ball, and desperately. He knew that even though this was our very first game, there would be no better opportunity. But even with the six-year-old out of the way, the ball boy looked beyond Ben for other children, always able to find a gleeful preteen waving a glove. The ball boy had so much power. What it must have felt like to be the boy with the ball.

We left our seats in the fifth inning to grab a bite to eat, taking advantage of our newly elite status to gain a table at an all-you-can-eat buffet that came included with the tickets. Not far behind home plate and fully ornamented with chefs in too-tall hats, the buffet was a great deal if you had a huge appetite and had gotten your tickets for free. Amidst a veritable feast of seafood, sushi and cured meats, the salad line was by a wide margin the longest, curving around the prime rib stands and filled start to finish with slender women in sunglasses. The sun had set, though no one would dare point it out to them, and few seemed intent on watching much of the game. Safe inside from the threat of baseball, they took full advantage of the buffet by doubling down on the cheapest item offered.

We were not as inclined to put expensive-looking free food to waste. Eric headed straight for the seafood section, where a chef guarded plates of lobster and crab.

"Crab, please," Eric said.

There were eleven crab legs remaining. Eric only counted because the chef gave him every single one of them, filling his entire plate with a constantly toppling supply of disembodied legs. With no room to fit anything else, he headed back to the table.

A waiter appeared before he'd cracked the first one open.

"May I take that for you?" he asked, indicating the plate.

Eric stared at the eleven uneaten legs. There was clearly some sort of crab embezzlement ring operating behind home plate, and Eric wanted no part it.

"Still eating," he said.

When Eric left to use the restroom five crab legs in, he returned to find an empty plate. They were relentless. He felt bad for the ocean.

On the way back to our seats, we discovered a section of particular interest: bins upon bins of all the classic ballpark food, free for the taking. Unsure if such an opportunity might ever present itself again, we stuffed our pockets with peanut bags and cotton candy. Always looking out for his friends, Eric took a handful of giant swirl lollipops and gifted them to Ben.

"Start licking one of these," he recommended. "Next time the ball boy looks in the stands he'll mistake you for a little kid."

Ben was not pleased with the concept, even if he had to admit it had merit. At five feet five and adorably round-faced, he had the confounding talent of simultaneously looking like he could be eight or 80 years old with equal likelihood. All that was certain was that he did not look 22.

Back in our seats, Ben quietly tore the wrapping off a lollipop and took one long and anguished lick. Eric had never seen an 80-year-old man with a lollipop before. Neither had the ball boy. Ben did not receive any balls.

But whenever you felt down at a ballpark, there was always the Jumbotron to cheer you up. Yankee Stadium didn't disappoint, offering a flurry of inexplicable mid-inning games to keep the waning crowd entertained. In a feel-good shout-out to baseball's booming multiculturalism, we were treated to "Pronounce Today's Hard-To-Say Spanish Term." Today's word was *chancleta*, Spanish for flip-flop. Americans of all races and ethnicities laughed pleasantly as Japanese player Ichiro Suzuki gave it his best shot. There was nary a heart that was not warmed.

Another gem was "Who's That Baby Boomer," a game where one lucky contestant was given the task of matching players' baby pictures with their current likenesses. The real kicker was the grand prize, a case of Poland Spring water. We can only assume that the contestants from other games who only won wads of cash must have felt horribly slighted.

The real spectacle, of course, was saved for the kiss cam, where bickering couples across the stadium were given the chance to pretend like they loved each other as 50,000 people watched. It was the usual affair: a camera would home in on a man and a woman, the man would be eating a hot dog, the woman would be staring at her nails, the fan in the row behind them would tap them on the shoulders, the couple would notice the whole world was watching, the man would lean in and pucker up, the woman would let herself be kissed. They would smile, the kind of smile you gave when someone who didn't know how to operate a camera was taking your picture. And finally the Jumbotron would move on, and we'd do it all again.

This was a Saturday night, however, and a rivalry game to boot, which could mean only one thing: totally original proposals.

Once the kiss cam ended and birthday messages had their turn, the simple request materialized in plain white letters: "Monica—Will you marry me? Chris."

The crowd cheered in approval. No one knew where Monica was but it could only be assumed she said yes. Get asked at a Mets game and who knew what could happen. But at a Saturday night Yankees game? There was no such thing as a surer thing.

After ten seconds, the engagement message disappeared. To everyone's delight, it was replaced by another proposal.

"Haley—Will you marry me? Johnny."

The crowd cheered. Haley and Johnny lived happily ever after. The message disappeared.

"Tiff—Will you marry me? Simon."

The crowd cheered. Our collective hands were starting to hurt.

"Vanessa—Will you marry me? Tom."

It wasn't Tom's fault that he went last, and he clearly hadn't discussed the matter with Chris, Johnny and Simon, but he had to understand that we as an audience could only do so much. Our food was getting cold, our bladders were getting full and our hearts were getting very spiteful at all these unidentifiable lovebirds flaunting their eternal happiness.

Tom received cordial though muted applause.

Once everyone was done putting rings on things, we returned our attention to more important matters.

"I can't believe I haven't gotten a ball," Ben said in the eighth inning, the Red Sox still up 5–1.

"You're still thinking about that?"

He would probably never stop thinking about it. He stood, climbed out of the row and thought about it all the way to the bathroom.

Eric stretched out in his seat, all alone.

Boston third baseman José Iglesias came to the plate. He hit a foul ball. The ball boy picked it up and sidestepped toward the dugout, glancing into the stands.

"Could I have that ball?" Eric asked.

The ball boy tossed it to him. He put the ball in his cup-holding trophy case.

Ben returned and did not need to be informed of its arrival.

"What happened?"

"I caught a foul ball."

Ben glared at him in disbelief. Eric shrugged. It was a foul ball, and it was thrown to him, and he'd caught it. It was technically true. If Ben was going to have fun watching baseball, then Eric was going to do all he could to have fun watching Ben watch baseball. At the end of the day, every day, there wouldn't be much else to watch.

The Red Sox added another six runs in the last two innings to cap the blowout 11–1, an embarrassing defeat for the Damn Yankee Evil Empire Bronx Bombers. Ben headed promptly for the exits, his beloved Red Sox winners and his psyche irreparably damaged. And Eric, having looked forward to the end of the game for some nine or so innings, tossed his priceless treasure through the warm night air as he put Ben's promptness to shame.

Game Two:
Pittsburgh Pirates

We had 14 hours till the Pittsburgh game the following afternoon, and needed only six hours to make the drive out of New York and through New Jersey toward the southwest corner of Pennsylvania. It was Day One. We were well rested, young and almost even strong. We headed for Atlantic City.

Because it was so early in the trip we weren't sure how to handle detours. It was unclear how many hours we actually needed to get from one place to the next or how many sights to be seen were not worth the forfeit of an extra hour or two of sleep. On some drives we'd barely have time to stop for gas. On others, we'd have nearly an entire day to ourselves. Atlantic City was a two-hour detour, turning a six-hour drive into an eight-hour endeavor. Eric had always wanted to visit the boardwalk. An extra two hours did not seem so terribly bad.

We pulled into an isolated parking lot with the strip of flashy, peeling casinos glimmering in the distance. Our nearest suitor was the Trump Plaza Hotel and Casino, a magical place that Eric thought had already gone bankrupt. He could distinctly remember his father sitting him down one summer morning, handing him the business section of the *LA Times* and at long last having the talk. Collateralized debt, unpaid loans, Chapter 11. It was a seminal moment in any child's life.

Eric hailed from a gambling family. He'd never heard of anyone being diagnosed with an addiction, which he'd once explained was what happened only when you gambled and *lost*. The goal then, which often grew surprisingly easy to forget, was to gamble to win. That was the family joke, and sometimes it was true, and sometimes it was too true. But if gambling was in the family genes, so was moderation and incisive care. No one played the cards recklessly. No one bet more than they could afford.

Walter, his maternal grandfather, was a poker player and nothing but. Living in Chester, West Virginia, he made a living at the table when there was legally no living to be made. He was married to the first certified female optometrist in the state. Together they had four daughters. He never spoke of his work if he could avoid it. When he lost he said nothing and when he won he said less. At the age of 65, with everyone grown up and moved out, he set off to Vegas. Housed in a small two-bedroom apartment a mile off the frenzy of the Strip, he drove to the Mirage Casino every afternoon and played Texas Hold'em till he ran out of tourists to defeat.

Eventually health dealt him a raw hand. Time called his bluff. In January 2013, Eric's father Phil made the four-hour drive from Long Beach out to Vegas and brought Walter home. Until now, that drive had seemed so long.

Eric hadn't been back to Long Beach since Walter moved in. All he knew for certain was that he wouldn't be receiving any poker tips upon arrival. Walter refused to teach Eric his lifetime's worth of secrets. "You don't want to do this," he once said with a butter knife in one hand and a lox bagel in the other. "You can do better things than this."

So Eric had to take his biological predisposition elsewhere. His father's father had been an avid horseplayer, which led his father to becoming an avid horseplayer, which led Eric to becoming an avid horseplayer. The tradition was the closest thing to a family heirloom he had. His kin were all too big to jockey, never rich enough to own. But they could watch like no other. And now and then, for the fun of it, bet.

Eric played little league as a kid along with half of the American male population. He was by no means destined for the major leagues, but he could hold his own at the plate, a reliable batter with a knack for drawing walks. His father came to every game, drove him to every practice, pitched with him in his backyard.

But baseball was nothing more than an athletic activity. Father-son bonding occurred at the racetrack, where they'd arrive in the mist of morning to watch the horses train in the still-damp dirt. His father would hoist him up on the railing and together, with no bet to place, they would watch.

It didn't take much deduction for Eric to guess this might be one of his fundamental problems with America's self-declared pastime. Fathers took their sons to games until those sons became fathers and did so with their own. It had happened to Eric too—Friday nights at Dodger Stadium, Dodger Dogs for dinner and dessert, an endless quest to amass as many bobbleheads as possible. He'd collected four: Kirk Gibson, Fernando Valenzuela, Éric Gagné and Adrián Beltré.

But he had six horse-racing bobbleheads, which most people didn't know were a thing. The first five jockeys, Laffit Pincay Jr., Patrick Valenzuela, Chris McCarron, Julie Krone and John Velazquez, were not household names anywhere outside of Eric's house. He was one of the select few ten-year-olds in the country with no direct connection to the racing industry who could rattle off two dozen jockey names. And as the kicker, his favorite bobblehead in his collection: the prolific trainer Bob Baffert. It was a bobblehead of a sunglasses-wearing white-haired man in a suit jacket and jeans.

Baseball wasn't his pastime.

Ben loaned Eric a crisp $100 bill and we sat down at a blackjack table. It was one game where Eric knew the odds by heart, having memorized long ago the proper way to play every situation that was dealt out.

"You're not playing?" Eric asked Ben, who was making no move for his wallet.

"The odds are against you."

"The house only has a half-percent advantage."

Ben nodded. "The odds are against you."

"Ad infinitum," Eric corrected. "The variance can go either way in the course of a couple hands."

"Strong words for a guy without a degree in statistics," Ben said.

Eric won his first hand. He lost his second. And then the next nine. It was a remarkable statistical feat, one that Ben could only smile at.

"Told you," Ben said.

"You know better than anyone that a single isolated sample tells you nothing."

"Told you," Ben said.

With enjoying the coastal view the only remaining activity Eric could afford, we headed for the boardwalk.

For months now we'd seen the pictures — storefronts flooded alongside ice cream shops in shambles, wrecked like docked ships by the force of Hurricane Sandy. It was as if some child somewhere was given a voodoo Monopoly board. Flipping it over in a fit of rage, all the properties were drowned.

But six months out, the community had risen from the sea foam, the old-timey facades beside the ocean again touting "Free Lunches" and attorneys who notched "Acquittals in Most Cases." The strip of sand-strewn cement pulsed with inebriated life, filled end to end with drunken twentysomethings in no particular hurry to leave. A backlit expanse on the beach itself hosted a seaside nightclub, filled to the brim with gyrating hands that conducted a meandering wave.

The shore was alive again. America, slurring with a blood-alcohol level on par with the ocean's salinity, had once again conquered the earth's attempt at tragedy.

Then it started to rain. For some of our boardwalk companions, this was welcomed. See-through clothing now offered more to see. But with each drop of rain that hit Ben's impressively wrinkled brow, he looked toward the starless sky with the lonely eyes of a man who had no one but his numbers.

The number of the moment was approximately 1/3. According to historical June averages, there was a one out of three chance that one of our games would be rained out. The odds were in our favor by a breathable margin, but if the clouds decided to collude on one of our parades, the entire trip could be wrecked. Recovering from a rainout was a matter of catching it before it happened. If we could foresee one in advance, it might be possible to reconfigure the schedule and stay on pace for 30 in 30. The new schedule would no longer adhere to the standards of Ben's optimal path, but it would still keep the trip alive. If a rainout was not called until right before a game, or even worse, postponed in the middle of play, there would likely be no chance of reconfiguration.

Though well aware of the monthlong threat, we hadn't expected the trip to be jeopardized before the end of the first day. As the rain continued to fall, we sprinted back to our car, dried off our clothes and looked up the weather report for Pittsburgh. It was a 1 PM game. At 1 PM, the forecast declared a 40% chance of rain.

As children we had both read the Choose Your Own Adventure stories. They were books where every chapter ended in a choice, leading you to a new chapter of your choosing. In general, all but one exact set of choices led to a grisly death.

We now had two choices: continue on to Pittsburgh with a 40% chance of rain, or reroute to a game in Baltimore, a move that would cost us several hours of sleep the following day as well as Ben's optimal schedule.

"We've got to go to Baltimore," Ben said.

"Great. Pittsburgh it is."

"It might rain."

Eric held out his hands, his own tried-and-true strategy for weather forecasting. "Forty percent rain is lazy rain. It's 'Eh, I guess I'll fall out of the sky today' rain. It's not angry rain. They only cancel games for angry rain."

"I don't know if we can afford to take the risk on this one."

"Trust me. I have a good feeling about this one."

"You just lost one hundred dollars in ten minutes playing blackjack."

Eric got behind the wheel. It was four o'clock in the morning. We drove to Pittsburgh.

Crossing a trademark yellow bridge into the Steel City, it appeared we were leaving a Monopoly board for the game of Life. Perched upright like game pieces inserted into the soil, the downtown skyscrapers stood against the edges of Pittsburgh's three rivers, a model city blown up to larger-than-life proportions. And fortunately for our purposes, the towers pointed toward a cloudless sky. Eric's gamble had paid off, paving the way for the chance at 29 more days of financial losses.

It took only three wrong turns to find a parking lot. A brilliant yellow footbridge led us straight to PNC Park.

The first sight to behold was The Great One, a looming statue of Roberto Clemente guarding the centerfield gate. Eric's grandfather Walter had lived for decades on the Pennsylvania border and was a Pittsburgh fan through and through. "They'd called him the great one," he'd told Eric, "but that was a lie. He was The One. He was a saint."

Among other things. A Pirate for life till the day he died, Clemente was the once-a-generation athlete who could unify sports with a cultural movement and bridge the gap with fans. Owner of every award Major League Baseball could think to hand out, he was the best player on any field in the nation, and he was Puerto Rican. By the time he went down in a charter plane on his way to delivering earthquake aid in Nicaragua, he'd melted straight through Pittsburgh's steeled exterior. The Pirates former home, Three Rivers Stadium, was opened in 1970. Clemente lived till the end of 1972, more than long enough to make it the House Clemente Built. He was the sort of player baseball hadn't quite had since, a man who took baseball and made it something more.

"His stats were good too," Ben said.

"No kidding."

We found our seats up in the nosebleeds a few rows below the top of the stadium and what felt like a few hundred rows above third base. We were joined by Girl Scout Troop 50460, a lively bunch that had somehow managed to overlook two seats in its group-ticket cluster. Eric had been a Cub Scout once upon a time, but never managed to make it to the title of Boy. Ben was the rare special talent who could neither start a fire nor put one out. It went unspoken between us that these Girl Scouts could threaten our manhood. Ben was quickly growing tired of the young girls who seemed to haunt him everywhere he went.

The Pirates were playing the Reds, a team that math had fated us to watch four separate times—once in Cincinnati and in three away games. If fandom was a simple formula of proximity and frequency, Ben was poised to fall deeply in love with the Reds. Eric still needed to open his heart to let love in.

The Reds didn't waste any time getting down to business. Reds center fielder Shin-Soo Choo was hit by Pirates pitcher Jeanmar Gómez in the first at bat of the game. That was promptly followed by a triple from shortstop Zack Cozart. Then a walk. And a single, and a single, and a single, and a sacrifice fly. Gómez was pulled from the game in the top of the first. It was looking to be a long game.

The Reds headed to the bottom of the first inning with a 4–0 lead. It had been less than a half hour and their win probability, according to Ben's stats, already stood at 85%.

It was the second game in two days where the away team sprinted off to a commanding lead, a ready-made recipe for a deflated crowd. Add to the mix the languid heat of a summer afternoon, and it could only mean one thing. Sad people eating ice cream.

It is difficult to understate the beauty of sad people eating ice cream. Surely some of it has to do with ice cream's hallowed spot in Americana, the feel-good food if there ever was one. Long walks on the beach, backyard barbeques, school, spring, church. They all have a happy ending: the consumption of ice cream. It is an unimpeachable fact that happy people live their lives with a cherry on top.

Which makes sad people eating ice cream all the better. They lick and lick, and when they move the cone away, the evidence is plastered all over their frowning faces, above their lips, in their dimples, on the brims of their noses. To hold such a happy thing and be so sad, and to watch the happy thing melt into a sad little puddle because it is so difficult to eat quickly when in such a low mood — that is baseball beautiful.

With the Pirates down 4–0, the sad ice cream connoisseurs came out in full force, buying out the vendors' supplies before they could make a well-honed sales pitch. There must have been a thousand sad people eating ice cream that day, dutifully dampening the mood all around us.

Neither the ice cream nor the sadness would last long. The Pirates added a run in the second, then another in the sixth. A two-run deficit seemed far from impossible to overcome. To Eric's terror, the possible happened. A two-out single by Pirates center fielder Andrew McCutchen brought first baseman Garrett Jones to the plate. Jones then left the plate, touched all the bases and returned to the plate with a home run to deep right field.

It was a tie game.

Ben could root for the Red Sox on the rare occasion we intersected with them. Eric, some twenty days from now, could halfheartedly root for the Dodgers. But for the vast majority of the games we lacked a rooting interest — or a team to root for, at least. No matter who was playing or where we were, there was one thing and one thing only we would consistently have to cheer on: brevity.

We showed up at games so we could root for them to end. A short game meant more wiggle room in the schedule. More wiggle room meant more sleep. After trading in sleep the night before in the name of the shortsighted Atlantic City adventure, we were already feeling the wear and tear of the trip. Before reaching Pittsburgh we'd crashed at a motel for just long enough to shower and take a short nap. From check-in to checkout we were there a total of three hours. Ben had managed a little shut-eye in the car on the way into Pittsburgh, but Eric was already faltering. In the span of less than 24 hours we were already physically wrecked with 29 days left to go. But we'd learned our lesson. Seven hours of combined game time plus eight hours of driving did not check out against three hours of sleep. So maybe we were mortal.

In the meantime, we had the pleasure of suffering the consequences. The ninth inning came and went without a run. In only our second game, we found ourselves headed to extra innings. On the wrong day, extra innings could be a death sentence, but today led into one of the more lenient journeys. The next game was not until 7 PM the following day in Philadelphia; if extra innings in Pittsburgh were going to do us in, they'd also have to rewrite the record books.

Instead, they had to settle for wreaking havoc on Eric's sanity. Ben was taking the extra at bats in stride, revived by the sudden intrigue of the game and the reinvigoration of the crowd. After the disastrous four-run first inning, the Pirates had not allowed the Reds a single run. If momentum was something more than a statistical fallacy and actually existed, it was on the Pirates' side. The Jumbotron playing an inspirational speech from Keira Knightley in *Pirates of the Caribbean* was more than enough to do the trick. Ben was on his feet.

Eric remained in his seat.

He doesn't remember much. The top of the tenth inning went by without a run. Somehow, if Eric's memory serves him right, the Pirates tallied three outs. The game then headed to the bottom of the tenth. Eric remembers flying above a highway, soaring past a traffic jam. Then a deafening sound. He startled awake.

The commotion, like all things evil in a ballpark, was Jumbotron-induced. In flashing capital letters, the Jumbotron did not ask. It demanded. "MAKE SOME NOISE!" Play resumed and the cheering subsided.

Eric fell back asleep.

Eagles flew with him above the highway, their beaks tattooed with stars and stripes. Then a roaring boom.

"MAKE SOME NOISE!"

The fans obeyed. Eric vaguely recalls somebody getting called out.

The Eagles swooped down toward the stalling cars, swiping at windshields with razor-sharp talons. Eric flew as high as he could go.

"MAKE SOME NOISE!"

Eric rubbed his eyes. Even Ben was in a fit of noise-making.

"What happened?"

Ben pointed incredulously at the Pirates players charging the field. "It's over. We won!"

Eric looked at the scoreboard. Pirates 5, Reds 4, bottom of the 11th. "It's over!" He started making some noise.

Game Three:
Philadelphia Phillies

It was a five-hour drive across Pennsylvania, but we still hadn't nailed down the concept of going straight from Point A to Point B. No matter where the alphabet took you, there always seemed to be a Point A.5, which amounted to a lot of points for one location.

Eric wanted to dovetail into Chester, West Virginia, the nine-street town his mother grew up in that started on First Street and ended on Ninth. It was a thirty-minute detour out of Pittsburgh, but we had 27 hours between games. Even factoring in eight or ten hours of sleep, there would still be time to kill.

"It's out of the way," Ben said. "We're headed the other direction."

"But we have nothing else to do." It was home to a sturdy piece of his family history, a quiet corner house just off the Ohio River his grandfather purchased 40 years ago.

He slept there through the afternoons before stints of poker at night.

"We'll come back this way," Ben said. "It doesn't make sense to go backwards."

So we headed forward. We cruised down the turnpike at ten miles an hour over the limit, the official speed for the entire trip. Ben had gotten his hands on a radar scanner, a device that beeped maniacally whenever a radar signal was in range. Its purpose was to catch policemen before they caught us, saving us from the constant threat of ticketing. With an expected total distance of some 18,000 miles and several drives that would inevitably cut it close, we knew the threat of tickets might slow us down. It seemed irrelevant that this was the entire point of tickets. What was clear was that they must be avoided at all costs. It was also clear that we would have to speed. This posed a problem.

On paper we could go the limit for the entirety of the trip and get everywhere on time. That was how the algorithm operated, at least. But it was a matter of course that reality would get in the way, clogging us with traffic jams and quixotic quests for gas stations in the middle of nowhere. Neither of us wanted to speed, but we knew that if we were to finish the trip there would come a moment when we'd have to lean heavy on the pedal. The key was avoiding speeding tickets on the days when we were in no hurry. It would be a waste to get written up in vain. It was a strange mindset to be intent on getting ticketed during certain stretches, or at the bare minimum to be prepared for the worst. Neither of us had ever been ticketed in our lives, and neither of us expected it to stay that way.

The radar scanner was in theory supposed to help prevent that from happening. But it had to be plugged into a cigarette lighter to work, which severely limited the abilities of our operations base. Knowing we'd be living out of the car for the better part of the month, we'd come prepared. A cord plugged into the lighter led to a thick black adapter box, which in turn offered us a three-pronged outlet. Of course one outlet would not be nearly enough, so the adapter was jammed with a splitter that offered up another six. While Eric had the 21st-century standards everyone his age was expected to possess—a Mac laptop and an iPhone—Ben was not so cutting edge. He lugged around a hulking PC laptop along with an ovular black phone that Eric never managed to identify. All he knew for certain was that it almost never worked. The result was four unique chargers between the two of us, plus a GPS charger, plus one cord whose purpose was never deciphered by either of us.

Since we could only reach the outlets if the adapter box made use of the front seat cigarette lighter, the radar scanner was relegated to the one we'd discovered in the trunk, then clasped onto the back window. The scanner had advertised 360-degree protection, but rarely did we hear it *beep* or *boop* until we'd already passed the radar source we were trying to evade.

About 200 miles in, we passed a cop car pulled over on the side of the road. As we watched it shrink into the background in the rearview mirror, the scanner started to sound.

"Brilliant," Eric said. "We have a radar scanner that will tell us when we've been pulled over."

Ben kept his eyes on the road. "Semantics."

Aside from two cameras and their respective chargers, our final and most treasured gizmo was a GoPro camera we'd purchased the first day before the Yankees game. Designed to take photos and videos in "extreme situations" such as from the base of a surfboard in the water or the head of a golf club, the camera had a time-lapse function that would take a photograph every few seconds. Since we were going to be spanning every region of the country, we figured it'd be worth the trouble to create a time-lapse video of the trip. Using a specially designed suction mount, we were able to place the camera on the hood of the car. From there it would take a photo once per every ten-second period during which its battery wasn't dead, which tended to be just about always. Encased precariously in its mount on top of a vehicle traveling at earth-shattering speeds of ten miles an hour over the speed limit, the device looked like a miniature Mars Rover that had gotten very lost on its way out of the atmosphere.

The eyesore produced a reliable supply of stares from other drivers on the road, who often pointed at it with a delicate mix of curiosity and confusion. When we drove with the windows down and the car's interior was readily viewable, the combined effect of the GoPro, radar scanner, laptops and six or seven wires convinced more than one driver that we could be nothing but undercover cops. Cars began driving slowly when we neared them, fearing the speeding ticket that we feared so desperately ourselves.

After three hours on the road, Ben pulled off the turnpike and merged onto a separate highway.

"This is the wrong way," Eric said, spotting a sign to Philadelphia fade away behind us.

"We need to make a pit stop."

"We just filled up."

"Not for gas," Ben said ever so mysteriously.

Eric picked up Ben's GPS, solving the mystery. "What's in Williamsport?"

"My dream."

"You have a lot of dreams."

"At least I don't have them during the ballgames."

Eric scrutinized the map. "It's an hour-and-a-half detour!"

"I know how time works."

"You wouldn't let me drive a half hour to visit the place of my mother's birth. What could possibly be in Williamsport?"

"The place where my dream went to die. I told you about this months ago."

"And then never again," Eric said, suddenly realizing.

"Don't tell me you never wanted to."

"I never wanted to."

Ben shrugged. "I'm sorry you had to live through a childhood that you spent lying to yourself."

Williamsport, Pennsylvania, is a former lumber town, population 30,000, now known for its production of airplane engines. It used to be home to more millionaires per capita than anywhere else in the nation, a fact that led the local high school's sports teams to go by the Williamsport Area Millionaires. Things had changed a bit since the late 1800s.

In 2008, an eight-screen movie theater opened up. It looks pleasant from the exterior and is still in business.

The city also happens to be the birthplace of Little League Baseball.

Every year, the world's best little leaguers travel to Williamsport at summer's end to compete in the Little League World Series. Tears are shed, puberty is hit, champions are made.

Sixteen teams — eight international and one from each of eight different regions in the U.S. — make the pilgrimage to the town whose crowning achievement is the crowning of 12-year-olds. A Who's Who of future college standouts and major leaguers, the tournament features all the drama of the big boy World Series with the added chaos of everyone being 12 years old. Far from honed professionals, it is a venue for baseball insanity, where anything can happen and all but a select few hearts are broken. Just reaching the tournament is a remarkable achievement, defying odds too embedded in Ben's soul for him to calculate.

Eric had never played for a team that won even a rec league. He'd never set his sights higher than the local arcade where teams always ordered too much pizza and held their end-of-season parties.

But Ben had higher aspirations. Even as a child he was a realist. He knew he would be too small to ever cut it in the major leagues. He didn't fancy himself with grandiose ideas of hitting walk-off home runs for the Red Sox as sold-out crowds cheered. Instead, he imagined himself sitting in the GM's box with a knowing grin as the statistically efficient player he'd acquired for scraps hit that walk-off home run.

Little league was a different story. It was in the name. Everyone was little. He was still only short. He wasn't yet really short. And skill levels varied wildly; an average player could wander onto a better-than-average team and hold his own. Ben was no future Hall of Famer, but he could swing a bat respectably. The Little League World Series was certainly implausible, but unlike the big leagues, it wasn't impossible.

Until it was. Not selected for his town's all-star team, he would never even get to compete in a qualifying match. Instead, it was less efficient players with lower on-base percentages and more impatient swings going in his place. It was not the team Ben would have crafted.

The team advanced to the state championship without him, an impressive feat mitigated only by the size of New Hampshire. They failed to reach regionals. Ben turned his TV back to the Red Sox.

At last, his pilgrimage could be made. We found a Williamsport motel for the night and arose the next morning to make the trek that never was. The complex was headlined by the Howard J. Lamade Stadium, a 40,000-capacity ballpark built to be two-thirds the size of a major-league field. Covered in groomed checkered grass and carefully raked dirt, the stadium was a baseball kid's candy land.

Overlooking the stadium behind left field stood a monstrous sculpture of Casey at the Bat, the eponymous subject of the Ernest Lawrence Thayer poem that stands as baseball's foundational epic. It's a curious thing that the sport's most notable piece of literature is about a man who strikes out. There is no glory to be had for Casey, though he goes out with a bang, shattering the air with his blustering Swing and a Miss.

"If only you liked poetry," Eric said. "Now what?"

"Now what we're here for. I run the bases."

Ben marched solemnly down the hill to the outfield fence. There was no clear entry point onto the field. There was no mistaking it was not a field for public use, too precious to be left at the hands of ordinary 12-year-olds.

On the other side of the fence a groundskeeper rode a lawn mower methodically across the grass. There was no one else in sight. The mower traveled at a sauntering pace, easily beatable on foot. When the driver was nearest the outfield fence, Ben would be able to hop the barrier and make a break for the bases. He would almost certainly reach the infield. Whether he could make it all the way around the bases would depend on if the groundskeeper felt like leaping from his mower and chasing Ben down. The groundskeeper was clearly aware of our presence, tracking us with tired eyes. There was little else to be aware of in an empty compound at the eight in the morning.

The groundskeeper reached the infield dirt and turned the mower around to make the next cut back toward the fence. Eric had been less than eager to lose another several hours of sleep for this detour, but now that we were here, he was looking forward to the sight of a gleeful 22-year-old man running a 12-year-old's set of bases.

The groundskeeper neared the outfield fence. "Now!" Eric whispered. "Go!"

Ben ran down the incline. A life's contemptuous quest all came down to this moment.

"Excuse me," Ben said.

The groundskeeper shut off the mower.

"Would you mind if I ran the bases once?"

The groundskeeper rubbed his eyes. "Are you kidding me?"

"It's always been my dream."

"*No* running the bases."

Ben returned to Eric. "I wasn't able to run the bases."

"You are banned from detours for the rest of your life."

Just like the fearsome Casey, fearful Ben had struck out.

We drove straight to Philadelphia, notching our first thousand miles on the odometer. The opening legs of the trip bounced back and forth across the Northeast, making for trips of hundreds of miles in length. It was a trip around the block compared to what was to come, but we were beginning to feel road fatigue already, spending more hours in the car than anywhere else. Eric's right leg was beginning to cramp from its endless stretches on the pedal. Ben's leg had the pleasure of stretching every time it reached for the pedal.

"Buckle Up For the Next Million Miles," declared a road sign a few minutes out of Williamsport. A million miles was supposed to mean "for the rest of your life." It was starting to feel like "for the next week or so."

We did buckle up, and we drove with increasing care. According to crash averages per mile driven, there was a 0.5% chance we would have a vehicular accident over the course of the trip. Factoring in night drives, highways and the sheer number of consecutive hours we'd be on the road, we both knew that number was a gross underestimate. We'd already seen enough crashes on interstates to make us feel lucky. Given the number of hours we'd be putting in, it was more than unsettling to think of driving as a game of luck.

Eric's mother worked at a company specializing in same-day deliveries, featuring a fleet of 3,000 drivers who transported supplies on a daily basis. In the past three months, three had been killed in road accidents, all victims of semitrucks that had lost control. Three thousand was a lot of drivers, but three was a lot of deaths. The road suddenly seemed like a tangibly lethal place. Upon seeing the trip's schedule a few weeks before Day One, Eric's mother begged that he back out of the trip.

"How'd you get her to let you go, anyway?" Ben asked.

Eric shrugged. "Every now and then I can be persuasive."

But it kept us cautious. If a chain was only as strong as its weakest link, a road was only as safe as its worst driver. It might not matter how careful we were. Safety could be a question of the carelessness of others. On a normal drive on a normal day—that is, one that did not take place in the middle of a maniacal road trip—the thought of crashing never came to mind. It was a drive to the dentist, not a drive to the dentist without a crash. But when driving was the foremost activity of our day, every day, the prospect of crashing felt like a legitimate threat that was never more than a lane away. Caution, we promised ourselves. We would be as cautious as we could possibly be.

And Ben maintained he was being cautious when he nearly ran a man over in Philadelphia. Backing into a parking spot in the heart of the city, he neglected to look behind him, one of the most useful directions to look when backing up.

"You're going to kill a man," Eric declared matter-of-factly in the nick of time. Still unconvinced he could trust Ben behind the wheel, he'd been quietly scanning the area every time Ben attempted to do anything other than go straight. Like many statistically uncertified hunches, it was a good one.

The balding man in a collared shirt leapt out of the way, barely avoiding contact with the back bumper. He caught his breath and raised his arms, bewildered by how anyone could drive a car so poorly. Ben caught his breath and raised his arms and agreed.

"Put your hands back on the wheel."

Ben returned his hands to the ten and two and ever so cautiously parked.

A policeman approached and tapped on our passenger window.

"Hello," Ben said to the officer.

"Did you notice you nearly just hit a man?"

"I noticed."

The officer chuckled pleasantly. "Be careful, will you?"

"I will."

"Have a good day now."

The cop returned to his post at the nearest corner.

"That's it?" Eric asked. "A polite request to be careful?"

"They can't arrest you for almost killing someone."

"You just keep almost killing people and see what happens."

We had a little over two hours to definitively kill before the game. Since it was Eric's first time in Philadelphia and the city was vaguely relevant to American history, he was adamant we do as much sightseeing as possible. Ben, who'd been several times before, claimed to know the lay of the land.

"We can start with the Liberty Bell, if you want to see that," Ben offered.

Eric did. A dozen different units throughout elementary school warranted reason enough to give it at least a passing glance.

"But I've got to warn you," Ben advised, "It's just a bell that doesn't work. You get there and it's just a bell."

This was not an issue for Eric. "I haven't seen a bell in weeks."

"That's extremely doubtful. Just think about it. Somewhere, at some point, you've definitely seen a bell."

"Just drive," Eric said. "And look both ways."

We arrived at the Liberty Bell Center at 4:50 PM, which was important to keep in mind, the security guard informed us, because the center would be closing in ten minutes.

"It takes seconds to see a bell," Ben reassured everyone.

Eric stopped at the first placard in a long exhibit explaining the history and significance of the bell.

"Bell's this way," Ben said.

"Do you walk into an art gallery and ignore the inscriptions?"

"I don't walk into art galleries."

He forced Eric along to the end of the wide-windowed hall, stopping finally at the bell itself.

"It used to ring for freedom," Eric read from a brochure. "Now it silently reminds of the power of liberty."

Ben yawned. "That doesn't even make sense."

"The center closes in five," a guard said. "Please make your way toward the exit."

A handful of other stragglers took their photos and did as they were told. As Ben suddenly forgot his list of grievances and busied himself with a selfie of his own, Eric slipped back toward the history exhibit. He'd have much rather stayed shored up in Liberty Bell Center for three hours than waste his time in Philadelphia at a baseball game between the Phillies, who he couldn't care less about, and their unknown opponent, who he would care even less about as soon as they had an identity. So he was going to read some placards, even if it was the last thing he did before 5 PM that day.

"Exhibit closes in two," a guard shouted.

Ben located Eric behind a partition bearing a transcript of the bell's engraving.

"1753," Ben said.

"What?"

"MDCCLIII. The Roman numerals. 1753."

"That's what you get out of this proclamation of 'Liberty throughout all the land unto all the inhabitants thereof'? The roman numerals?"

"There's no roman numeral for zero, which is how long we have to get out of here. You can read about bells online at the game."

Eric relented and we circled back to where we'd entered.

"Sorry," the guard said. "You can't get out this way."

We retraced our steps back to the rear of the center. "Sorry," another guard said. "You can't use the exit." He pointed back toward the entrance.

We retreated once more. The first guard gave us a scowling look—nothing had changed in the last 30 seconds.

And that was how we got held prisoner in the cradle of liberty.

We spent another few minutes wandering in confused circles before a third guard, possibly a freedom fighter, found us in the middle of the exhibit and escorted us to a side exit that was less self-evident than most of the truths our nation held. "Don't worry," he reassured us, "people get trapped here all the time."

Needless to say, we were reassured.

We continued on to the Phillies' stadium, reaching our seats at the very top of the nosebleeds. It was a large field with an enthusiastic crowd, a phenomenon easy to come by for a team that had consistently reached the playoffs in recent years. Grown men clung to their Phillies jerseys as they jeered the Miami Marlins players on the field and occasionally each other. Baseball outfits were such an integral aspect of the game that it was difficult not to take their existence for granted. In isolation, however, there were few other venues to watch clusters of men—all supposedly representing the epitome of masculinity—as they ran around in stretchy pants and knee-high socks. The idea of eager fans dressing up in player's uniforms was no saner. No one went to the doctor's dressed up like their favorite doctor, even though it made far more sense to root for the success of your favorite doctor than it did for your favorite player.

The game moved at a nefariously average pace, producing little of interest until Domonic Brown and Delmon Young of the Phillies combined for back-to-back home runs in the sixth inning to extend a 3–2 Phillies lead.

"Who's up next?" Eric asked.

Ben shrugged. "I can't read the jersey."

"It's ridiculous. The players really do look like ants from up here."

"Correct."

"Correct? What's that supposed to mean?"

"Correct, they really do look like ants from here. Just do the math."

"Not this again."

Ben had lectured Eric on this one before. Factoring in our vertical height and horizontal distance, we were about 550 feet away from home plate. The average baseball player was just over six feet tall. An ant, meanwhile, was in the vicinity of two-thirds of an inch long. If the ant was right next to your shoes and you tilted your head down to look at it, then, depending on your own exact height, it would be around five feet away. From where we were sitting, the players on the field looked proportionally smaller than an ant would at the base of our feet.

"I'll keep that in mind," Eric promised. "So next time I see an ant, I'll remind myself that it looks just like a two-hundred-pound catcher with muscles the size of my face."

Ben wasn't sure. "I haven't run an analysis on their muscles."

Cementing their lead with another two runs in the sixth, the Phillies held on for an easy five-run win.

We embarked on a night drive for Boston, eager to return to familiar territory. Eric took the first shift in the car, carefully watching the vicissitudes of the speed limit as we drove from county to county. After two full days of crisscrossing the Pennsylvania turnpike, we breached the paradisiacal lands of New Jersey, free at last of cluttered city traffic.

It lasted a few tranquil minutes. Then, without warning, a deafening *beep* erupted in the car and Eric instinctively sped up. We were on a highway. There were no cars in sight. There was nothing to stop for—having never heard the noise before, it was his jerk reaction to escape whatever danger we were in.

Then a siren blared and red and blue flashed in our rear window. We were being pulled over.

He instantly realized what the beeping had been. Our beloved radar detector, which up until now we had assumed did not work properly. Eric had been so spooked by its sudden and foreign ringing in the total silence that he'd pressed down on the pedal—at the exact moment he drove by the hidden cop, whose radar the detector was detecting.

The officer sauntered to our window.

"You know why you were pulled over?"

"Speeding," Eric brilliantly guessed.

"I got you going eighty-five in a seventy. Why were you going so fast?"

"Because of my radar detecting device" was clearly not the correct answer. He'd never been pulled over before. He'd never had to argue with a cop.

"You like baseball?" Eric asked.

The cop stared at him.

He was out of ideas. "We were in a hurry to get to where we were going."

"Why were you in a hurry?"

"You'd have to like baseball to understand." Which was Eric's way of saying that not even he understood.

The cop wrote him up for a $180 ticket. We got back on the road at a blazing 60 miles per hour.

Eric tempered his anger. "You realize that your device whose sole purpose is preventing speeding tickets caused me to get a speeding ticket?"

"At least now we know it works," Ben offered, always the pragmatist.

Eric went wild and sped up to 65. "Glad I could be of service."

We drove in silence.

"You know," Ben said, "you've lost a lot of money in New Jersey."

We went back to the silence.

Game Four:
Boston Red Sox

"It's nice to be going back to Boston," Ben said as he steered the car onto the I-95. "Feels like a homecoming." The most beautiful thing about the I-95 was that it was a highway he could name.

"You know, you've only been gone a long weekend."

It seemed impossible, but the calendar vouched for time taking its time. We were a mere tenth of the way there on the game calendar's count, and a twentieth in terms of miles. There would be several legs of the trip where we'd eclipse one thousand miles in a single day.

Still, it was nice to be headed toward some welcome familiarity, even if for only a pit stop dinner and a three-hour ballgame. While Eric had only spent the last three years of his life in Boston, Ben was as Nor'easter as a storm. After a lifetime of worshipping the Red Sox, every trip back to Fenway was a walk down memory lane, a lane which was heavily congested with traffic on weekdays from 5 to 7 PM.

At over 100 years old, Fenway Park was arguably the most historic major league ballpark still in use. The Chicago Cubs' Wrigley Field could give it a run for its money, but it was still a certified baby at the ripe age of 99. With a 37-foot-tall wall nicknamed The Green Monster—the sort of lovable architectural quirk that cuts into profits by impractically prohibiting a standard outfield viewer area—and entire sections that faced the outfield instead of the actual field of play, Fenway should have in no way still existed in its current form. It was historic and charming in the same way a real estate agent knew a cramped studio apartment to be cozy.

It was that lack of conformity that made a visit memorable. Ben could vividly remember the first time his dad brought him to watch Pedro Martínez strike out 11 as a manual scoreboard operator hoisted zero after zero in the opposing team's stat line.

Nonetheless, most of his memories of Fenway came from watching games on television. For years, the stadium had the lowest seating capacity of any ballpark. This, combined with a crazed New England fan base, meant ticket prices were the highest in the league. With an average price of over $40 and essentials like parking and food fit for price gouging, a trip from New Hampshire to Fenway could easily run in the neighborhood of $300. Visits to the park were therefore saved for rare special occasions like 50th birthday parties, which Ben had been waiting all his life to have.

With no alternative, he watched nearly every game from home. By his own estimation, he never missed more than two games a week, meaning he'd watch approximately 175 hours of Fenway Park each year. That worked out to more than seven days. Ben would spend seven entire days of his childhood, every year, staring at images of Fenway Park.

This level of obsession with baseball was difficult to explain to anyone who had not also fallen into the abyss of super fandom. The need to watch every out and know every detail of *your* team can become so engrained in your psyche that it becomes confusing how a person could possibly *not* care if Trot Nixon would get out of his slump. Rooting for the Red Sox became like rooting for Ben's own family, except this was a family that could hit balls 400 feet and never cut him in on their paychecks.

One year, when Ben's little league team made it to the town championship, his father landed free tickets to a pivotal Red Sox-Yankees game that was being played on the same night. His father chose to go to Fenway instead of watching his biological son suit up and battle for glory. At Fenway, he had nine sons taking the field. What was more, this seemed completely sensible to Ben. Why watch *me* and a bunch of 11-year-olds when you could be watching Nomar Garciaparra and the Red Sox take on the Yankees? Ben tried to skip the championship game to attend the Red Sox game himself. In a confusing blend of sportsmanship and parenting, his father made him play.

True fandom did not just take place when the home team took the field. If he wasn't watching the Red Sox on TV, he was playing a makeshift game of baseball in his own backyard with a friend. If he wasn't playing baseball in his backyard, he was playing his favorite computer game, appropriately titled Backyard Baseball.

And every night he dreamed of compiling their roster and leading them to success. He maintained that his peers who seriously thought they'd make it to the MLB as players were deluding themselves. After all, with less than 125 players making their big league debut in any given season, the chance that a kid grew up to be a pro was 1 out of 32,000.

On the other hand, there was Theo Epstein, the youngest, smartest and coolest general manager to ever hit Boston. Ben was never quite able to hide his knack for math, and his classmates teased him relentlessly, lobbing insults about how he was a nerd and would be "the next Bill Gates." For some reason, being compared to the world's richest man merited bullying. It also did not intrigue Ben in the slightest. But when Theo took over and the newspaper grew littered with stories of how math and statistics were being used to win a World Series, he knew where he wanted to end up in life. Ben had always been a fan of batting averages and strikeout tallies, but the idea that the Red Sox would *need* someone to use *math* in order to win a championship was earth-shattering.

Furthermore, Theo was awesome. He was declared the most eligible bachelor in Boston. He was making millions for running the numbers. And he did win a ring in 2004, and again in 2007. Theo was the reason Ben could finally wear his mathlete T-shirt with almost as much pride as his Kevin Youkilis jersey.

Only in retrospect did his dream of becoming the next Theo Epstein seem just as outlandish as becoming a star slugger. Given that there was just one general manager position for every 25 players, it suddenly occurred to Ben on the drive into Fenway that his own dream might have been the real pipe dream. He might have been facing odds just as steep, if not far steeper, than 1 out of 32,000.

Before reaching Fenway we took a short detour to pick up a friend, unhelpfully also named Eric, and generously gave him a lift to Fenway. It was only a coincidence he'd gotten us free tickets to the game.

"You remembered the tickets?" Ben asked immediately.

He fanned them out for us to see. We let him enter the car.

"So how's life as a college grad feel?" Eric 2 asked Ben.

"Well . . . it's been busy. And baseball. Mostly baseball."

It'd been less than a week since his graduation and now he was zipping through his alma mater's campus for what had to be one of the quickest and most uneventful college reunions of all time. Even so, he leapt at this first chance to reminisce about the Good Old College Days, spent mostly in his dorm room studying math. He'd always found a way to tie his affinity for math and statistics back into sports. His thesis, the pinnacle of his academic career, was no different. While classmates studied cancer cells and dissected the philosophy of Heidegger, he spent his sleepless nights developing "An In-Game Win Probability Model for American Football." His extracurricular life was dominated by a club called the Sports Analysis Collective, an organization dedicated to the study of sports from a quantitative point of view. One day there was beer.

At the end of junior year, Ben's analytical work landed him a job as a summer statistician for the Jacksonville Jaguars, an NFL team under new ownership. Sure, the Jaguars played with a ball made of pigskin instead of cowhide and measured scores with points instead of runs, but it was close enough to Ben's dream to make him forget to ask how much he'd be paid.

The Jaguars were one of the worst teams in all of professional sports, and he was there to change that. At long last, he was part of a professional team—maybe not a part of the Jaguars per se, but he was the third member of the Football Research Department, which had been founded just months prior by the franchise's new owners.

By embarking on this road trip, he'd delayed his return to the Jaguars and a chance at a Real Person job. It was one dream clashing with another—his dream of being the next Theo pitted against his dream of visiting every park in America. Ben had never felt so dreamy in his life.

We picked up Renee, another college friend of ours, near Fenway's gates and headed for our seats. Fifteen rows behind home plate, they were some of the best seats Ben ever had at Fenway. He held his tongue so he didn't say anything too sappy.

His good vibes would get greater. On the very first play of the game, Elvis Andrus of the Texas Rangers hit a high pop fly into foul territory near first base. Mike Napoli of the Sox tracked the ball toward the stands till his hips collided with the dugout barrier. Steadying himself with his right hand, he extended his glove deep into the dugout to successfully bring in the ball.

Eric was still at the beginning of his three-inning routine of settling in and convincing himself to pay attention, but Ben erupted in jubilant applause. It was possibly the best play we would see all day.

Moments later, the Jumbotron confirmed it. The catch was replayed and labeled "Official Play of the Game." It was literally the only play of the game, but there was nothing to be done. It was official.

It was possible the man in charge of picking the play of the game was trigger-happy. Or, as Eric hypothesized, picking the play of the game was his sole responsibility and he got to go home to his wife and kids as soon as it was chosen. Even though the "Official Play of the Game" had zero impact on the outcome of the game and was not even recorded in the annals of baseball statistics, selecting it before any of the other (at minimum) 53 plays could not be condoned by any self-respecting sabermetricians. It was like crowning Miss Alabama as Miss America before giving any of the other contestants a chance to strut their evening wear.

Despite the imposed limit on the quality of any remaining defensive plays, the Red Sox were still able to provide some offensive dazzle. A quick two runs in the first inning were followed by six in the second. It reminded Ben of when he used to turn his video game difficulty level to "easy." By the end of the third inning with a 9–0 lead, there was less than a 1% chance the Rangers would come back to win the game. There was still two-thirds of the game left to pad their averages and run up the score, and the players had no intention of letting up. In the fifth inning on a deep fly ball to right field by Mike Carp, Rangers right fielder Nelson Cruz was so intent on robbing him of the home run that he flipped over the short outfield wall, somersaulting the four-foot-tall padded fence in one fluid motion, and landing on his back in the bullpen. At the time of the play, not only were the Rangers behind 10–2, but it was also officially impossible to snag a better catch than Napoli's in the first. Even so, an athlete whose health was worth millions of dollars a year crashed over a wall while failing to prevent a run that was both inevitable and meaningless.

It was such a one-sided affair that it brought into question the merit of a mercy rule, a hallmark of mismatched youth league games. According to rule 4.10 (e) in Little League Baseball's rulebook, a game was declared over if, after five innings, one team was up by ten or more runs. Like many aspects of little league, such as aluminum bats and snacks brought by Mom, this rule did not exist at the pro level. On extremely rare occasions, major league teams could be forced to forfeit, though usually due to unruly fans endangering players on the field and not for any scoring reasons.

In the sixth inning, the Sox went up 13–3 on a sacrifice fly.

"Wait, isn't that ten?" asked Renee. "Is this game still going on?"

The lack of a mercy rule made emotional sense to Ben. If there was no crying in baseball, then there could also be no mercy. But perhaps Renee's instincts were right. Why did they bother finishing games? Why did fielders keep colliding into walls? In the eighth inning, with the score at 17–5, Mike Carp of the Red Sox was ejected for arguing balls and strikes. The players still cared, and the mostly full stadium of fans shared their sentiment. After all, they'd paid to see a nine-inning game. And you could never be sure when a miracle might play out before your eyes.

The only problem with baseball miracles was that, statistically, "miraculous" was a kind way to put it. In the past 50 years, out of 14,542 games in which a team was down ten runs after five innings, only three of them had come back to win. Mercy had a good argument.

On the other hand, there was at least one irrefutable argument that even Eric acknowledged to justify the continuation of blowout games. If, hypothetically, the feeling of pleasure was physically achievable at a ballpark, then part of the pleasure of seeing a game was that no matter how many you'd witnessed, you might see something you'd never seen before. Whether it was some odd combination of throws to record an out or an obscure pitching record broken, baseball was so chock-full of statistical anomalies that independently rare events occurred with remarkable frequency. The newness factor held true for passing spectators and lifelong viewers alike. The notion of "This has never been done before!" was addictive like a drug, luring fans like Ben back to the ballpark again and again. He'd seen hundreds of games in person and on TV. In many ways, things were always the same. The players changed slightly each year and stadiums were renovated little by little. Three strikes made an out, four balls drew a walk and a ball hit into the next ZIP code meant a fist-pumping trip around the bases.

Yet even today, it seemed we were poised to witness something that few throughout baseball history ever had.

With their steady offensive blitz, the Red Sox had scored at least one run in each of the first seven innings and now had a runner on second with no outs in the bottom of the eighth. Since it was a home game and they held the lead, they wouldn't bat in the ninth. If the Sox could bring the runner home, they would become only the 13th team since 1900 to score at least one run in every inning. The crowd was on its feet.

The batter struck out looking. Dustin Pedroia watched the first out from his vantage point on second. Still two more chances. The second batter slapped a sharp liner straight at the left fielder. A single could still be enough. Then, a routine fly ball to center. Three outs. Pedroia was stranded on second. Incapable of *not* scoring in the previous seven innings, the Red Sox had deftly managed to avoid the history books. It was just another ballgame. Officially.

Eric watched the road signs pass with growing unease. "You lied, didn't you. Cooperstown isn't on the way."

"Technically, the only thing that's ever on the way is the highway," Ben assured him. "It only adds another three and a half hours to get there."

Our driving endurance was finally coming into form. When driving six hours a day, an extra three and a half seemed like a reasonable detour, at least to Ben. For Eric, it just turned a potential night of eight hours of sleep into four.

"Remember when we didn't visit my mother's childhood home because it was thirty minutes out of the way?" Eric asked. "Because I remember that."

Cooperstown was often called the mecca for baseball fans, a destination all diehards needed to visit at least once before dying. A baseball fan in Heaven who hadn't been to Cooperstown could not be self-respecting.

Ben subscribed to this theory, but was not adding the trip to the itinerary for his own benefit. He'd already been once before with his father. But he wanted Eric to see it. Here was the perfect place to start shifting his perspective about the game. Eric was a student of history, and Cooperstown was nothing but. Ben knew that unless he was trapped in a car that was headed there, Eric would never visit on his own.

We spent the night at a motel in Schenectady, New York. It was a location chosen in part because it was on the way to Cooperstown, but ultimately because both of us just loved the name. Wheeling our suitcases to the room, we looked up and discovered something we had not yet witnessed on the trip: stars.

Eric tilted back his head. "What's that constellation? Orion?"

"No. That constellation is just a bunch of baseballs. Every constellation is just a bunch of baseballs."

"Don't ruin stars for me."

"What, you've never heard the legend? Among hardcore baseball fans every star is a piece of baseball lore. See that superbright star up there? It's the baseball Carlton Fisk clobbered over the Green Monster in the '75 World Series."

"And that one?"

"That's just the moon."

It wasn't the most absurd form of hero worship baseball fans had used to honor their idols. After all, we were headed to a Hall of Fame that was essentially a collection of shrines to old players. To be able to come within a few inches of a ball that Ted Williams hit was a downright honor. It wasn't a ball. It was a mystical orb. Players were built up like Greek gods. Stories of their prowess were passed down from generation to generation. A swing of a bat that landed a ball ten feet to the left of an outfielder instead of directly at that outfielder was enough to ordain one a holy saint of the sport. In World War II, the United States government named a 422-foot ship the SS *Christy Mathewson* after the legendary Giants pitcher. The military, which surely should have no shortage of its own heroes to draw from on the battlefield or in the halls of Congress, chose to honor a man who threw a ball a shorter distance than a soldier could throw a grenade.

So the idea of each star in the sky representing a baseball did not seem terribly insane. Visually speaking, none of those collections of stars resembled anything close to bears or lions, and even Eric had to admit that each star did look exactly like a tiny glistening baseball.

When we at last reached Cooperstown the next day, it was like walking into a stadium, a feeling that was growing familiar. Though the museum more closely resembled a library than a ballpark, the first sight to be seen was still a giant gift shop. Once stadiums finished merchandizing the present, Cooperstown could merchandize the past.

The cashier at the ticket counter handed us our "souvenir tickets" in exchange for $40 and showed us into the exhibits.

"So we cash these in for souvenirs at the gift shop?" Eric asked as he carefully stashed his ticket stub in his wallet.

"Even better. The ticket itself is the souvenir," Ben explained.

Despite Eric's complete lack of desire for a souvenir upon entering Cooperstown, he still felt like he'd been robbed. Just as baseball parks could turn trash like plastic cups into "souvenir collectible cups," the Baseball Hall of Fame had turned a receipt of purchase into a "souvenir ticket." Eric removed the ticket from his wallet and gave it to the first trash can he could find.

Ben, for his part, held onto his souvenir. He reasoned that one day when the Baseball Hall of Fame ran out of worthwhile baseball artifacts to show, they would probably decide to build an exhibit of past tickets to the Hall of Fame itself, and the ticket would therefore have value.

Our first stop was the actual hall of the Hall of Fame, the long expansive room where each player's contribution to the game is memorialized with a unique plaque. The plaques featured an engraved portrait of the player along with a short description of their playing career, essentially making them glorified versions of trading cards. The amount of information on each plaque was scarce — Babe Ruth's inscription was a terse 38 words. To put this in modern terms, the career, life, and impact of the greatest player of all time was summarized so briefly that it could be told in the span of two tweets. This made the hall a less than ideal place to learn about the rich history of the game. Striding past the crowded plaques, Eric could type "Ted Williams" or "Carl Yastrzemski" into his phone and in seconds find a

Wikipedia page complete with an encyclopedic description of the man and the myth, along with links to pages featuring career statistics and photos. Eric did concede that the plaques were useful for spelling "Yastrzemski."

Ben thought Eric was missing the point, although in fairness, he already knew about all the players. It would not have mattered how long the inscriptions were. He would have known most of everything they could have declared. It was a grand hall, and to walk it filled Ben with a sense that he was close to greatness, even if upstate New York was most likely hundreds of miles away from any of the honored players, living or dead.

Eric found the very concept of a Hall of Fame bewildering. In the abstract, it was perfectly logical as a symbolic destination for players to strive to reach. Entry was a validation of a lifetime's worth of work. Just about every sport had one, a cemetery built to haunt the players still young enough to play the game.

But this was his first time visiting a Hall of Fame, and it had never before occurred to him that the Hall of Fame was literally a hall in which people deemed worthy of being famous were allowed to hang their names. It wasn't the Hall of Skill. It was a man-made corridor in which the barrier to entry was a matter of renown. The pertinent question was not "Were you one of the greatest players to ever grace the field?" but rather "A hundred years from now, do you deserve to be remembered?"

What was a hall for famous players to do with people like Mark McGwire? He embodied the latest controversy to infiltrate the game, posting record-breaking seasons only to be undermined by allegations of steroid use. Love him or hate him, McGwire represented a turning point in modern baseball, exposing the rampant presence of performance-enhancing drugs and provoking a massive operational over-haul. Regardless of how much of his talent was artificially induced, his significance was certainly worth remembering. It would be hard to vouch for him in a whitewashed, plaque-polished Hall of Talent, but this was a Hall of Fame.

"Just take it all in," Ben promised. "Cooperstown is the home of baseball history."

"I think I understand what you're getting at," Eric said. "Being here is like visiting the childhood home of your mother."

Ben ignored that perspective and continued on through the hall, finding all his favorite Red Sox players of genera-tions past. Eric pointed out the oddity of being a fan of players whose entire careers were over before either Ben or Eric was even born. Indeed, Ben had never seen Carl Yastrzemski pick up a bat, but what did it matter if he be-came a retroactive fan, long after Yaz hung up his socks? A win was a win, no matter what century it was in. It was in the shadows of legends past that tomorrow's legends were made.

There was one person in particular to whom Ben felt the need to pay his respects, and of course that person was not a player. General Manager Branch Rickey was best known for signing Jackie Robinson and helping to break the MLB color barrier, which was not a bad line on a ré-sumé. But he was also a business revolutionary, inventing the concept of a minor league system to grow talent for future years. The Theo Epstein of his time, Rickey had thought outside the box, a fact that went unmentioned in his plaque's terse inscription.

"Don't worry," Ben assured Eric, "there will probably be a whole exhibit to him upstairs in the museum."

Since Ben had the car keys, Eric followed him upstairs.

Expecting to find an inspiring exhibit discussing the accomplishments of the enterprising baseball executive, we instead walked immediately into an exhibit on hot dogs. Hot dogs did have a deep connection to the game, surely rivaled only by broken color barriers, but the exhibit was still a disappointment. Ben had pledged to down a hot dog at every single ballpark we visited, but even he found the display unappetizing.

Exhibits at Cooperstown were designed to please small children, featuring an abundant use of knobs and buttons that made baseballs light up for no apparent reason. We were witnessing business as usual when twenty summer camp children in a guided tour jumped up and down for the chance to hold one of the used bats tethered to the wall.

"They don't get it," Ben complained. "They just don't appreciate the history." He turned his head to see Eric aimlessly walking around the exhibit checking email on his phone.

He redoubled his efforts to sell Eric on the museum's countless perspectives. There was now a large exhibit dedicated to players from Latin America, which two Japanese businessmen examined in perhaps the perfect metaphor for the internationalism of the game. On a nearby wall was displayed the T206 Honus Wagner baseball card, known to be the most valuable card in existence. It seemed obvious to Ben that if people flew in from all over the world to Cooperstown or paid millions of dollars for a piece of paper made a hundred years ago, there was something in baseball for everyone.

Eric had a lot of emails in his in-box.

On our way out, we passed a tour group of 60-year-old men walking in together. At 10 AM on a Tuesday, the Hall was all but empty for our visit. Still, other than a couple of families spotted passing through, the vast majority of visitors were either kids under 13 or men over 50. A memorabilia shop next to the museum displayed a sign vouching that "We Have All the Cards Your Mother Threw Out." It was Cooperstown at its core, a fanciful intersection of old and young. Kids dreamt of becoming baseball stars and old men relived the years of dreaming. Ben, sandwiched somewhere in the middle, had one cleat dug into both.

Part II

Strike Out Sleeping

Game Five:
Washington Nationals

If Cooperstown was the baseball capital of America where almost no baseball was played, then Washington, D.C., was the legislative capital of America where about as much legislation was passed. One brisk six-hour drive later, we were left with just over an hour and a half to spare in D.C. before that night's Nationals game. It was Eric's turn to get to see an historic monument for five minutes, so we put "US Capitol Building" into our GPS device.

"In one hundred feet, turn left," the woman inside the GPS device instructed us. "Then, you have reached your destination." We rounded a corner and entered what more closely resembled a strip mall than the National Mall.

"This isn't the Capitol," Ben informed the electronic machine. "It's a laundromat."

"In one hundred feet, make a U-turn. Then, you have reached your destination," the GPS device fired back.

It soon became clear the device had taken our directive of "US Capitol Building" and chosen to lead us to the Capital Laundry Mat, a small laundromat about five miles from the Capitol. It provided us the always useful reminder that "capitol" spelled with an "o" referred to the Capitol building, while "capital" spelled with an "a" and followed by "Laundry Mat" referred to a small run-down building that two tourists would never drive six hours to visit.

Clearly, explaining spelling to the GPS device was easier said than done, and fairly difficult to say. Every time it attempted to send us to New York Mills, Minnesota, instead of New York, New York, we had to remind ourselves that we needed each other. We couldn't get anywhere without the GPS device, and the GPS device couldn't turn on without us.

We reoriented toward the actual U.S. Capitol building. Eventually managing to locate the dome, we snapped a quick photo to send to Eric's mother to prove he was alive and went in search of food. We hadn't eaten since that morning in Cooperstown, and were determined to find dinner in our remaining forty free minutes and avoid overpaying inside the ballpark.

The search for a quick meal quickly proved difficult. The only buildings to be found were imposing government behemoths. The clock was ticking, so Eric gave in and asked a policeman where the nearest source of nutrition could be located. The cop pointed behind his back.

"Fastest meal around has got to be the café in the congressional office across the street."

We stared at each other. We were thinking he'd point us to a Subway or Chipotle, but a stop for dinner in a branch of our nation's actual government would do as well.

We were naïve, of course. There was no such thing as a government meal without red tape. D.C. was perhaps the only city where "the fastest meal around" involved removing your belt, shoes and jacket and emptying your pockets. Surviving the metal detectors, we found only signs for congressional offices. Interesting, sure, but not as interesting as a sandwich. A high-heeled aide promised there was food to be found in the basement. We promptly learned that the proper follow-up would have been, "Which basement?" Two basements later, a sign on the door assured us that the cafeteria had been closed for two hours.

Members of Congress already dealt with mountains of bureaucracy on a daily basis, but if any of them had the foresight to fight to keep the café open, they would have guaranteed themselves the support of two wandering Americans who would most likely be passing through their district sometime within the next thirty days. If anyone passed a law making it illegal for police officers to direct time-limited tourists to winding basements in search of a café already closed, they would easily secure a donation to their 501(c).

We had burned so much time looking for dinner that we had only twenty minutes to spare by the time we sighted the park. Finding parking close to a stadium is not a science but an art, in the sense that almost no one is as good at it as they think. When approaching a park there are always available spots and signs for "ten-dollar parking" that seem to go on forever. You can choose to press your luck and creep closer and closer to the stadium, usually being rewarded with steady prices and a shorter walk. But venture too far and prices will skyrocket as open spots disappear.

It was an inconvenient day to play the part of suckers, but suckers need no schedule. By the time we circled back to where we knew there were empty spaces, those spaces were filled, and by the time we circled farther and put the car in park we had eight minutes until the first pitch. This would have been perfect timing were we not a half mile away. We had vowed before this 30-day 30-game trip not to miss a single pitch of any game, and we were not going to let the government stop us. It was the first time our perfect attendance was at risk. There was no choice but to run.

We sprinted toward the stadium as fast as anyone could expect from two guys whose leg muscles had been slowly atrophying for days. We hurdled over concrete barriers and jaywalked at any chance we had.

"Would we make it on time?" Eric wondered aloud in his voice-over voice.

Yes, easily. There would be no classic top-of-the-first-with-no-outs drama. We covered the half mile sans ankle sprain and there was no line at the ticket check. The first pitch even commenced a few minutes late. Just like a fan standing up to cheer on his favorite batter in a clutch situation only to watch him strike out, we had exerted a lot of energy for nothing. It could take weeks to recover.

We found our seats and were welcomed by the most patriotic Jumbotron message yet: "Welcome to the First

Annual Congressional Night with the Nationals," a special evening where Congress members were invited to come watch a baseball game at Nationals Park. It was relieving to see that our nation's leaders, who too had suffered at the hands of the congressional café's early closure, had a warm and comforting place to spend their night. We would live vicariously through their executive suite buffets.

In any game, an astute observer can learn a great deal by paying careful attention to the Jumbotron. Knowledge comes often in the form of statistics or trivia about each player, or perhaps a summary of a memorable game played exactly 20 years prior. But a game at Nationals Park was about more than baseball. It was about educating the electorate. For example, who knew the word "wonk" was "know" spelled backwards, implying that a wonk was someone who knew things forwards and backwards? We were not aware of this, and were not expecting to learn this fact at a baseball game. In no other ballpark would the Jumbotron be ceded to a political science professor to give minilessons. In D.C., where the city industry was "civics class," it was natural that the mascots were eleven-foot-tall presidents named George, Tom, Bill, Teddy and Abe. The fans adored the government references, apparently finding nothing odd about past presidents joining the echelons of other mascot luminaries like the green blob from the Red Sox or the green blob from the Phillies.

It was a good thing that the employee in charge of fan services was doing such a dedicated job to entertain us with political factoids. By the third inning, the New York Mets had taken a commanding lead and would go on to win 10–1.

With four of our five games thus far devolving into certified blowouts, the grave importance of mid-inning trivia contests was becoming readily apparent. They threatened the game itself for the title of most exciting event at the ballpark.

Even the Nationals' ballpark proved to be relatively dull. Round, concrete and vaguely stately, it looked as if a video game animator had been given the template for a stadium and forgotten to add any customizations to make the stadium unique. Opened in 2008, it was designed like a piece of legislation. Built to be as compact and efficient as possible, it passed muster but did little to enthuse the public.

So when the game ended in a nine-run Nationals loss, we wasted little time fleeing the capital. It would take an eight-hour drive through the night to reach the next game by its 1:00 PM start time. We were traveling from the bailout issuers in D.C. to the bailout recipients in Detroit, and Eric was wondering how he might get someone to bail him out of this journey.

Game Six:
Detroit Tigers

Detroit was bleak. Unlike the refined rigidity of D.C. or the visible wealth of cities like New York and Boston, Detroit's skyline looked as tired as its economy, bruised and in need of repair.

It turned out our car also fit into that description. When the "Maintenance Required" light turned on as we entered the city, we figured there was no better place for an oil change and tune-up than the home of the automotive industry. We dropped off the car at the first service shop we passed and waited in a restaurant across the street. The puffy-eyed waitress served us with a smile, the sort of smile you wore in a restaurant where the manager posted a sign reminding you to do just that. At least we'd contributed to the Detroit economy ever so slightly, even if we ordered water and drove a Japanese Toyota Rav-4. But what could you do if you stopped at an Irish pub in a Japanese car on the way to a ballgame starring a Venezuelan player. It was that kind of all-American road trip.

Surprisingly, the one building in town that was alive and well was Comerica Park. Despite Detroit being hit hardest by the 2009 financial crisis, their attendance numbers escaped unscathed, managing to edge out over half of all major league teams in tickets sold in 2010. However, it was unlikely that their bottom line had been faring as well. We'd purchased our tickets online for $3 apiece, which was cheaper than the StubHub service charge. The act of purchasing the tickets was more expensive than the tickets themselves. This day an impressive 36,000 fans turned out to watch the Tigers take on the Tampa Bay Rays, or at the very least turned out to the park to do *something*. Comerica featured an impressive array of amusements to help some fans have a good time in addition to the game, and others in spite of the game.

"Look, it's a Ferris wheel," Eric said. "You should give it a ride."

"I'm not riding a Ferris wheel while there's a game going on. Let's just find out seats. Wait, is that a merry-go-round?"

It was indeed a merry-go-round. A cluster of kids circled it gleefully, possibly completely unaware they were at a baseball game.

We meandered to our section, passing by a video game station where you could stand in a tunnel and play as the players you'd paid to come see.

We never ended up on the Ferris wheel, but as Eric sat bored in our seats and put on his philosopher's cap, he said one of the few things Ben would agree with over the course of the trip.

"Ballparks are judged by how much fun you can have by not watching the game."

Even Ben, who was still wearing his Red Sox cap, realized this was true. An interesting game was an interesting game regardless of its stadium, but an uninteresting game was only as uninteresting as its stadium. Baseball teams had smartly figured out that if they could make a visit to the ballpark fun, fans would return regardless of what happened on the field. Detroit was by no means the only team to invest in out-of-place amusements. Arizona had a pool in its outfield. Baltimore had bounce houses and playgrounds. Almost all parks now had in-stadium restaurants. Tickets were becoming less about the seat and more of a cover charge. You paid and had unlimited access to three hours' worth of a stationary circus, with the promise of baseball in the center ring.

It was unclear if this was good or bad for the game. It seemed obvious that anything to get people into the stadium was good for baseball. Most stadiums rarely sold out, so anything that got people through the door offered a chance to grow the fan base, but the antics came at a price. For diehards like Ben, the flourishes threatened to destroy the dignity of the ballpark experience. What did a merry-go-round have to do with the nation's pastime? There came a point when a ballpark stopped being a ballpark and became a park where ball was played.

And it would have been a shame to miss this particular game because you were sitting on a plastic horse a hundred feet from your seats. For one, both teams had respectable records placing them in contention for playoff spots. More important, the game featured Miguel Cabrera. The season before, in 2012, the Tigers third baseman had hit for the triple crown, a feat achieved by leading the league in home runs, batting average and RBIs. It was a feat that had not been accomplished since Carl Yastrzemski did it in 1967. Doing so in today's game, where there were designated hitters paid for their power, placed Cabrera's 2012 season as one of the best of all time.

In his first plate appearance, Cabrera hit a hard line drive past first for an easy single. Four innings later, he did it once more for an RBI single. He then reached base yet again on an infield single, stealing second for stealing second's sake. It was another predictably amazing performance by a player who came around once in a lifetime. He was so good it was a disappointment not to see him hit a home run. Four days later and 750 miles southwest in Kansas City, we would run into Cabrera again. There would be more than enough time to see the best player in the league hit one over the fences.

By virtue of going to every stadium and seeing every team play at least once, no active position player in 2013 would escape our sleep-deprived stares. Just over 24 hours prior we'd been in Cooperstown staring at plaques of the greatest players who ever played the game. Now we were watching the greatest currently playing it. We would see every much-discussed rookie, every much-maligned slugger, every much-adored All-Star.

For Ben, this was like trading in his collection of baseball cards for a collection of baseball humans. He knew he could tell his grandchildren about the time he saw Miguel Cabrera round the bases, or when Ichiro Suzuki made a diving catch, or when Lance Berkman struck out.

Eric was skeptical. "I thought you didn't want children."

"But everyone wants grandchildren."

No matter how many games you watched on TV, there was nothing quite like actually being there. As was true with most sports, baseball was admittedly better viewed on television. The bevy of angles and replays offered a fuller perspective of the game. Unless you had front-row seats, which we hadn't been able to swing since Day One, your view was about as good as the establishing shots they played on TV when the program came back from commercials. And half the time those shots weren't inside the stadium. But physically being there with the players and fans was a feeling a TV could never offer. If you spilled beer on yourself at home, it was always your fault. At a ballpark, it always got to be someone else's. Which was what made the concept of kids playing as Miguel Cabrera in the video game booth when they could walk 50 feet and see the real Miguel Cabrera so saddening.

To his credit, Eric watched the entire game from the grandstands. Ben was unsure if this was out of respect for him and his views, or simply because riding around on a horse in circles was not his thing.

"Race tracks are ovular," Eric confirmed.

In truth, he was simply engrossed by the field of play. Again and again, his gaze returned to center field. There, two Chevy cars were on display, facing each other on downward-sloping ramps. It was a nod to the city's prevailing industry, a notion reinforced by almost every ad in the stadium. But the two cars in the outfield were something else entirely, spaced at an unnatural interval and tilted toward the ground for no visible structural reason. The net effect was an image of impending destruction, the two cars headed for a cataclysmic pileup on the outfield below. At a time when the auto industry was still bandaging its wounds, the industry's self-constructed symbol was itself a freeze-frame picture of the moment before the crash. It was harder to watch than the game.

Ben found himself distracted too, glued to his phone, rememorizing the schedule ahead of them. An 8:10 game in Milwaukee, 7:15 in Denver, 4:10 in Phoenix. The future glistened on the phone's LED screen.

Detroit pulled away 5–2, fueled by Cabrera's slew of singles. We returned to our own car, reinvigorated by the oil change, and began our six-hour drive to Milwaukee that we had 28 hours to complete. We would be able to pit stop in Chicago and catch up on much needed sleep.

Waiting for us there was Tony, Ben's boss from the Jacksonville Jaguars. His apartment offered not only a free place to crash, but for the first time on the trip our own beds in our own rooms. The night before, we'd slept three hours on a shared bed in an Econo Lodge. Eric could hardly imagine a world where he did not have to share a bathroom with Ben. Despite numerous, increasingly direct hints, Ben had still not managed to figure out what towel went where and why.

Eric went to freshen up as Ben told Tony about the trip.

"And then Cabrera got another RBI. Comerica Park had a lot of new stuff in it too."

"I just can't believe you two haven't started to kill each other yet, being stuck in the car together 24/7."

"We're having too much of a blast to be upset with each other," Ben said. He headed for a bathroom.

Eric emerged from his room refreshed and with a new set of clothes.

"Ben says you guys are crushing the trip. That's amazing you two are holding up so well together."

"I guess you could say we're holding up in the sense that we haven't completely fallen apart," agreed Eric as he found a water bottle that no one was going to charge him $6 for drinking.

"You sound a bit more exhausted than Ben."

"I'm too tired to argue with that."

So maybe we were on different pages. As two people were wont to do, despite seeing, hearing and eating the exact same things for the last six days, we had a tendency to arrive at exactly opposite opinions. The majority of each day was spent in a car together where we were never more than three feet apart. This held true for our seats at every stadium as well. Restaurants were a shell-shocked break that allowed us to face each other instead of sit side by side, with the exception of one diner in Pennsylvania whose waiter thought we were romantically involved. In many ways we *were* like a married couple, the kind that had been married 29 years and had lost all physical desire until all that remained was the question of which one of us would do the laundry. Conversations devolved into the musings that we normally confined to the comfort of our own heads. *Isn't that a weird-looking highway sign? The water they serve here is almost room temperature, right? Should I pull over now for a bathroom break? Yes, of course you need to go too, I forgot we were on the same bladder cycle.* Despite traveling parallel paths, we were having perpendicular reactions. The trip was surpassing Ben's expectations, with every new ballpark feeling like the opening of a present. And the trip was surpassing Eric's expectations, with every new ballpark feeling like he was gift wrapping a present for Ben.

Eric went to bed while Ben and Tony delved into every detail of the trip. At last Ben had found someone who would put up with his recitations of box scores. Ben could already not wait for five days from now, when we would return to Chicago for a doubleheader. An afternoon with the Cubs at Wrigley, now home to Ben's idol Theo Epstein, would be followed by the White Sox in the South Side at night. The doubleheader selected by the algorithm was pivotal to completing the journey in 30 days. In the four metropolitan areas with two franchises, it was rare for the two teams to both play at home on the same day but at different times. Generally, teams played night games during the week and afternoon games on the weekend, making it impossible to attend two whole games in a day. A doubleheader in Los Angeles would have been impossible—between all the 81 Dodgers home games and 81 Angels home games in the 2013 season, none of them were scheduled for the same day and were at least three hours apart. The Cubs' antiquated ways were what made this modern slog possible. Once a park with no lights where only day games were played, Wrigley still featured many afternoon contests to appease early-to-bed homeowners in the surrounding residential neighborhood.

The doubleheader in Chicago would give us one day off, between San Diego and Houston, on the 27th day of the trip. We already had grand plans for our single day with no baseball. Plan A on the itinerary was a pit stop in Vegas, a four-hour detour that would allow us to stop watching baseball and start betting on baseball. If we were lucky, we could cash in our month's worth of baseball knowledge at the casino sportsbooks and recoup a few costs for the trip. More likely was Plan B, which involved spending the entire day hibernating in a bed. Both options were unspeakably exciting. Either way, thanks to the upcoming Chicago doubleheader, we'd be able to finish the trip with 29 days of stress instead of 30. Leaving Tony's apartment for Milwaukee, we drove straight past the White Sox stadium. It seemed a smidgeon ridiculous to go directly past an MLB ballpark on a trip whose purpose was to go to MLB ballparks, but the algorithm said what the algorithm said. We would be returning soon enough.

Game Seven:
Milwaukee Brewers

Our trip odometer neared 3,000. We'd maintained an ungodly rate of driving over the course of the first week, but the worst stretch of the journey was just about to begin.

Ben had been warning Eric about this section of the trip since the algorithm first spat out the schedule. Starting tonight in Milwaukee on Day Seven, we would drive over 1,000 miles in 15 hours to Denver. The 7:15 game in Denver would be followed by a 13-hour drive through the night to Phoenix for a 1:10 PM game local time. From Arizona, we would embark for Kansas City, 1,200 miles and 19 hours away. We would then stop in Minneapolis on the way back to Chicago for the doubleheader. In five days, we would drive 4,000 miles and be in the car for over 60 hours.

It was the equivalent of having a two-hour commute each way to a job with a forty-hour work week, and the job was driving. It was by far the largest and longest scheduled

stretch of the trip. Upon first seeing the results of the algorithm, neither of us could hide our concerns. We weren't
sure it was possible for us to complete, and specifically we
weren't sure if it was possible for us to complete without
perishing in the process.

But our anxiety was nothing compared to the uncon-
trollable worry of our mothers. The trip was mathematically
designed to be the optimal way to visit all 30 major league
ballparks, but it also seemed to be the optimal way to increase the blood pressure of two worrisome moms. Ben's
mother was the type of mother who would make her son
call when he got to the movie theater safely. Eric's mother
was the type of mother who questioned the psychological
ramifications of the movie. Unlike their often irrational fears
in the past, their concerns had legitimate merit this time, as
Eric's mother had made crystal clear.

We did our best to allay their fears as we secretly tried
to calm our own. To admit to a mother that you were about
to do anything with even the tiniest risk of harm was a risk
in its own right. Ben hoped running the numbers might calm
some nerves. The chance we would die in a car accident on
the trip was 0.04%.

To Ben, a one in 2,500 chance of dying was totally
acceptable. This trip was his dream. Maybe not everyone
would feel the same way, but a 2,499 in 2,500 chance of
surviving his lifelong quest was well worth the risk. You
only lived once, not 2,500 times.

Eric didn't trust the number, having heard long ago
that three-fourths of statistics were completely made up.
For once he questioned Ben's methods. The 0.04% risk was

based on the death rate per mile of all drivers in the United States combined. It was an average. Our driving was far from average. We were driving through the night with low visibility, often sharing the road with drunk drivers. We would be driving on little rest and through places we had never been. We were also young, which was never good news when it came to driving statistics.

The problem with trying to accurately calculate the risk was that there were no applicable data points. Almost no one ever drove as much and often as we would. Those who came closest were truckers. The US DOT FMCSA (better known in pop culture as the United States Department of Transportation Federal Motor Carrier Safety Administration) had regimented regulations dictating how long a commercial driver was allowed to be behind the wheel within a given time frame. Their first rule was that a trucker must be given ten hours of rest for 14 hours on the road. On 16 separate occasions we would be breaking that regulation. Truckers could also not drive more than 60 hours in a seven-day period. We were about to drive 60 hours in the span of five. There was not a single seven-day period in our trip when we would not break 60 hours. In fairness to truckers, we had the liberty of alternating with each other.

Taking matters into her own hands, Eric's mother intervened by buying us a Christmas present six months early: a flight for one of our college friends to take to Chicago. This friend, also unhelpfully named Ben, would join us just before the Milwaukee game and stay with us through Denver, Phoenix, Kansas City, Minneapolis and finally Chicago before flying back home.

Ben was more than happy to have Ben 2, under a few conditions. He had always envisioned this trip as a strictly two-person mission. Consequently, Ben insisted that Ben 2 couldn't drive. Sure, Ben 2 could help with navigation, but Ben 1 firmly believed that the spirit of the trip would be lost with a third driver.

Eric was skeptical of this idea, in the sense that he thought it was one of the stupider ideas he'd ever heard. A three-driver rotation meant someone could always be napping in the back while the person in the passenger seat could work the all-important job of keeping the driver awake and alert. On the other hand, a two-driver rotation with a third person sitting in the car amounted to two drivers and a 150-pound breathing radio. Furthermore, it was common decency to allow a friend who was willingly accompanying you on a hellish cross-country frenzy to get a little time behind the wheel. Ben 2 had signed on to drive through the middle of nowhere while the two of us snored. He hadn't come to sit in the passenger seat for five days while the two of us bickered.

We picked him up at Chicago O'Hare on the way to Milwaukee, still in disagreement over whether he would drive. Undisputed was his role as official energizer of the trip.

"What's up, wildcats!" Ben 2 screamed as he threw his bag into the backseat. "Let's go for a ride!"

Neither of us could have been described as overly enthusiastic in a normal context, and driving 3,000 miles in seven days had not helped the cause. Eric, already someone who preferred to spend his days on the couch at home reading or watching movies, was running on exhaust fumes. The trip activities that got his blood pumping—visiting historic

monuments, exploring uncharted terrain, standing up—
were few and far between. And though Ben's passion for
completing the trip kept him going when the going got boring, it did not always translate to fun-loving enthusiasm. He
was too obsessed with the mathematical dynamics, calculating and recalculating travel times and estimated arrivals until
there was no time left to travel and we had arrived. Updated
weather reports, traffic notices, construction zones—there
was too much to worry about to waste any time singing
along to the radio.

Ben 2 lived on a different plane of existence. A wreck-
ing ball of energy, he was a revelation to our dreary silver
sedan. He was not on the trip to cross off a lifelong dream
nor to once and for all visit Minnesota. He was here solely
for the free ride and the good times. He was enough of an
adventurer to believe that a five-day journey of 4,000 miles
could be defined as exciting, even if he still considered our
30-day, 18,000-mile journey the most idiotic way the month
of June could be spent. Unlike Ben, he was not a baseball
fan, and unlike Eric, he was not an antifan. He didn't really
care either way. He was just here to have fun.

With at least one of us enjoying himself, we drove north
into Wisconsin in search of dinner. The first restaurant we
found was named Cheese.

"That's the most Wisconsin thing I've ever seen," Ben 2
noted, "and we've only been in Wisconsin for five minutes."

We reached Milwaukee's Miller Park an hour ahead of
schedule. With nothing else to do, we parked our car and

played a game of catch in the parking lot. Ben and Ben 2 were thrilled to run around the one paved area free of both cars and port-a-potties. Eric was less enthused. Always an efficient packer, he'd embarked on a trip to 30 baseball games without bringing a mitt. While Bens 1 and 2 brought gloves, no one had thought to pack a ball. The only ball we had was the foul ball Eric had "caught" at Yankee Stadium. More than happy to damage it beyond repair, Ben 1 seized it from the car and proceeded to toss Ben 2 grounders against the coarse gravel pavement.

"Petty much?" Eric asked as Ben 1 let another fly ball drop from his glove.

He sidearmed another ground ball. "You wouldn't have gotten this ball without me."

"I'm guessing you want me to ask how."

"You would have never gotten to Yankee Stadium without me. I had to both drive and do the directions."

"You didn't ask. And I could have driven."

"You're the worst. I always do the directions when you're driving. You never do them for me."

"I thought you liked doing them."

"I hate it."

"You fall asleep with the GPS wrapped up in your arms. You don't let me go near that thing."

Ben bounced the ball hard off the gravel. "Because I know you'd break it."

It was about as trivial of an argument as we could have, but it was the first time we'd butted heads outside of our thoughts. We could both see it was the tip of the iceberg, a sign of things to come. We were coming unraveled.

When it was just the two of us, we were completely dependent on each other. We were trapped in one of those movies where the misfit pair is forced to work together once they realize it's the only way to save the day. Neither of us could drive a day alone, and during three-hour stints behind the wheel through unknown terrain, help was always needed. We couldn't alienate each other without alienating ourselves.

Once Ben 2 showed up, the dynamic was flipped on its head. We were no longer mutually dependent. If Ben 1 refused to grab Eric a granola bar from the trunk while he was driving, Ben 2 could do it. When you had two Bens, one was always replaceable.

Even more dangerous, Ben 2 could now serve as arbiter of all claims, determining for every point of contention who was right, who was wrong, or if both of us were delusional. For the past week we'd been sweeping things under the rug while quietly building loads of pent-up anger. With a living human suddenly there to tell us "Yes Ben, Eric should download a fourth navigation app if the first three didn't work," and "Yes Eric, Ben should not lie to you about how long a drive will take," it became a nuclear arms race to see who could file the most grievances. It wasn't pretty, but it was cathartic.

Ben 2 was starting to realize just how long the next five days would be.

We did our best to minimize our bickering once inside Miller Park, a cozy new stadium featuring a retractable roof. A yellow spiral slide twisted around the upper echelons of left field, providing the cartoonishly mustached Bernie

Brewer a means of celebration after every Brewers home run. This gimmick captivated both the hard-core fan like Ben, who saw it as a trademark of the Miller Park experience, as well as the casual fan like Eric, who knew to pay close attention when a mustachioed man got on a slide amidst a crowd of children.

We were joined at the ballpark by Eric's friend Zena, who was a godsend by virtue of being a good conversationalist and not being named Ben. Eric had quickly discovered a very straightforward pattern: the games he enjoyed were those attended by outside friends. Attending a baseball game could mean many things to many people, but the one thing it always meant was a three-hour conversation with the person next to you. Batters came and batters went. The occupant in the next seat over never left you. For Eric, a good game was defined by a good conversation.

It'd been a while since we'd had one.

Eric knew going in that Ben was a man of few words and a lot of numbers. But as the days went by, the words grew fewer and the numbers overwhelmed him. Eric would go hours on end without managing to elicit more than a grunt or a nod of the head from Ben. Open-ended questions like "What do you want to eat for lunch?" received yes or no answers. Yes or no questions sometimes received no answer at all. It was making Eric stir-crazy. The only thing worse than talking to a wall was talking to a wall that could do math. There were nights when the inability to carry a conversation began to threaten our safety. In no-man's-land without radio service and malfunctioning iPod cables, talking was all there was to keep Eric awake at the wheel. Ben, whose humanity was gradually eroding away, could last at the wheel for hours in total silence without saying a word. Eric was admittedly not as good at driving at 4 AM in dead quiet in the tenth straight hour on the road. It was inevitable that Ben began to openly resent him for it. This led to even less talking, which led to more resentment, which would have led to even less talking had there been any talking left to lose.

Which was why Ben 2's presence would either save us or destroy us. We desperately needed a sounding board to make sounds on. Whether it drove a bigger wedge between us would be a matter of opinion, something both of us were certain to have.

In the meantime, Eric caught up with his friend Zena. It was the first time we hadn't sat next to each other at a game. We were both excited.

Zena was a Wisconsin native, and she agreed with our scientific analysis that Miller Park was a great stadium. There's no such thing as a free stadium, though, and the locals here had to pay for this one. From an owner's perspective, the ploy was simple: if you build it, we will stay. If you don't, someone will build it for us elsewhere. It was a self-perpetuating trump card, one that existed because it has existed in the past. Most teams made enormous profits and were owned by billionaires or groups of multimillionaires. More often than not, the money was there.

Yet it was painfully easy to convince a mass of voters to vote for subsidized stadiums. Though teams were owned by wealthy individuals, the fundamental principle of fandom rested in the conceit that each was a community's team.

Owners had no problem with this tendency. The public's heart was good for the owner's wallet. It was why Ben said "*We* won in the ninth last night" when the Red Sox pulled away. "The team owned by Fenway Sports Group won in the ninth last night" didn't roll off the tongue. It was a dangerous imbalance of monetary fact. Fans in budget-strapped communities found themselves paying for the construction of stadiums and parking lots that they were then expected to pay more to enter. The public saw a financial return on its investment so rarely that it *never* made economic sense for the public to foot the bill. There were potential positives from building a stadium, like an improved sense of community or even a safer community, but the economic benefits never outweighed the economic costs. An entire genre of movies was founded on the premise of teams giving hope and camaraderie to a downtrodden populace. It was part of baseball's unimpeachable lore. But the economic reality was that camaraderie came with a price tag that most communities could not afford.

It was hard to fault the owners, as it was their job to maximize profit. The way Ben saw it, gouging the public's pockets was necessary. As a Red Sox fan, he would of course preferred to not have to pay $40 to sit in the outfield. But he also wanted the Red Sox to win. Charging $10 for a beer would never stop being annoying, but it would never stop being smart business. Profits were useful to pay for good players who were needed to win.

If hope was priceless, winning was worth even more. Everyone loved a winner, and there was no clearer winner than on a playing field. Sports fed into the national desire for victory, adding a local flavor. On the surface, it made no sense for the citizens of Milwaukee to clash with the citizens of Philadelphia. But as the two teams squared off in Miller Park, the players on the field gave fans a socially valid reason to verbally assault each other. Each was trying to prevent the other from winning, and victory was sacred. The hometown team was inseparable with hometown pride. When Wisconsin residents opened their morning paper the next day, the headline would not read "Mark Attansio's Brewers Win." Most people had no idea who Mark Attansio was, which was fine, because Mark Attansio had nothing to do with the ethos of winning. Instead, the headline would declare "Milwaukee Wins." Not the Brewers, but Milwaukee. Not the team, but the city. If a team demanded payment for a stadium, then you paid. Without a team, you didn't get to compete.

After completing seven innings, the Brewers trailed the Phillies 4–2, and it didn't matter to anyone in the crowd who financed their stadium. They simply wanted to see their Brewers come back to tie the game. With a runner on first, Brewers shortstop Jean Segura hit a triple to right field. One misplaced throw later, he scored to even the score at four. We always tried to root for the home team, as it was the path of least resistance and sociopathic tendency. But we already had only 20 hours, until 7:00 PM the next day, to complete the upcoming 15-hour drive to Colorado. It was not a good day for extra innings. Surrounding fans began to look on with confusion as we proceeded to root for *both* teams. We were strictly on the side of whoever was up to bat. We wanted a run. We wanted a winner.

In the top of the eighth, this meant the Phillies. With a promising two runners on base and only one out, Delmon Young could uneven the scoreboard with a single. We instantly became the world's biggest Delmon Young fans. He repaid us by swinging at the first pitch and hitting into an uninspired inning-ending double play.

That was that. We moved on to being Brewers fans.

The bottom of the ninth still saw the score knotted at four. We prepared for the worst.

The first out came quickly. But next up was Jean Segura, the man who'd already dashed our hearts by tying the game in the first place. It was thanks to him that Ben was doing the unthinkable, rooting for a ballgame to end as quickly as possible—even if it was only so he could make it on time to another one. None of us had ever driven through the Midwest, and an extra inning or two could be the difference between making the next game and ruining Ben's whole life. There could be traffic leaving the stadium, traffic coming into Denver or of course the infamous 3:00 AM traffic in Iowa. There was no way of knowing what might occur, so we did not take kindly to Jean Segura. Until, with two strikes against him, he hit a single and became the potential game-winning run. Then we loved him very, very much. Ryan Braun followed with another single, advancing Segura to second. As Aramis Ramírez came to the plate, the crowd rose to its feet. They were ready for a walk-off and we were ready for a walk-out. He connected on the second pitch, sending a rocket over the infield. Segura chugged his way around third and high-fived his way through a

Brewers mob to notch the game-ending run. Milwaukee won! We could leave and start a 15-hour drive!

Eric took the first shift behind the wheel as Ben 2 rode shotgun. Ben 1 found himself in the backseat for the first time all trip. The backseat was large and Ben was small. Nine times out of ten, being small for a man is awful. It was disadvantageous personally and socially, as all the women who refused to be his girlfriend could attest.

The exception was when it came to traveling. Horribly cramped airplane seats became only regularly cramped seats. Compact Toyota RAV-4 backseats became luxurious bumpy beds. He was small enough to lie down horizontally from door to door. It was a revolutionary discovery for his sleep cycle. If Eric ever tried to lie down similarly, his tall frame would force him to bend his legs and hunch his back, which was exactly what he deserved for having a six-foot-something stature. Little Ben went to sleep dreaming big dreams.

And awoke in a daze. The car was pulled over on the side of the road in an unlit gas station that had gone out of business. He had no idea what time it was or what state they were in.

He sat up and rubbed his eyes. He wasn't seeing things. Ben 2 was in the driver's seat.

"Have you been driving?"

"I've been driving countrywide, wildcat," Ben 2 replied.

Just like that, the road trip as he knew it was over. Its purity was forever ruined. Eric had pulled a slow one over the course of three hours, all while he was asleep. The moment Ben 2 drove a single mile, it was no longer a two-man affair. Eric knew Ben 1 would never have allowed it, and he also knew it was a reckless, pointless, self-imposed rule that accomplished nothing. He didn't take pleasure out of shattering Ben's lofty ideals, but he would happily accept the extra hours of rest it would now provide. What was more, his mother would be pleased. It was the end of a very strange battle between Ben and Eric's mother, two people who had never met but would have mortality to talk about.

Now that Ben 2 had already logged miles, Ben 1 knew there was no point in kicking him out of the driver's seat. Even he could see there was now no logic in fighting against the opportunity to milk Ben 2 for every mile he had in him. Completing the trip would require stamina, and as of yet we'd only mastered stubbornness.

He gave Eric a long look in the front seat.

"Go back to sleep," said Eric.

He went back to sleep.

The drive was a beeline down I-80 West through Iowa, Nebraska and Colorado, featuring 100-mile stretches that in turn featured no change of scenery. There were farms, and then farms, and then four gas stations, and then three fast-food restaurants, and then farms. We stopped every few hours to rotate seats and fill up the tank, a system that worked until Colorado turned storybook rural. Passing signs with reassuring promises of "No Services Next 40 Miles" and "Do Not Trespass," we'd pull onto the barren land off the side of the highway and circulate positions and blood.

We made good time, reaching the Denver city limit at 3:30 PM for the 7 PM game. It was the first time Eric was keeping close watch of the clock, and though barely able to keep his eyes open, he was ecstatic about our early arrival. The date was June 8—or, as Eric knew it, three weeks after two weeks after the first Saturday in May.

The first Saturday in May, as was acknowledged world-wide, was the most important day of the year, especially if your world was Kentucky. It was on that day every year when the Kentucky Derby was run, the pinnacle of American horse racing. Known as "The Two Most Exciting Minutes in Sports," it was in stark contrast with baseball, "The Three-and-a-Half Most Boring Hours of Sports Every Day" as Eric knew it. Following 20 years of watching the Derby from living rooms and college dorms, he'd finally made it to the Run for the Roses just a month ago with his father, skipping two days of school for two days of mint juleps and hats not meant for heads. If Cooperstown was Ben's sporting pilgrimage, then Churchill Downs was Eric's. It was his version of a trip of a lifetime. Family and friends at *the* Kentucky Derby—and it only took four days.

But the Derby was only leg one of the Triple Crown, the devilish three-race combo filled out by the Preakness and the Belmont. The Preakness was always run two Saturdays after the Derby, and the Belmont three Saturdays after that. This year, that was June 8. Post time was 5 PM local time.

Eric scanned the cityscape for a place to watch the race. He'd never thought much of the fact that motels always advertised having rooms with TVs, but now he understood that there came a day in a man's life when he needed to watch the premier event of a dying industry in a run-down compound. It could have peeling walls and it could have poisoned water, but it also better have a TV.

After getting turned down by four motels with green vacancy signs that told white lies, we found a Super 8 motel just two miles from Coors Field, home of the Colorado Rockies.

It was the happiest we'd been in days. Ben would get to the game with time to spare, Eric would get to watch the Belmont and we would all get to sleep.

We found our room. Ben claimed he'd purchased a room with two beds for the three of us, but if this was the case, we were unable to locate the second bed. Too tired to return to the front desk for an argument, he cut his losses.

"You guys can have the bed and I'll take the couch."

"That's nice of you," Eric said, genuinely surprised by Ben's unprompted generosity. "We appreciate it."

"Just remember we need to be out of here by 6:15. I want to get there by at least a quarter till seven to be safe."

Eric showered and set his alarm to just before 5 PM so he could wake up for the race. He lay on one side of the bed and instantly passed out from exhaustion. Ben 2 then took his turn in the shower. He lay down on the other side of the bed and passed out immediately from exhaustion. Last and least in size, Ben 1 took his long-awaited shower. He lay down on the couch to pass out immediately from exhaustion. He did not.

The couch was too small for Ben, which meant it was probably technically a wide chair. He stood and gazed at the queen bed. Eric and Ben 2 looked so comfortable. *So* comfortable.

There was a sliver of space between them, clearly ear-marked as the no-touch zone. There was little choice to be made. He was but a sliver wide. He squeezed in, settled down and passed out.

Ben's cell phone buzzed. Six eyes struggled open and discovered twelve entangled limbs.

"Seriously?"

"Really?"

"Seriously?"

Ben's presence in the bed received a lukewarm reception.

He reached for his phone to turn off his alarm. But it wasn't an alarm—according to the clock, it'd only been ten minutes since he'd climbed into the bed. The screen flashed the number of Tyler, our friend from Colorado who was meeting us at the game. Eric and Ben 2 went straight back to sleep.

Ben begrudgingly answered. "Hello, Tyler." The nap he'd been waiting twenty-four hours to take was swiftly slipping away.

"Hey! I'm outside Coors Field. On Blake Street. Where are you guys?"

"Super 8. Napping until the game. Or at least we were trying to."

"Oh, well the game just started. Are you guys coming soon?"

"It's 5:15. The game doesn't start for two hours."

A pause. "No it doesn't."

Ben yawned and returned his head to the pillow. "It starts at 7:15. I distinctly remember double-checking the schedule in Detroit—"

And that's when Ben realized he had made the most foolish, avoidable, predictable mistake imaginable. He stared at the clock in astounded silence.

When he checked the time in Detroit, the schedule did say 7:15 PM, which was 7:15 PM eastern. Denver was in mountain time, two hours behind. It was 5:15 here, but it was 7:15 eastern.

The game had already started. We'd driven fifteen hours to a motel two miles from the stadium only to fall asleep and miss the opening pitch by ten minutes.

And it was all his fault, 100% his own doing and no one else's. It was his schedule and his confirmation. It was his time frame and his alarm. Eric and Ben 2 had endured a 15-hour drive at his behest just so he could forget how the United States of America operated time. Eric had checked to make sure he double-checked the schedule, and he'd managed to check it wrong twice. It was a rookie mistake, and he'd made the mistake of taking himself for a road trip professional. He had no one to blame but himself. Seven days of perfect attendance and sleepless nights were all for naught. The entire premise of the 30-day trip was shattered. We could still show up at the Rockies game, but not for every pitch. Not even for every inning. It just wasn't the same without seeing 30 complete games. Anything less was a cop-out. A failure. We could see 29 games in 30 days or 30 in 31. It would never be 30 in 30. His dream was done.

Ben did not know how to emote such anger. He flung his phone against the too-small couch, breaking off its case. He threw his hands up and threw his hands down. He paced from sink to bed to sink.

"Where have you gone, Joe DiMaggio!" he screamed, our euphemism for less family-friendly expletives.

Eric startled awake. He squinted at Ben clenching his fists in his boxers. He put two and two together.

"What time is it?"

"5:15."

"Oh my god," Eric whispered. It was true. "We slept through the Belmont!"

Ben stared at Eric in disbelief. "The game. We slept through the game."

"Where's the remote control? There might still be post-race coverage." He leapt at the remote on the bed stand and flipped on the TV. He flipped through the channels in search of any mention of the Belmont.

"Go back."

"What?"

"Go back to that last channel."

Eric flipped back. It was a live broadcast of the Rockies game two miles away. It was the top of the first inning.

Eric put the other two and two together. "That's today's game?"

Ben nodded in mourning.

"What happened?"

"I made a mistake."

Part III

It's Zero, One, Two Strikes You're Out

"I made a mistake," Ben said again, not sure if Eric understood the immense and unbearable gravity of the situation.

Eric clapped his hands with a smile. "Finally!"

"Come again?"

"Now we can have some fun."

Eric found it obvious that this was the best thing that could have possibly happened. Every minute of the trip Ben had carried with him a crippling burden, the incessant fear that the littlest detail might go wrong. He'd constructed the perfect schedule with the perfect itinerary. All that was left to do was be perfect. Bags formed under his eyes. Wrinkles doubled his chin. He began to drag his feet and mumble as he spoke. The trip was physically debilitating for Eric, but psychologically toxic for Ben. It was his baby and he wasn't ready to be a father.

He spent his life leaving nothing to chance and now he'd made the most careless of unforced errors. Eric couldn't help but laugh. Though a mathematical masterpiece, the schedule was constantly threatened by acts of God and nature. It was only natural that the trip be thwarted by an act of stupidity from the only man smart enough to conceive of it in the first place.

And now there was no numerical sanctity to waste our days preserving. Now we could relax, take a deep breath and enjoy ourselves. We could have fun.

Ben 2 rolled over and pulled the covers off his face. "It's baseball time already, isn't it."

That was one way of putting it.

And it was. We still had a game to go attend. Ben could barely bring himself to exit the motel, but our friend Tyler had himself driven four hours to meet us at the game. Even if we'd wanted to flee and recoup the game at another park, there was no feasible Plan B. The Rockies were based about as far from another stadium as a team could be. Only the Seattle Mariners were more isolated. With the sun already setting over half the country, there were no other games to catch. It was a lost day.

We dropped Ben 2 off at the stadium to locate Tyler while the two of us went in search of cheap parking. Since we'd already missed the first inning, there was no need to hurry. We were just two friends meeting other friends at a ballgame.

But overcoming a baseball addiction was a multistep process, and Ben now entered his rationalization phase. "Technically," he declared, "five innings constitutes an official ballgame. And we'll see more than five innings today."

"Doesn't count," Eric said.

"We saw an extra-inning game. And odds are we'll see a couple more. We'll wind up witnessing an average of nine innings a day."

"Doesn't count," Eric said.

Ben couldn't stand to look at Coors Field as we approached on foot. "I can't believe I did this to us."

Eric watched Ben walk the streets of Denver a defeated man. As much as he tried to convince himself otherwise, there was no denying it. Ben was genuinely heartbroken. And he would never forgive himself.

Eric couldn't think of the trip as anything but a silly, frivolous quest. We were two guys with a month of summer to kill and just enough cash to kill it with. There was nothing at stake aside from an artificial, abstract achievement. It meant nothing to the world or even baseball if we finished. No lives were at stake. No one was counting on us. It was a foolish thing to do while we were still young enough to get away with being fools. And now unbound by the torture of 30 in 30, we were liberated. We could enjoy each day for what it was, instead of a day that led to the next. We could finally have the road trip Eric had always wanted.

But he had on his hands a friend in need.

"June twenty-seventh," he said.

Ben looked up from his stupor.

"June twenty-seventh. Our off day. We drive from San Diego on the twenty-sixth to Houston on the twenty-eighth. Right?"

Ben nodded, processing.

"Denver's as close as it comes to in the middle."

He discarded the idea immediately. "The twenty-seventh is a Thursday. Every team rests on either Monday or Thursday. The odds they'd be playing at home on a Thursday are twenty-five percent."

"That's better than zero."

"Except I checked for that possibility months ago. I checked for that exact scenario. Colorado doesn't have a game on the twenty-seventh."

Ben tried to return to his self-pity, but Eric whipped out his phone. "Sorry, buddy, but you've lost your authority on the schedule."

He pulled up the Rockies schedule and scrolled to the month of June.

"I have good news and bad news."

Ben took the bait. "What's the good news?"

"You're not completely out of your mind. You were right when you checked that scenario months ago."

"And the bad news?"

"You're still wrong. The Rockies had a rainout against the Mets in April. A rainout at home. Guess when it got rescheduled?"

Ben stopped walking. "Impossible."

"No, improbable."

"What are the odds?"

"You tell me, you lovable buffoon."

Ben got busy on his phone. "Times and distances. We need times and distances."

"The twenty-seventh is a 4:10 eastern game."

"The twenty-sixth and twenty-eighth are both evening."

"Drive from San Diego to Denver is fifteen and a half."

"We'd have sixteen to do it."

"Theoretically possible."

"Drive from Denver to Houston is fifteen and a half as well."

"We'd have sixteen to do that one too."

"Theoretically possible."

Ben remembered how to smile. The trip was alive. Theoretically.

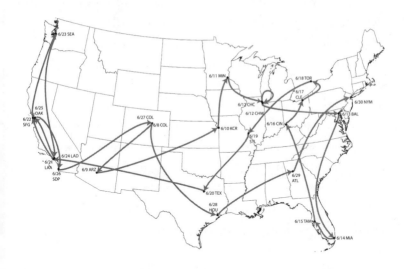

We entered Coors Field by the end of the third inning in good spirits. The trip resurrecting itself from certain death to probable death was like witnessing a car swerve three lanes across a highway only to regain control inches before slamming into another car, something we had witnessed several times. Seeing his dreams balance on the tip of ruin put Ben in a meditative mood, or as close to meditation as a computer nerd had ever come. Which meant he was quiet and thinking.

Coors Field overlooked the Rocky Mountains, giving fans the same picturesque view featured on Colorado license plates and beer cans. It was a sad day when scenic panoramas came to remind you of nothing but grueling 15-hour drives, but Ben had already promised himself this was now a happy day so there was nothing we could do. Gazing out romantically into the distance, he thought of how far we had already come. This landscape was so foreign and yet everything within it so familiar. He had a beer and hot dog in hand. If he looked to his right, there was Eric. If he looked to his left, there was another Ben. But looking out over the field and purple mountains filled him with a sense of accomplishment that reasonable people only felt when they are on top of the mountain looking the other way. He was proud to have gotten this far, and to have convinced his friends to join him on an adventure so immense and so ill conceived. Ben hadn't moved mountains by convincing Eric to join him on his journey, but he'd moved Eric to the mountains, which was possibly the more difficult feat of the two.

Though our self-imposed rules gave us no obligation to stay for the duration of the game since the affair was officially a lost cause, we remained through the bitter end to catch up with our friend Tyler. We recounted our tales of road trip hijinks to him in detail, and he was clearly jealous that he wasn't on the trip. He tended to spend less time at baseball games and more time in coffee shops listening to music by artists we had never heard of while reading the works of poets most bookstores had never heard of, but he was enamored with the extremity of the trip. The prospect of being forced to complete double-digit drives day after day enchanted him. Ben hoped his envy of our trip would rub off on Eric and make him doubt his intractable belief that every minute spent in the car was pure agony. But Eric knew Tyler well, so there was no convincing him that Tyler was anything other than completely out of his mind.

The sun had set on the Rockies by the time we left Denver. Our GPS device gave us two options for getting to Phoenix. We could drive south into New Mexico and west through Arizona for a trip that would take 13 hours and 10 minutes to complete. Or, if we decided to complete the trip in 13 hours and 17 minutes, we could drive west into Utah and then south to Phoenix. Since we'd be cutting across New Mexico the next day en route to Kansas City and would have no other chance to hit Utah, we headed west for what we all lovingly knew as the Beehive State, a reference we could all totally understand.

Seven minutes was a small price to pay to see a new state, and it only took us seven minutes of driving to realize what Utah would look like when we saw it. Blackness. Pure darkness. It would still be predawn by the time we crossed from Utah into Arizona. We'd traversed amazing vistas all throughout the country. We'd seen the prairies of Nebraska, the Appalachians in Pennsylvania, even a glimmering view of Lake Michigan from a Chicago skyscraper. We'd seen so much it was becoming hard in our minds to keep track of which beautiful mountain we saw on which leg of the trip and in which state. But even before things started to blur together, much of our countrywide viewing had blurred into the darkness of night.

We made our way into Utah and within the first hour saw exit signs for Arches National Park. "It looks beautiful at this time of day," Eric remarked. "Almost as pretty as those mountains and canyons we probably passed earlier that were also covered in darkness."

Ben did not get the chance to snicker, as he had fallen asleep in the backseat the moment his head hit the cushion. After darkness, sleep was the second leading cause of missed vistas. Eric had skillfully slept through the entire state of Indiana on the way to Detroit. He'd never been to the state before, resulting in a sleepy-tree-falls-in-a-forest dilemma as to whether or not he could cross it off his list. Ben set an alarm for a few minutes before we were scheduled to cross the Utah border so he would not face the same predicament.

We drove south on route 160 toward Phoenix, blowing by the signs for Grand Canyon National Park. It was Eric's worst nightmare. We were seeing America via exit signs. One of the most stunningly beautiful sights known to man was within our reach, and we had to drive right by because we were on the verge of being late to a concrete dome.

Game Eight:
Arizona Diamondbacks

We arrived in 100-plus-degree Phoenix and marched into the air-conditioned stadium that was Chase Field. Before the trip began, Ben emailed many of the teams' public relations departments explaining that we were going on a 30-game trip, hinting that complimentary tickets would be nice. To no one's surprise, very few teams responded to a request for free things from two no-names who were capable of buying 15-dollar tickets on their own. The Diamondbacks were the lone exception, not only giving us two free tickets behind home plate but offering us the chance to walk around the field before the game began. There was something in the water in Phoenix, or more likely, there was a lack of water and the dehydration was making the Diamondbacks front office delusionally kind.

The fan services director greeted us above third base and led us onto the field. We walked up and down the dirt toward home plate and into the dugout, acting as if we belonged and had been given similar access in all of our previous stadiums. Although Ben had been honest in his emails, it still felt as if we were somehow perpetrating a scam. In most other stadiums we were relegated to the absolute cheapest of cheap seats. Here we were handed first-class treatment, no questions asked.

It was nice to be treated like VIPs by an MLB team, given that the entire trip was one big mobile shrine to baseball. We were somehow given free rein of the Diamondbacks' dugout, which was strikingly bare and not yet littered with the remnants of chewing tobacco. It featured a single bench extending across the pit, packed with a few bat holders and Gatorade containers but nothing more. There were no televisions or electronics and nothing that screamed "2013." The modern dugout was as distraction-free as it would have been a hundred years ago. We wandered around its confines for a few minutes. Eric enjoyed a rare view of the field as Ben checked under the benches and around the corners for anything a real live ballplayer might have left.

The two seats provided to us by the Diamondbacks were fantastic, just ten rows behind home plate. With an all-encompassing view of the field and servers coming around every half inning to take food orders, there was never even a reason to leave our seats. We had a direct line of sight on the Jumbotron and were provided multiple versions of the game program. All of this combined for a more stimulating spectating environment than what any of the players had in their own dugouts. Players weren't allowed to use cell phones during gameplay, and other than gum, tobacco, sunflower seeds, Gatorade and water, it seemed as if dugout cuisine was prohibited. Sure, they were on the job, but who didn't pass the time between pitching changes these days by checking updates on other games around the league? Players were being paid millions to get bored to death inside a cage for three hours every day. Perhaps it forced them to maintain an excruciating focus on the task at hand, or maybe being held in the same conditions as Babe Ruth ninety years ago was reason enough to avoid a redesign. But they were public figures living public lives. They must have been getting so many emails.

Ben 2 had not been lucky enough to receive a free seat, as we had written the team before we knew there would be three of us. We offered to trade off every couple innings so he didn't have to suffer alone, but he was more than content in his nosebleeder seat. He was behind on *Dollhouse*, a TV show neither of us had ever heard of, and was looking forward to firing up his Netflix app on his phone and logging some quality viewing hours. Not unlike the dugout, sitting alone in the farthest-away seat on the uppermost deck provided him a distraction-free zone where he could focus on the task at hand.

The Diamondbacks were playing the San Francisco Giants, a fact that an army of Giants fans made abundantly clear. Coming off a World Series win, the Giants had garnered a dedicated fan base nationwide. Undercover San Franciscans emerged from hiding everywhere the team went.

The dynamic made for a clap-happy stadium. Each time someone got a hit, half the crowd applauded. Each time someone got out, the other half applauded. While soccer stadiums could segregate fans by team, baseball stadiums were a stirring pot of allegiances. The net effect was a crowd that seemed to love everything. Ben could hardly agree more with the notion, for what was there not to love?

The Giants took an early lead and never looked back to win 6–2. Though division rivals, there was little personal beef displayed between opposing fans. Most cheers consisted of polite standing ovations and syncopated clapping per the Jumbotron's instructions.

The only time during the game when the fans really got into it, when they rose to their feet, when they demanded their voice be heard, when they yelled as loud as they could without concern for those around them, was in the sixth inning when the gates to the outfield opened up and a hundred-strong parade of puppies marched across the warning track with their owners at hand. It was Puppy Day in Phoenix. Puppies brought the world together. Everyone could cheer on a puppy.

Game Nine:
Kansas City Royals

"How far did you say to Kansas City? Twelve hours?" Eric asked as we returned to the car.

"Something like that," Ben agreed.

"Something like that? Is it twelve or isn't it?"

"A little more."

"How much more?"

"Seven hours."

"It's only seven hours to KC?"

"Seven more hours."

"It's *nineteen* hours?"

"Right," Ben agreed.

"You kept saying our drive to Denver was the hardest we'd have to do!"

"Well, I was trying to motivate you. And it worked."

"By lying. You lied."

"And it worked," Ben said, focusing on the important part. "This really shouldn't be a surprise. If you ever got your GPS app to work, you'd know all the distances. Or just look at the pillow."

The pillow was not just any ordinary pillow. It was a spherical squishy globe. Just a few years ago, the idea of a nationwide road trip without the use of a single physical map in the car would have been nonsensical. Gone were the days of Thomas Guides. Now it was all electronic satellites and one extremely comfortable pillow that happened to feature a map of the world. A friend had given it to us while we were in Boston and we tossed it into the burgeoning mess in the car, figuring it could only do us good.

Eric stretched out the pillow, flattening the divide between Colorado and Missouri. He frowned. He had only himself to blame. "I should have checked the pillow."

Nineteen hours was a painful endurance test, but a 25-hour window meant we should have little trouble with its completion. Arriving in Kansas City on time would simply be a matter of keeping each other company at the wheel and avoiding disaster at the hands of Mother Nature.

At 3 AM in New Mexico we stopped at a gas station to rotate positions and revitalize ourselves with drinks. A gas station at 3 AM in the middle of nowhere was a desolate sight, populated only by insects swarming low-hanging lights and one solitary cashier. Conversations with them were always memorable, featuring gems like "Find everything you need?" and "Oh, Gatorade, nice choice. Did you find everything you need?"

This particular gas station was in the desert in the northeast quadrant of New Mexico, remote even by our new standards. We pulled in to the sight of a hunched man clutching a broom, sweeping away the sand and dirt that would blow back in the moment he stopped sweeping.

Ben found his Gatorade and put it on the counter. The sweeping man returned to his post behind the cash register.

"Find everything you need? Where you fellas heading tonight?"

"Kansas City," Ben told him as he handed over a wad of bills. We were past the point where telling a stranger in New Mexico that we were headed to Kansas City struck us as strange.

"Oh, Kansas City." The man's eyed lit up. "Watch out for tornadoes. I heard there are lots of tornadoes."

"Right now? Is it on the news?"

"It wasn't on the news, but there are always tornadoes in Kansas. Be careful . . ." The man's voice trailed off as he handed Ben his receipt for the $2.19 drink. The way he said it left unclear whether it was a sincere warning or the placing of a curse. Either way, Ben returned to his car for another few hours of driving through the beautiful tornado-free desert in the blackness of night.

Luckily, gas station attendants in New Mexico were just as clueless about the weather as professional meteorologists. The drive into Kansas City was as sunny and warm as could be. After hours of suffering through a single-lane highway in the thick of Kansas, we arrived at Kauffman Stadium on the Kansas-Missouri border.

Kauffman Stadium, built over 40 years ago in 1973, was now one of the oldest ballparks still in use. Its most distinctive feature was a giant crown, visible from both the seats within the stadium and the highway outside, placed atop a Jumbotron abnormally designed with a unique vertical orientation. The ballpark sported the Royal's team color of blue, a hue easy to spot on the backs of the many empty chairs. Although it was "Value Monday" at the ballpark — everyone's favorite kind of Monday — the stadium still remained less than half full.

Even so, it was a decent showing for the Royals. The last year the Royals had finished with a winning record was 2003 and the last time they'd reached the playoffs was 1985. The Royals were not just trapped in a streak of bad luck. They were trapped in a decades-long cycle of abject failure. Kansas City was the second smallest metropolitan area to host an MLB team, garnering the Royals only 300,000 total "likes" on Facebook. This was the fourth-lowest of all teams, and millions behind teams like the Yankees and Red Sox. It was the downward spiral of professional sporting. There were not many fans so attendance remained low. Attendance was low so revenues were low. Revenues were low so payroll was low. Payroll was low so the team could not afford high-priced athletes. No high-priced athletes often meant no competitive team. No competitive team meant low attendance.

It was a franchise's worst nightmare. A handful of teams had managed to buck this trend — Billy Beane's 2003 Oakland Athletics and the 2008 Tampa Bay Rays among them — but these were exceptions to the rule in long-term analyses. While everything had to go wrong for big-market teams like the Yankees to badly miss the playoffs, the Royals needed everything to go right to make them. The tenets of Michael Lewis' *Moneyball* could certainly help a team rise in the standings every few years, but in the long haul, frugality was no match for teams that used both moneyball *and* money.

If nothing else, unpopular teams at least made for comfortable viewing. The seats in front of us were footrests, the seats beside us armrests. Despite having respectable seats just a few rows up from the foul line in left field, the nearest fans were several rows up. In games where there was minimal on-field action, we resorted out of habit to our nation's other favorite pastime: eavesdropping.

Of course, listening in on conversations could be as dull as the events on the field. It was hard enough to suffer through hearing about your own niece's piano recital. Someone else's niece thrust you into another circle of Hell. But after nineteen hours on the road, it genuinely felt like there were no remaining possible conversations left to have in the world. The people behind us became by default the most interesting people we knew.

"So yeah, Joe Carter is up in the box behind home plate right now. If you want, just let me know and we can go say hi," one stranger said to another.

"Oh wow, that would be awesome. I'll let you know."

We looked at each other. Interesting just got really interesting. An accomplished player with five All-Star appearances to his name, Carter was best known as one of only two players in the history of Major League Baseball to hit a walk-off World Series–winning home run. In other words, he was one of two people on earth to live the recurring dream of every boy to ever pick up a baseball bat.

Eric leaned over to Ben. "Who's Joe Carter?"

"Seriously? I thought we just had a moment."

"What are you talking about?"

"They mentioned Joe Carter and we looked at each other and had a moment. You don't even know who he is?"

"All I heard was 'up in the box behind home plate,' so I just assumed it was someone important."

Ben glared at Eric. Eric searched "Joe Carter" on his phone. "Oh," Eric said. "*That* Joe Carter."

"He's a legend."

"Then go meet him."

"How am I going to do that?"

Eric had an idea. The plot was more straightforward than conniving. It was built on the premise that someone who loved baseball might take kindly to our trip, and secondly that midwesterners were as kind as they claimed.

"I don't know," Ben stonewalled. "You just want me to start up a conversation with that stranger and then eventually ask to tag along with them?"

"It's not that complicated. Just tell them Joe Carter was one of your heroes growing up."

"But that's not true."

"Did you idolize him?"

"Well, sure."

"Then I promise you that counts. You have a chance to meet walking baseball history on your baseball extravaganza. All you have to do is ask."

Ben was hesitant. Some in life might have called him shy. Those who knew him less well might have called him mute. Having a conversation with a stranger was not his idea of a good time. On the other hand, having a conversation in binary code with an inanimate object was an epic time. The "What's the worst that could happen?" argument had been thrown his way countless times, but all Ben saw was the probability of getting rejected. Sure, he would love the chance to meet Joe Carter, but the last thing he ever wanted to do was make a fool of himself in front of people he would never see again in a city he might never visit again.

The man who knew Joe Carter rose from his seat and headed up the aisle.

"He's leaving!" Eric whispered. "Now or never."

"It'd be awkward."

"What would?"

"Just going up and introducing myself to him."

"It's called meeting new people. He's about to reach the top of the stairs."

"He'll think I'm crazy."

"Right now *I* think you're crazy."

"But you know me."

The man disappeared into the crowd.

Eric collapsed in his seat. His partner in wholesomely legal activity was hopeless. Nothing could penetrate his protective shell. If Joe Carter couldn't do it, Eric wasn't sure what could. Watching Ben glance nervously at the humans around him, he silently vowed to turn Ben into a human in his own right by the trip's end. He had his work cut out for him.

"I'm going to go get a hot dog, and a beer also," said Ben, standing from his seat.

Eric nodded. "Then everything will be okay."

Having now consumed ten beers and hot dogs in as many days, it was becoming increasingly indisputable that they were all the same. Almost every ballpark had a name for their signature sausage, be it the "Fenway Frank" or "Brewers Bratwurst." But they were all just a piece of processed meat in a bun. Though they varied slightly in size, shape and how badly they were undercooked, they were the tasteless opposite of a unique dining experience.

The beers were likewise disappointing. The default draft beer was always Budweiser or Miller Lite, leaving Ben to sample the same beer he'd sampled throughout college, except now at six to nine dollars a cup. If he wanted to try the local flavor, which he attempted as often as possible, it was nine to eleven.

Ben returned to his seat with hot dog and beer in hand.

"You know," Eric said, "I can't wait for the game tomorrow, when we'll get a hot dog and beer and Joe Carter again. They serve beer in Minnesota, don't they?"

Ben took a long and bitter sip.

Game Ten:
Minnesota Twins

We retreated to a motel on the outskirts of Kansas City after the 3–2 Royals win. With our pockets quickly emptying, we reserved one room with two beds for the three of us. We drew straws and Ben 2 emerged the victor, winning the right to sleep in his own queen-sized bed for almost eight continuous hours.

"All right, so we should leave here at 7 AM if we want enough time to go visit the Field of Dreams in Iowa on the way to Minnesota," Ben said, checking over the travel times online.

"And if we don't go to the Field of Dreams?" asked Ben 2, tucking himself away in his tightly made bed.

"What do you mean?"

"I think what he's trying to say," Eric explained, "is in the crazy universe where we *don't* take a massive detour to see a patch of dirt that was in a movie twenty years ago, how long would we get to sleep?"

"Well, I guess something like 11 AM. But we need to stop at the Field of Dreams. I mean, it's *the* Field of Dreams," Ben argued in the most uncompelling way possible.

Eric fluffed his pillow. "So it's a choice between a field of dreams and the chance to dream actual dreams." He turned to Ben 2. "I think this makes you the deciding vote."

Ben 2 crawled into his bed. "See you at eleven."

The kerfuffle in Denver had completely altered the dynamic of the trip. Before Denver, Ben stood as the ultimate captain with unquestionable authority. He was the master of the schedule. The car went where he wanted it. He'd planned detours to the Hall of Fame and Williamsport, slipping them by Eric's tired eyes before there was anything that could be done. If Ben declared that we needed to leave a hotel at four in the morning, Eric did not resist. He didn't want to be responsible for destroying the trip over a few minutes of lost sleep. Soon he'd relinquished all responsibility.

But with the time zone flub in Colorado, Ben had lost his high ground. He'd committed an error more detrimental to the trip than anything Eric would conceivably ever do. He was no longer the all-powerful overlord, and Eric let him know it.

"But it's our only chance to see the Field of Dreams!"

"I'll buy you the DVD," Eric offered. "Now go to sleep and wake up eight hours later of natural causes."

And so against Ben's wishes, the drive to Minnesota was relaxed and peaceful. The sub-seven hour trip made it the shortest in three days. The I-35 led us to one of the Twin Cities, and though it was never clear which, we found our way to Target Field.

The term "Minnesota Nice" is often used to describe the polite and reserved demeanor of people from Minnesota. While we found kind strangers in most parts of the country, "Minnesota Nice" let its presence be known on the Target Field Jumbotron. In all other stadiums, the camera's movement from fan to fan would evoke the same reaction. The lucky fan would be chatting with a friend or checking their phone. Then someone would tap them on their shoulder or shake them out of their innocent obliviousness, and they'd discover they'd made the big time. They would be stunned and overjoyed. And why wouldn't they be? They'd just won the honor of being shown to 20,000 strangers. It was like winning the lottery, but even better, because you didn't come away a millionaire. They'd jump out of their seat and flail their arms with abandon. It was a combination of "I can't believe I'm on the big screen!" and "I'm moving my arms in this weird pattern to confirm that's really me." It was how the first caveman must have felt upon seeing his own reflection: a mixture of amazement, confusion and concern that he'd gained ten pounds.

Before Minnesota, the lone exception to this tendency was Kansas City's Oblivious Cam, a fan favorite that timed how long a fan was shown on the Jumbotron without realizing the entire stadium was watching. The camera operator had found a young woman absorbed in the abyss of her cell phone as thousands of people cheered her on. She clocked in 27 seconds of total obliviousness before the camera had to cut away to the start of the next inning.

But Minnesota was a world of its own. Unlike the rest of the country where fans seeing fans induced fanfare,

Minnesotans expressed a complete lack of interest in having their likenesses displayed. The most they could summon up to the Jumbotron Gods was a polite wave or a nod of the head in the cameraman's general direction. It was the reaction normally reserved for when you passed someone you knew on the street but did not want to have to stop for a conversation. There were no jubilant body dances or painted chests to be had on the streets of Minnesota.

This was not to say that those present weren't enjoying themselves. The most excitable person in our section was a 60-year-old ticket attendant who guarded the bottom of the aisle.

When we went to grab food a few innings in, she stopped us in our tracks.

"You can't leave now! We have a runner on second! You're going to miss it!" She was somehow still gripped by the same enthusiasm that infected six-year-olds seeing their first game. It was hard to believe no cynicism had crept into her when it was her job to stand there as game after game was played. Most ballpark workers looked worn down by the daily screaming and cheering, content to check out of the game barring anything remarkable on the field. Witnessing the games was their job, and if baseball was America's pastime, resenting one's profession had to be a close second. When we returned to our seats, she was still jumping up and down.

"You missed it! Two more doubles! Two doubles in a row! We're winning now! Enjoy your hot dogs!"

We were seated at the top of the right field upper concourse, the worst seats that money could buy, but difficult viewing was more than made up for with quick viewing. The Twins' 3–2 victory over the Phillies was over in a mere two-and-a-half hours. We squeezed out every minute we could muster, standing by the exits in the ninth to get a jump on the crowd the moment the game ended.

"You can't be going already!" the attendant cried in disbelief. "Who knows what can happen next!"

"Baseball. More baseball," Eric promised.

"Well, let's hope so," Ben said, He had just checked the weather report for Chicago on his phone. "As long as lightning doesn't strike once."

Game Eleven: Chicago Cubs

It was time for our doubleheader. The afternoon would see us at Wrigley for the Cubs game and night would take us across town to the White Sox. The weather report warned of a 70% chance of rain, but the hour-by-hour forecast suggested nothing would be getting wet till after the night game's first pitch.

We retreated to Tony's apartment, our makeshift Chicago headquarters. Eric and Ben 2 immediately crashed on the first flat surfaces they could find. But Ben's neuroses were only enhanced by the mistake in Colorado. Instead of taking the few hours of sleep, he read through every weather report he could get his hands on, knowing full well there was nothing he could do about any of them. His sudden powerlessness to ensure the trip's safe completion was crippling. There were no remaining days in the month when the Cubs and White Sox both played together at home. There was no averting the 70% chance that water might fall from the sky. If either of the two games was postponed, the trip would come to a screeching halt.

He sprinted to the window when he awoke later that morning. It wasn't a particularly beautiful day in Chicago, but it didn't look like the makings of a torrential storm, so it was beautiful enough. There were a few clouds dotting the skyline, but nothing dark and stormy. He scrolled through the weather reports again. The evening still stood at 70%, but the afternoon was only at 40%. He would take it one game at a time, the only way he could. He took a deep breath. Everything was going to be all right, probably.

Before heading to Wrigley, we first had to update our roster. Chicago marked the end of Ben 2's five-day, 5,000-mile loop around the western half of the United States.

"You know," he decided, "I think I did this trip for the perfect amount of time. You guys are idiots."

He headed for the airport.

In his place arrived our newest companion, someone who would help embody the mythic romance of baseball and its American tradition, and would also serve as Eric's mother's eyes and ears: Eric's father. Phil had been deployed by Eric's mother to join us for the next four games, which encompassed another demanding stretch of driving. He was a casual fan of the game, a regular attendee of the little league circuit who'd taught Eric how to play the game in his backyard. He'd also been a master of the ill-advised road trip back in his day, hitchhiking back and forth across the country multiple times and surviving with enough tales to tell to fill hours of driving. He'd accepted the call to duty with little hesitation, looking forward to getting back on the road. On paper, nothing could possibly go wrong. It was father and son and baseball. And Ben.

With our new crew acquainted, we proceeded to Wrigley Field. Constructed in 1916, it was the second-oldest ballpark still in use, trailing only Fenway. And though Fenway had undergone major renovations in the last decade to accommodate the 21st century, the Cubs were the Amish of baseball. In 2013, about thirty years after the first Jumbotron displays started popping up around stadiums, the Cubs were in an all-out battle with local owners over installing their very first. They were the only team left in the country without one—and the advertising revenue that came with it.

The Cubs further lacked electronic screens of any kind, leaving spectators to squint at a manual scoreboard straight out of another era. The outfield was famous for its ivy-covered brick walls, which was either a dazzling aesthetic choice or the result of one lazy groundskeeper who declared, "Eh, looks all right to me. Tell them it's a tradition here."

The exterior of the stadium also lacked advertisements, giving the crowd nothing to watch but baseball. Ben, who had been tallying the number of ad displays above the field at every stadium, found the average to be an astonishingly high 39. Wrigley offered only 16 advertisements within the stadium. It was a jarring throwback compared to other ballparks.

Yet for all its old-time feel, it still boasted Ben's new-age idol Theo Epstein as its general manager.

"It's his second year with the team," Ben explained.

"I know."

"He's looking to break another curse."

"I know."

"They have him on a five-year contract."

Eric groaned. "Ben. You've told me this a thousand times. I know."

Our seats were far from the action, a fact that left Ben slightly stressed as he had invited his boss from the Jaguars to attend the game. We were also joined by our college friend Ari, who was soon to join the Israeli military, but in the meantime could spend a day like a prototypical American. Ben watched nervously as his boss's eyes stayed glued to his phone, ignoring the events on the field.

At last he looked up from the device.

"So I've been emailing back and forth with the Cubs' front office," Tony said. "I think I may go up to their box and talk analytics."

"You're going up to meet with the analytics team?" Ben squealed. It was the only time in history that question had been spoken enthusiastically.

"Yeah, I think after the next half inning."

"To meet . . . Theo? Theo Epstein, will he be there?"

"Yeah, I just got an email from one of his guys."

Ben's puppy dog eyes came out in full force.

"I'll see what I can do," Tony said. "No promises."

The possibility of meeting Theo face-to-face left Ben speechless. Tony soon went up to the box while Ben remained in the bleachers, calculating the odds he'd be able to follow him up. Epstein may have never hit a home run to win a World Series like Joe Carter, but to Ben, that was all the more admirable. He'd been able to win a World Series without ever picking up a bat.

The game proceeded in a low-scoring fashion, with both the Cubs and Reds struggling to produce any runs. Ben tried to enjoy the game, but it was no use. He couldn't keep his eyes off his phone, desperately waiting for news from Tony. Surely he would be telling Theo about the road trip. But with every passing inning, Ben knew the odds were dwindling. His phone didn't make a peep.

The seventh-inning stretch rolled around. The Wrigley crowd, known for their organ-led renditions of baseball's anthem, rose to their feet and started singing.

"Take me out to the ball game, take me out with the crowd." Ben joined in with the crowd, singing it like a dirge. *"Buy me some peanuts and Cracker Jack…"*

He felt his phone vibrate in his pocket. His hand shot down and he thrust it out. A text from Tony: "Come up. Suite number forty-four."

It was happening. He grabbed Eric and lugged him out of his seat. Ari followed. Ben rushed through the concrete tunnels as though in a dream, a dream that he had actually had. He sprinted up the ramps to the suite level like a knight determined to rescue his princess, or at least shake her hand and tell her how much he looked up to her as a kid.

But like any fairy tale, there were obstacles. A collection of ticket attendants in a security booth stood guard over the suites' entrance, ensuring drunk fans couldn't sneak into booths for a better view or find their team's upper management to complain.

"Hello. Tickets please," the attendant said.

"We don't have tickets," said Ben out of breath, "We were invited up to one of the suites."

"Okay, which one?"

"Number forty-four."

The attendant's eyebrows rose in unison. She shared a skeptical glance with her coworker. "Who exactly are you here to see?"

"Theo. Theo Epstein."

"You're here to see Theo? Our team's president?"

Eric nodded. "Yep. That's the one."

She tried not to laugh. "I'm afraid you're going to have to wait for someone to come let you in."

"Of course," Ben said understandingly. "I bet you get a lot of crazy fans trying to sneak into his box."

"Exactly."

"Well, that's not us. We're totally legitimate."

"Right."

It occurred to Ben then that we were three college-aged guys with no credentials requesting to walk into the most exclusive suite in the most famous ballpark in the nation. It further occurred to him that the odds of getting past the attendant were not looking so good.

He texted Tony again and again, receiving no response.

"He's probably having too much of a good time with Theo to bother checking his phone," Ben assured the attendant.

She nodded sympathetically.

After exactly seven minutes, all of which Ben counted, Tony appeared in the corridor.

"They're with me," he told the attendant. She eyed us, surprised that we weren't entirely out of our minds. She let us pass.

And in we walked through the glorious door to suite number 44. Ben saw him immediately. Toward the back of the box, standing over a computer opened to Excel. Theo Epstein in the flesh. He watched one of his own players strike out on the diamond below and shook his head.

"He's hurting against righties lately," said one of Epstein's deputies. Ben was more transfixed by the men leering into their computer screens than any of the men on the field.

Theo turned around and saw the diminutive man with awestruck eyes staring his way, alongside the tall man with eyes staring at a refrigerated case of bottled water.

"You must be the two guys on the road trip," Theo said, extending his arm to Ben.

"Uh, yes," Ben stammered after processing that Theo's arm was extending for him to shake. "This is Day Twelve. It's beautiful here at Wrigley."

What a stupid thing to say, Ben thought. *Everyone probably tells Theo that Wrigley is beautiful. It's not even his job to make it beautiful, although I'm sure he could figure out the best way to do that if he wanted to. Why didn't I tell him about the rest of the trip, or the doubleheader, or a stat study I've run in the past. I've ruined it. He'll think I like gardening.*

Theo leaned back against a table covered in laptops running spreadsheets full of data. "Well, I've got some bad news for you two," he said. "The White Sox game tonight was just canceled."

Other than the information that all humans must eventually die, it was the worst news Ben had ever received. He had never felt so confused and conflicted, because it was also delivered by his favorite person ever.

Unbeknownst to us, the forecast warning of a chance of rain had been upgraded to "Storm of the Century." Cancellations were usually a game-time decision. Canceling a game over four hours before it was scheduled to begin was only done when the weather was projected to turn biblical.

Even if the city of Chicago survived the storm, our trip would be destroyed.

For a man short on emotion, Ben now had too much running through him. He looked at Eric, tragically, but Eric still thought it was just a joke that Tony had put Theo up to. The sky outside was clear. Nothing was suggestive of an impending doomsday. Ben did his best to remain cool, a task made more difficult by the fact that you had to be cool in order to remain cool.

"The trip sounded like fun though," Theo said, already discussing it in the past tense. "I'm assuming doing it in thirty days is hopeless now that the White Sox are canceled?"

"We'll rerun the algorithm," Ben muttered.

Theo cracked up. "Rerun the algorithm," he repeated.

The truth was that the algorithm would take hours to rerun. By the time we got back to Tony's apartment, accessed Ben's computer, reconfigured the algorithm and let it run to completion, we'd have already blown our chance to set off for the next necessary game. Not even the algorithm could save us now.

Ben stared ahead onto the field, entirely unable to appreciate the view from the luxury suite behind home plate. With every at bat someone in the box would recite a different stat line for everyone to process. They cheered their team on like everyone else, but they were also lost within the numbers on their screens. It was Ben's dream among the broken pieces of his other one.

Eric leaned over to Ben and whispered in his ear. "So wait. That *wasn't* a joke?"

Ben pointed to a TV screen that flashed a weather update. "It's over."

Eric scoffed. "Screw that. I didn't waste all this time just to fail. As Yogi Berra once said, it's not over till it's over."

"But it's over," Ben said.

"But not until it's over," Eric corrected. He pulled out his phone and started looking up ways to fix the schedule.

"It's not possible," Ben droned. "Remember how lucky we were after Denver? That's when we still had an off day to burn."

"What about San Francisco and Oakland? Could we pull off a doubleheader there?"

"No. Impossible. Already checked."

"The LA teams."

"Nope."

"Texas?"

"Not even close. There's no way we can finish by the Mets game on the thirtieth. To hit all thirty teams would take until July first."

Eric scoffed, unconvinced. "There must be a way we can still finish in thirty days."

Ben looked on without flinching. "I'm telling you. It's hopeless. We'll have to go to a game on July first." He spun around.

"What is it?"

"Wait a minute. July first. Who plays on July first?"

Eric pulled up the schedule. "Giants in Cincinnati at 7 PM, Milwaukee at Nationals at 7:05 PM, Tigers at Blue Jays at 1:07 PM, San Diego at—"

"That's it! Are you thinking what I'm thinking?"

"Ben, I don't think there's been a moment in my life when I've been thinking what you're thinking."

"We started the trip on June first at 7:05 PM when Phil Hughes threw out the first pitch at Yankee Stadium."

"And that helps us how . . . ?"

"That pitch did not occur on Day One. It happened— on Day Zero."

"Oh god."

"It happened on Day Zero! We forgot about Day Zero! By the time we saw the end of the second game of the trip in Pittsburgh less than 24 hours had eclipsed. June thirtieth isn't thirty days after June first. It's only twenty-nine."

"So you're saying—"

"Thirty days after the first pitch at Yankee Stadium at 7:05 PM on June first—thirty twenty-four-hour periods— is 7:05 PM on July first. We can still complete the trip in thirty days!"

Eric shrugged. "What is time but semantics, anyway?"

"Thirty days is 720 hours. And 720 hours after the first pitch of our first game, the Toronto game will be done. Is that the only day game on July first?"

"Yeah. So I guess we have to go to Toronto then?"

"Correct! I can't believe we forgot there was no Day Zero!"

"I know, right? Unbelievable. Who forgets about Day Zero."

Ben hunkered down at a table. Now that he'd remembered Day Zero, he'd completely forgotten about his idol standing five feet away. "Now we just need a way to sub in the White Sox game for the Toronto game. Then it's once again possible."

Our schedule was far from rescued. Although the removed Toronto game left us with a free day on the 19th, we had to figure out a way to accommodate adding in another stop to Chicago. The White Sox were out of town until the 25th and we'd already visited all the other ballparks in the area, so we'd have to reconfigure multiple games to make the schedule work.

We stood in the back of the room checking and rechecking team schedules and driving times. Theo and his crew continued to spit out their numbers and run analyses on the game at hand, a world away from Ben. Eric's father had wandered up to the booth after finishing a business call, but Eric barely took a moment to register this fact and introduce him to the executives in the room. It was now or never to resurrect the trip. In a room full of computers churning through algorithms, we were scribbling out schedules on used napkins.

Finally, Eric had a breakthrough.

"Atlanta. We can reach Atlanta on the nineteenth when they're at home. That's in between Cincinnati and St. Louis, easily within reach by our standards."

"Yes! We can get there. And Atlanta was originally scheduled for the twenty-ninth, when the White Sox will be back home. So on the twenty-ninth we can come back here and at long last cross off Chicago."

"The twenty-ninth is an afternoon game," Eric confirmed. "Do the times pan out?"

"Well, if the Houston game on the twenty-eighth goes three-and-a-half hours, we'll have sixteen hours and thirty minutes to make the drive. How long is that drive?"

"Google Maps is telling me sixteen hours and twenty-five minutes."

"I repeat," Ben said. "Can we make that drive?"

"Do we have a choice?"

Ben shook his head.

"Then we will make that drive. We'll just have to make sure we're well rested. We won't have a minute to break."

Ben did not bother to remind Eric that resting beforehand would not be an option. The two days before that trip now also featured drives of sixteen hours in length, thanks to the fact we had slept through the game in Colorado. Eric would realize the scheduling nightmare soon enough and be angry with Ben for not telling him, but for the moment, hope was in the stormy Chicago air. It was a familiar pattern in our relationship: Ben would offer Eric the opportunity to do something while brushing over the uglier details, Eric would not fully consider the ramifications and commitment necessary before saying yes, and then Eric would feel immediate regret once he realized what he had signed up for. It was how Ben had talked Eric

into coming on the trip in the first place, and now it was
how he talked him into retracing our steps thousands of
miles in order to save it.

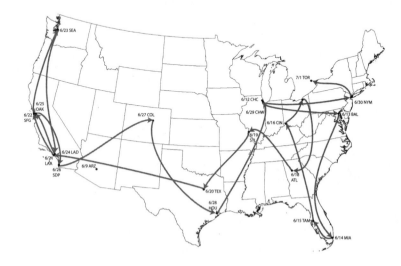

Ben turned his attention back to the baseball game,
only to see outfielder Alfonso Soriano hit a weak grounder
in the bottom of the ninth to seal a one-run loss for the Cubs.
Theo threw his arms up in the air, the gentlemen's version
of a curse, and immediately began packing up his laptop.
Ben approached Theo for one last time.

"Hey, thanks for inviting us up to the box. We sort
of reran the algorithm and it looks like we might finish in
thirty days still."

"Well, good luck. Even if you finish in thirty-one, I still
think it's a great idea," Theo said, making everything Ben
had worked for in life okay again.

"Thanks, Theo."

"Rerun the algorithm, that's great," Theo laughed to himself again. Ben did not understand why he found it so funny.

We overheard a tour guide on the streets of Chicago explain that its standing as "The Windy City" came not from the occasional billowing gust, but rather from all the hot air blowing out of its politicians. Perhaps. But hot air rose and this wind could have knocked a politician down.

The weather stations were declaring the incoming storm to be "historic." It was the first time on the trip that history failed to excite at least one of us. Huddled back in Tony's apartment, we watched from skyscraping windows as rain assaulted the streets below. In the span of two hours the blank blue sky had given way to a concentrated Apocalypse, with no sight of Heaven to mount an escape. The White Sox's U.S. Cellular Field looked less inclined to hold a ballgame than to blow off the face of the earth. There'd been a one in three chance we'd suffer a rainout, but Ben had neglected to calculate the odds of enduring the End of Days.

"Where are we supposed to be headed next?" Phil asked.

"Baltimore."

"The storm's headed east."

"Baltimore's east," Ben said.

Eric nodded, constantly impressed by Ben's unmatched ability to think aloud. He looked up Baltimore's weather report. "Ninety percent chance of rain tomorrow."

"But what does that even *mean*? It will rain ninety percent of the day? There's a ninety percent chance it will rain once?"

"Nine out of ten raindrops will fall from their clouds."

"Really?"

"Not at all."

We sat down at the window. Ben studied the schedule on his computer. "So we shifted Toronto to July first, replaced it with Atlanta and put Chicago in Atlanta's place. But it's all pointless if Baltimore rains out! The schedule was hypothetically able to support one botched game. And we already botched that game with Colorado. And the Day Zero Paradigm gave us one more get-out-of-jail-free card. So we can afford losing the White Sox today—but just barely. There's officially no wiggle room left. One more screwup and it really is over. We've reached our limit."

"So if we show up in Baltimore and it's a rainout—"

"We lose."

Eric gave Ben a pat on the back. "We lose with friends."

"We lose," Ben clarified.

"What are the odds Baltimore *is* a rainout? Even for games where it rains, only a fraction are actually rainouts."

"I don't know."

"What are the chances a ninety percent chance of rain converts to a game-day rainout?"

"I don't know."

"Is there an alternate route we could take avoiding Baltimore?"

"I don't know!"

Ben stood and walked away from the window. He approached Tony's liquor cabinet, remembered he was on a 30-day driving expedition and sat back down.

"I don't know these things," Ben said.

Eric laughed, which remained the clearest possible sign that the trip was on the verge of failure. "Calm down, bud. Can you rerun the algorithm?"

"No. It'd take too long. It's already five o'clock. We're running out of hours to drive to Baltimore. I wouldn't know if there was another route till we'd already been on the road for four or five hours, and by then it'd be too late to reroute to anywhere else."

"No parks within a stone's throw of Baltimore we could hit up?"

"We already covered the Northeast. All that's left up there is the Mets, and it's a ninety percent chance of rain in New York also."

"So there's nothing you and your computer can do?"

"It's hopeless," Ben declared.

Eric sighed and grabbed a pencil and paper. "All right. I'll do it then."

He wrote out the remaining schedule down the length of the page, factoring in the Toronto-Atlanta-Chicago rotation.

"There are too many permutations," Ben said, peeking over his shoulder. "Change one game and you'll have to change five. It's why we needed an algorithm."

"False," Eric said in Ben-speak. "The computer has to go through every permutation. I get to cheat."

He circled the block of games in California and Washington.

"No matter what we do anywhere else, we have to hit California all at once. You said last week that this was the only remaining cluster of days when all the California teams were home."

We removed the California stint, shrinking the editing floor to the rest of the country.

"And obviously, our new Colorado game is staying on the twenty-seventh, since we can only get there quickly enough from California. But we have options after Colorado." Eric sorted through the daily schedules as Ben paced the room. "What if we went to the White Sox on the twenty-eighth instead? Does Baltimore have a game on the twenty-ninth?"

Ben looked up the Orioles' schedule. "They do. 7:05 PM."

"Baltimore to New York is an easy drive, so the Mets stay the thirtieth, and Toronto is the only game on July first, so that solves that problem."

He crossed out the determined games, leaving the remaining assortment:

June 13: ?????
June 14: Miami Marlins, 7:10 PM
June 15: Tampa Bay Rays, 4:10 PM
June 16: Cincinnati Reds, 1:10 PM
June 17: Cleveland Indians, 7:05 PM
June 18: Atlanta Braves, 7:07 PM
June 19: St. Louis Cardinals, 8:15 PM
June 20: Texas Rangers, 2:05 PM
?????: Houston

"Pull up tomorrow's schedule. Which of these teams are home?"

Ben did so. "Not pretty. Just Tampa Bay and Texas."

"How far is the drive from Chicago to Tampa?"

"Seventeen hours. Not possible."

"Chicago to Texas?"

"Fourteen. And a half."

"Possible. How long from Dallas to Miami?"

"Texas to Miami just under twenty. Not possible. We have to get to the Florida teams before the sixteenth. They both leave town after."

"How long from Dallas to Tampa then?"

"Seventeen."

"Possible."

"Barely. It'd be seventeen in seventeen."

"Possible's possible. We flip Miami and Tampa. Atlanta had a game on the sixteenth and Cincinnati and Cleveland were just starting series. We bump Atlanta in front of them and we're done."

"We need to go to Houston."

"What day did we leave open?"

"The twentieth. When we were going to see the Rangers."

"Perfect. Does Houston have a home game?"

Ben checked their schedule. He shook his head.

"No?"

"No, yes. Yes they do. I can't believe that actually worked."

Eric folded the paper in half and handed it over. "You might be the human algorithm maker, but you shall hereby call me the Human Algorithm."

Ben compared the two schedules. He'd spent so long with the original version engrained into his mind that the slightest aberration was unsettling. The new version changed so many games it was like a different trip altogether. And while it did occur to him that it *literally* was a different trip altogether, he still felt a loving intimacy toward the original schedule. The original schedule was supposed to be the most efficient of the more than 265 'nonillion' possible routes. Eric had reoriented a smaller ten-game chunk of the schedule with such ease—it was simply unfair, unearned. Ben had put so much time and energy into his algorithm that losing its original output had the psychological effect of a physical loss. Sure, it had endured a slight altering with the Colorado fiasco, but that was his own doing. It wasn't the algorithm's fault. And even with the potential Toronto-Atlanta-Chicago swap, the vast majority of the algorithm's product remained intact.

In Ben's eyes, the addition of the Day Zero Paradigm only further glorified the mathematical insanity the algorithm manufactured. Only getting through 11 games of its deliberate schedule was like only getting to 11th base with a high school girlfriend and knowing you would never be destined to make it to all 30.

He honed in on the Dallas-Tampa Bay drive of the new schedule.

"A seventeen-hour drive in seventeen hours—we could just be delaying the inevitable. Throw in gas stops and we'd have to have a perfect drive. No traffic, no tickets, no time to spare."

"Won't be easy, but it's doable. We've picked up time on the last couple drives. A half hour here, forty-five minutes there. It would be a pain but there's no reason it's not feasible. Seventeen hours in seventeen hours makes a lot more theoretical sense than thirty games in thirty days."

"But is its success more likely than the odds we avoid a rainout in Baltimore? Because if Baltimore doesn't rain out, it'd be smooth sailing to Florida."

"So that's the choice. Do we take the weather and Baltimore or time and Texas?"

Ben took another long look at the liquor cabinet. "It all comes down to this. A complete, flip-a-coin guess."

Phil refilled a glass of water. "Let me get this straight. We're getting in our car in Illinois in fifteen minutes to drive through the night, and you can flip a coin to decide whether we go to Texas or Maryland?"

"Exactly," we both said at once.

Phil took an exhausted sip. "I don't know about this whole baseball trip."

We stared again at the schedules.

"Ninety percent chance of rain isn't one hundred percent."

"It was only sixty percent earlier in the day."

"It's hurricane season in Florida. The roads could be a mess."

"The roads *will* be a mess for the next three states out of Chicago. Just look outside."

"We could get a flat tire on the way to Tampa."

"We could get a flat tire on the way to anywhere."

"You can't trust the weather."

"You can't trust the road."

Outside, the rain fell harder.

"So?" Eric asked at last. "We both know how this plays out. You'll never forgive me if I decide and guess wrong. So which will it be?"

Ben pulled up a weather site one more time. The headline, in capital letters, screamed across the pages: "STORM COULD FLOOD MIDWEST TONIGHT."

"We'll drive to Texas," Ben said.

Eric nodded. "We'll leave in ten. Double-check the new schedule to make sure we didn't flub a time zone."

Eric and Phil headed for bathrooms to wash up. Ben went through the games one by one, comparing our notes with each team's season calendar.

When Eric returned, Ben was standing at his computer with his hands half raised in the air.

"What is it?"

"Baltimore got selected as the Sunday night game of the week on the thirtieth!"

"Translation?"

"They now play at 8:10 on the thirtieth. The Mets game on the thirtieth is at 1:10. It's a three-hour, twenty-minute drive from Citi Field to Camden Yards. If the Mets game didn't go longer than average and we didn't hit traffic, we could get there. Hypothetically."

"A New York-Baltimore doubleheader?"

"Hypothetically."

Eric rubbed his eyes and sat back down.

"Only if we headed to Baltimore tomorrow and it rained out. It'd come down to the minute, but it's a semblance of an insurance policy on tomorrow's game. We go to Baltimore, we have two chances. We go to Texas, we have only one."

"And then we'd head straight up to Toronto after Baltimore?"

"Three parks in the span of twenty-four hours."

"So. Baltimore?"

"So Baltimore."

Ben closed his computer. Eric stuffed his pencil back into his pocket.

Phil made his way back to the kitchen. He slapped a palm on the counter. "Let's hit the road. Texas, here we come."

"Maryland."

"What happened?"

"Math," Ben said.

"Luck," Eric said.

Phil shrugged. "Maryland, here we come."

Part IV

A Game Played By Nine Men and Nine Dads Doing Laundry

Game Twelve:
Baltimore Orioles

We had a long way to go if we were going to collect every animal for Noah's Ark. After a few hours on the road, we'd tallied two deer, two rabbits, two cats and two rodents, but still lacked some of the more extravagant creatures. And there was the problem of them all being dead. We also needed an ark, and Noah.

We had a flood though.

It's difficult to appropriate the exact moment a storm becomes "historic" from the inside of an air-conditioned sedan. There are telltale signs suggestive of something special—tires skidding on straight roads, wipers washing away an ocean a minute, roadkill lined up with eerily predictable spacing. And then the cars in front of you slow down, and the cars behind you stop, and the semitrucks roll over in ditches and play dead.

Eric was born and raised a California boy, and though he'd never stepped foot on a surfboard, his native habitat was still 72 degrees Fahrenheit. When it was 71 out, it was cold. When it was 73 out, it was probably still winter. It rained once or twice a season and sometimes school was canceled because the gutters would flood and the parking lot would get wet. One time it snowed, but that was in 1906.

Hurricanes were a phenomenon that happened on TV, blizzards a plot device in movies about Arctic exploration and thunderstorms a unit in seventh-grade science class. One morning in high school a bolt of lightning struck Eric's home and he assumed a bomb had gone off. At the time, a bomb seemed much more plausible.

The main natural disasters in his natural habitat were earthquakes. A few would hit every year, springing him out of bed in the middle of the night and sending his troop of jockey bobbleheads into action. They were principally dangerous for their suddenness, all but impossible to predict.

But a storm you could see coming. The clouds showed up, then the rain, then the lightning, then the thunder. It was incrementally orchestrated and wholesomely possible to predict. Weathermen never got all the details right, but none ever walked across a green screen to declare "There will be no storm today!" as a torrential downpour brewed outside.

So as Illinois became Indiana and Indiana turned to Ohio, Eric began to question the intelligence of driving into a death trap. He saw Ben sitting silently in the passenger's seat, and in the rearview mirror he saw his father dozing in and out of consciousness. He could see nothing else. The road in front of him was completely obscured. The side and rear windows were not even in the conversation. The world outside was a watercolor painting, a splotchy and meaningless mess. It was a four-lane divided highway, though he wasn't sure where any of the lanes was hiding.

"So, Baltimore," Eric said.

He swerved around what might have been an unidentified bloodied mass in what might have been the middle of the road.

"I can't find the hood of the car."

"Trust that it's in front you," Ben said. "We can ride this out. We still have eight hours ahead of us. We'd be tempting fate if we stopped now."

"It's entirely possible I'm driving through a cornfield right now, and you call *stopping* tempting fate?"

"We have a few hours to stop at a motel, but if the weather keeps up we can't risk getting stalled by road closures."

Eric continued on at 30 miles an hour under the speed limit. High beams lined themselves up on the side of the road, and it could be inferred that there were probably cars attached to them.

Then somehow the rain figured out how to pour harder yet. There was so much rain it became difficult to see the rain.

"Ben," Eric said.

"Now what?"

"At any moment, I could kill us all."

"So nothing new."

He caught sight of the white line on the side of the road splitting in two. He veered right.

Ben gripped the armrest. "What are you doing?"

"I think I'm taking an exit ramp."

"We'll never find the highway again."

"That's how you know it's time to get off the highway."

We pulled into a dimly lit town, confirmed by the presence of buildings.

"There has to be a motel somewhere around here."

After lapping a few blocks, we found one. We parked in the attached lot and ran for cover.

"One room, please."

The manager processed two key cards. "You guys just missed the evacuation."

"Evacuation for what?"

"The tornado."

"The tornado?"

"A town over. We're probably safe now."

"Probably?"

"You never know with tornadoes."

Guaranteed to dream nothing but happy dreams, we ventured to our room and pretended to fall asleep.

We arose four hours later to discover wet clouds and wet ground but no wetness in between. The storm had finally passed. We found our car in the parking lot, pleased to see it had not floated away.

It rained on and off for the remaining eight hours to Baltimore, and we in turn oscillated between being awed by our good fortune and being certain we were doomed.

We hit Baltimore with two hours to spare amidst a lazy drizzle.

"Nap in the car?" Ben suggested.

"But we're in Baltimore," Phil said.

"Is it not safe?"

Phil began to understand what his son had been putting up with for two weeks. "You can't come to Baltimore and not go out for soft-shell crabs."

We found a restaurant near the docks by Camden Yards, and Phil treated us to our first meal of the trip that did not include a hot dog or a drive-thru on the side of the road.

"I think your dad thinks we're crazy," Ben confided to Eric as we walked to the ballpark.

Eric elected not to justify that with a response.

Camden Yards was the poster child for a stadium mixing new with old, built at the turn of the 1990s to resemble the parks of a generation past. Constructed atop what used to be the Baltimore & Ohio Railroad rail yard, the station's redbrick warehouse was incorporated into the stadium's design to give the park a rustic bygone feel.

The modern spin on the historic permeated the park's traditions as well. A sign in a men's restroom reminded urinators that Baltimore was the birthplace of the national anthem, the lyrics written by Francis Scott Key after witnessing a bombardment in the Chesapeake Bay during the War of 1812. This fact was not lost to fans, who shouted a victorious Orioles' "O!" when the anthem asked leading questions like "O say can you see" and "O say does that star-spangled banner yet wave" that made clear America's baseball allegiance.

Watching the words of the anthem cross a Jumbotron for the 13th consecutive day, we both simultaneously took pause as the last line was displayed: "O'er the land of the free and the home of the brave?"

"It's a question," Eric said. "I never thought about it that way. One big question."

"What's it asking exactly?"

This question seemed treasonous on the surface, but it was deceptively difficult to provide a one-sentence response to the question of what the anthem was questioning. The first words that came to mind were those straight out of an American propaganda film—bravery, honor, freedom, liberty, bravery, star spangles, freedom. But what *exactly* did the anthem ask? And why did half the parks end the nation's song on a period, instead of a question mark?

We stood there, caps still over our hearts, dutifully embarrassed as we recited the anthem's words back to ourselves.

"So at last twilight, we saw the flag flying. Then there was battle. Now does that flag still fly?"

"Yes."

"Yes, that's the accurate summary, or yes, the flag still flies?"

America being America, we'd known the anthem by heart before we knew the alphabet. And everyone knew what the anthem was *about*, the sort of way all high schoolers knew that *The Catcher in the Rye* was about phoniness. The anthem was about America. And about the War of 1812. But what was it actually saying? After hearing it ten, a hundred, a thousand times at every sporting event, political gathering and public endeavor that supported loudspeakers, it was just words. Words that conveyed faith and respect in the United

States of America, and were then immediately followed by "Play ball!" The anthem before a sports contest was like grace said before a meal, a "Thank you, America, for giving us the freedom and opportunity to partake in this trivial and comparatively inconsequential game, Amen. Now let's go throw things at each other."

And so, actually pondering the precise placement of the precise words for the first time in a long time, it struck us as strange and beautiful that our country's anthem was a question, not telling, but simply asking the citizen if the brave were still free. It was a call begging for a response. In a moment of renewed patriotism, we were impressed by our own anthem, reminded again that America was pretty cool.

All of which made us feel an enhanced sense of idiocy when a nearby plaque revealed that the anthem in fact had three more verses, each of which answered the first verse's question and clearly delineated that the flag indeed still flew. Aside from expediency, we weren't sure why only the first verse was sung, but there was nothing more we would have loved to see than 40,000 fans cheer the line "O'er the land of the free and the home of the brave" only for the singer to continue on for another four minutes in what would probably be taken for heresy.

So it was nice to clear that up.

And long story short, that's when the game started.

Short story long, nine innings later, it was still not ready to end. A two-run seventh by Ben's Red Sox knotted the game at four, a tie that carried into extra innings. Still underslept from our tornado dreams the night before, we were not in the mood to watch our minimal downtime for the coming night dwindle away. The upcoming drive to Miami would take a solid sixteen hours, offering a generous three-hour rest if the Baltimore game ended in a timely manner. The tenth inning was not so timely, and the eleventh even less. By the twelfth inning we began to wonder if we'd suffered a fate even worse than a rainout. With the game dovetailing into extra innings, it could be the worst of both worlds — no downtime off the road as well as the possibility of driving all the way to Florida for naught. It would take an unwieldy amount of extra innings for us to reach that point, but crazier things had happened that very day in the MLB. A Cincinnati-Cubs game stretched out to 14 innings, and a Yankees-Oakland marathon ballooned to 18. Games like those were schedule killers, and though they didn't tend to happen every day, lately they were becoming implausibly regular. In the last week alone, a Toronto-Texas game lasted 18 and a Mets-Marlins whiff-fest made it all the way to 20, enough to become the longest game in three years. They all fell short of the longest in major league history, a 1920 game between the Brooklyn Robins and the Boston Braves that dragged on a mind-numbing 26 innings. And even that was nothing compared to a Triple-A game starring a young Cal Ripken that lasted 33. But the recent string of extra-extra innings weren't far behind. There was indeed something in the water this month, and to make matters worse, it tended to come in the form of rain.

The lone consolation for extra innings was progressively better seats. While park attendants stood with their shoulders high and eyes wide open at the beginning of games, their patrolling grew more relaxed as the innings passed. Ben, reverent of the ballpark experience to the bitter end, was always hesitant to attempt any seat hopping, gripped by a crippling fear of disrespecting unnamed baseball deities. We ritualistically found our proper seats at the start of every game, but Eric's eyes would begin to wander before the first inning gave way. In a minimum-security prison where the only alternative was watching baseball, a quest for better seats helped to pass the time. Some days he set his sights on a simple improvement—a little shade or a less obstructed view. The attendants in the upper echelons were less likely to put up a fight, usually letting you slip by without checking your ticket.

The lower levels were more of an art form, requiring a balanced combination of bravado and good timing. Most lower sections were in the practice of checking all tickets indiscriminately. But some low-grade scouting could often sniff out more vulnerable sections, where attendants pretended to recognize the faces of the fans belonging in the section over which they stood guard. With decent reliability, simply nodding and smiling as you strutted passed them— pretending that *you* remembered *them*—was enough to win you a $50 seat upgrade. The sections nearer home plate were a little more discerning, tending to require a confident smile aided by arms full of baseball paraphernalia that prevented you from reaching for your ticket. A tilted head and a knowing look of "You're not really going to make me put down this hot dog and take off my foam finger to find a measly scrap of paper, are you?" tended to do the trick.

The ultimate upgrade—seats on the bottom level, directly behind home plate—necessitated the perfect storm of inconveniences. Timing your walk down the aisle to coincide with wealthy-looking middle-aged couples that definitely did have legitimate tickets was never a bad idea. By walking close behind and nodding lovingly toward your brand-new mother and father as the attendant watched you pass, you could head on down to the very front rows and enjoy a family outing.

But slipping by the attendant was only half the battle. There was still the matter of selecting two seats that would not stir up any trouble. A keen eye could scan the section from halfway down the entrance aisle and pick out unoccupied seats. If possible, it was best to find a string of four or more seats showing no signs of life, as it was unlikely so many consecutive people who picked up after themselves were temporarily displaced. Ideally, you could find a pair that produced no one sitting directly next to, in front of or behind you, limiting the chances of an aggrieved fan complaining to the attendant. And finally, though it was tempting to nab two aisle seats for the sake of expediency, it was the last place you wanted to sit, a rookie mistake. Aisle seats screamed of opportunists, kids who snuck past the security post and plopped down in the first seats they could find. But no one questioned the authority of two guys who had the gall to make eleven people rise to their feet so they could reach their seats in the middle of the row.

If it were up to Ben, we'd have never moved anywhere, sitting tight in the seats we'd purchased. He was always afraid of being caught, a fear Eric considered to be irrational since the worst possible thing that could happen was winding up back where we started. No one was ever kicked out of a park for hijacking empty seats. Yet Ben could never get comfortable in seats that weren't ours, his chin glued to his shoulder as he endlessly sensed someone was on to us. Almost no one ever was. That night we were caught red-handed a few times in seats that constituted $200 upgrades, and Ben would mutter under his breath and swear "I told you so," and Eric would shrug and lead us into a section two aisles over.

In extra-inning games, however, there wasn't even a thrill. The end of every half inning incited a mass exodus, sending thousands of fans shuffling for the exits. Slinking down toward better seats became an inherent aspect of the ordeal. Attendants working overtime grew more concerned with getting home for bedtime than keeping devoted fans from a better view.

As the Baltimore game plodded along into the night, a distinct pattern emerged in the fan migrations out of the park. In the early innings, it was possible that fans came for the quintessential baseball experience, the peanuts and the Cracker Jack and the hecklers and the seventh-inning stretch. But by the 13th inning, fans — especially those who had sobered up since their beers were cut off in the seventh — were there for one thing and one thing only. They wanted to see their team win. Each time the Red Sox failed to score a run at the plate, masses of fans dressed in red flooded out of the stands. When the Orioles fared no better in the bottom half of an inning, a sea of orange filled the aisles. The concessions stands were closed and the Jumbotron was out of games. There was nothing left to do at the ballpark but win or lose. And no one was going to stay up late on a workday to suffer through a loss.

By the time MLB-leading home run slugger Chris Davis drove in a run in the bottom of the 13th, the crowd was so sparse we could have had our choice of seats. And with time growing shorter and our drive feeling longer, we'd selected what we considered to be the best seats in the house. The ones closest to the exit.

Game Thirteen:
Miami Marlins

With the clouds parting over Baltimore, things were finally looking up and our eyes could now look elsewhere. With Baltimore free of rain and rainout, we wouldn't need to rely on the dubious Mets-Orioles-Blue Jays trifecta at the end of the month. It had been improbable at best, a Hail Mary in a sport that didn't have one. Crossing Baltimore off the list on Day 13 instead of Day 30 bolstered our chances of completing the trip considerably. We now had before us a linear procession of games—there would be no more grandiose switching or swapping of schedules. Minor tweaks such as a Cleveland-Cincinnati flip-flop were possible, but would not have any overwhelming ramifications on the overall schedule. Our itinerary was now more or less set. The road we would travel, on the other hand, was anything but linear. Already lacking much visual logic from the get-go, the manual alterations we had to make looked utterly senseless when drawn out. From the algorithm's perspective, they were. Our corrected schedule would have never been proposed by the algorithm, as it now violated the driving-to-rest ratio it had been instructed to compute as sacred. As Ben 2 once put it, our route looked like what would happen if a drunk airplane decided to go on a baseball bender. But now that we'd been on the road for two weeks, we knew that a 16-hour drive in 18 hours was not desirable, but doable, and another one the following day less desirable, and perhaps less doable, but doable still. Doable, at least, if there were three of us in the car. A two-man rotation was all but impossible to uphold over long stretches of time. There inevitably came a point when both of us were too tired to drive and we needed to rest on the side of the road. Yet when there was literally no wiggle room, pulling over was not an option. We agreed that if we were going to have any chance of surviving the final week of the trip—assuming we made it that far—we'd have to once more enlist the services of a friend. But we could travel down that road once we zigzagged across it.

If nothing else, we now knew all the unknowns we were up against. The schedule was taut as it could be, unable to bend any further without breaking. One more rainout or time zone error and we were finished. All we had to do was go to 18 games in the next 18 days without messing up a single time. That was all.

"How could we possibly not even be halfway done?" Eric said, regretting his ability to do mental math.

Ben shook his head. "I can't answer that question without patronizing you."

Another drive through the night landed us in Florida, home to two MLB teams and a certain NFL team that had amassed a dazzling 2–14 record the year before. The Jacksonville Jaguars were a young team with great potential. It was a description that Ben was confident could apply to the Jaguars' statistical department as well.

Since the drive to Miami took us straight through Jacksonville, there was no debating the pit stop. Ben hadn't been back since the thick of the last NFL season, cheering the Jags on to loss after loss but nailing down statistical prediction after statistical prediction. Though he'd only worked there as a summer intern in the just-conceived analytics department, he was a diehard employee, hawking the merits of the team to anyone who would listen and doling out "Jag Swag," the fitting name for any article of clothing with a Jaguar on it.

As a resident of LA County, Eric had no strong NFL allegiance prior to meeting Ben, and it was hard to not be won over by a franchise that had gifted him a free hat, tee, long-sleeve tee, running shorts and even a zip-up polo that made anyone donning it look like an assistant coach. Ben's boss Tony was refreshingly genial and fun as well, so there wasn't much to dislike aside from their win percentage — a minor sticking point that Ben promised would be resolved in two to three years.

Even so, nothing could have prepared Eric for what he was about to witness upon entering Jacksonville's Ever-Bank Field. Still half conscious from the end of a four-hour driving shift, he watched in total confusion as his mumbling, neurotic, unshaven five-foot-five companion was greeted with a hero's welcome.

"It's Ben!" A fifty-year-old Jaguars employee, who, based on his body type, was clearly not an ex-player, shouted down the halls, sending a deluge of skinny men in glasses through their office doors to partake in the homecoming of one of their own.

Eric and Phil stood back and watched as the same man who could not set the car's clock was swarmed by grinning mathematicians.

"How many miles so far?"

"Any rainouts?"

"Best stadium?"

"Worst stadium?"

"Still like baseball?"

So they'd heard about the trip.

Soon Tony emerged from the office to greet us yet again. We'd stayed with him in his Chicago apartment only two days prior, and now we were standing in the same office in Jacksonville, Florida. The only difference was we took a 29-hour drive and he took a four-hour flight.

Tony gave Ben a slap on the back. "I'd say I was jet-lagged, but I've got to watch my words around you guys."

We marched off to lunch at the players' cafeteria, breaking bread alongside actual NFL players who needed a whole lot of bread to break. The buffet's spectrum of food was unlike anything we'd seen in weeks, a feat accomplished by virtue of it being a spectrum. Ben took his seat at the head of the table and recounted his detailed play-by-play of the trip, answering the statistical queries lobbed his way as he sped through each and every day.

But Eric had lived through it all, and did not have any particular desire to relive it all again. He sat down at the opposite end of the table next to a new summer intern, as far from Ben's gleeful renditions as he could get.

"The trip sounds pretty awesome."

"Well, that mostly depends on your inflection."

"I'd love to go on that. Thirty in Thirty. Man, that'd be amazing."

"You can take my place if you want," Eric offered, though it was clear from the intern's laugh that he didn't realize Eric was being serious.

"So," Eric said, "Do you know Ben well?"

"This is the first time I've met him. I've heard a ton about him though. He's a legend around here."

Eric choked on a grape. "That Ben? That Ben sitting over there?"

After lunch the posse of analysts gave Eric and Phil a tour of the facilities, ending with a chance to walk out onto the actual field.

"This is huge," the intern said, impressed.

"You say that like you haven't seen it before," Eric joked.

"I haven't. This is my first time too."

Eric turned around. "But you work here."

"You can build a whole roster without knowing what a field looks like," the intern assured him happily.

Eric was starting to see why Ben considered this home.

We said our good-byes and headed back to our car, weaving through a parking lot full of committed fans out to see a free summer practice despite the sweltering humidity.

"Why would you ever leave?" Eric asked, still overwhelmed by Ben's double life as the popular kid.

Ben looked at him as though the answer was obvious. "Away games."

As could only be expected, we entered Miami to the soundtrack of rain pounding against the car. For once, we didn't have to worry—the Miami Marlins ballpark was a covered dome. The same went for Tampa Bay the following day, assuring us of reaching the halfway mark without being thwarted by weather. Despite taking a beating on the last few drives, our GoPro camera on the hood of the car was holding up with impressive consistency. Aside from the battery almost never working, the suction pod had not loosened over the course of 14 days, and the weatherproof case kept the camera functioning through sunny days and tornado warnings alike. We became so accustomed to its presence at the front of the car that we felt like something was missing whenever we drove with it charging in the back. It gave the trip a tangible road-tripping feel, there to document every mile we traveled as the odometer clocked them one by one. Without the camera there, it was unlikely anyone would have guessed we were on a road trip. All there would have been to clue them in was nine charging cables, three Cheez-It boxes, two half-opened suitcases in the back and two grumpy unwashed men with bags under their eyes.

The Miami Marlins had the distinction of being the worst team in the major leagues, featuring a lot of players no one had ever heard of playing games no one wanted to see. It was nothing against the players themselves. It didn't matter what team you were on — the major leagues were the major leagues. Even so, one team had to be worst team in the major leagues, and it was them.

At any rate, it was never a good sign when the stadium was more striking than the team. Marlins Park was a creature all its own, the brainchild of either a surrealist artist or a 15-year-old kid who set out to build an arcade and accidentally constructed a baseball field. Splotched with vivid shades of green, red, yellow and blue, the color palette was in stark contrast to the concrete and brick of most other parks. An outfield featuring a nightclub, a swimming pool and an aquarium did little to help make it feel anything like a place where baseball was played.

Ben, still holding Fenway as the standard, felt like a classical pianist hearing rap for the first time. He wasn't sure if it was music, but it was what all the kids these days were buying.

"Today's Fireworks Friday," Eric read off a sign.

"Because all they need around here is more explosive coloring."

Eric was equally skeptical until he stumbled across the most magnificent museum he had ever seen. It was small for a museum, about fifteen feet long and ten feet tall. And there were no descriptions, nor historical documents, nor entrance fees. Just 609 bobbleheads, all bobbling away on a gyrating two-sided platform. He wasn't entirely sure what made the massive collection of bobbleheads constitute a museum, but he was more than willing to let it slide.

It was difficult to explain the allure of bobbleheads. They were like figurines, but clunky. Like trading cards, but clunky. Mostly they were clunky. In the last 15 years, the bobblehead boom had exploded across baseball, permeating even the smallest venues as marketing departments rushed to cast their star players' heads upon springs. They were fragile, often breaking without being touched. They rarely looked much like the human they were supposed to depict. They were extraordinarily clunky. But they were as adorable as pint-sized millionaires in stretchy pants. Regardless of the rest of the stadium looking like the venue for a rich kid's birthday party, the Bobblehead Museum was a quality production. Admiring the outlandish sculptures pitting All-Stars alongside managers and mascots, Eric bobbled his own head in enthusiastic approval.

We took our seats for the start of the game, pitting the league's worst team against the St. Louis Cardinals, who happened to be the league's best. Aside from the novelty of the matter, we were looking forward to this game for its statistical likelihood of its being a shorter-than-average game. When contests were close, games often dragged on past the mean length, elongated by an endless supply of mound meetings and pitching changes.

Blowouts, on the other hand, were less likely to drag on without end. When the score was 7–0 in the eighth inning, no pitching change or other stall tactic was going to save the day. Though baseball games were notoriously variable on a daily basis, the Cardinals up against the Marlins registered as the most likely blowout we would see.

The first inning lived up to expectations. Three quick singles and an unforced error provided the Cardinals an immediate 2–0 lead. With a single out in the game, the Cardinals already had designs on strolling through nine innings.

Until, at least, one inning later, when the Marlins knotted the score back at 2–2. We sunk a little in our seats, preparing ourselves for what might be an actual competition.

The next few innings surprised the Cardinals as much as anyone else. A double by Marlins first baseman Greg Dobbs gave the fish a 3–2 lead. Another double by right fielder Giancarlo Stanton served up yet two more runs. Now it was the Marlins who had a 92% win probability, producing a drastic swing of the odds in their favor. Seeming rejuvenated by their sudden offensive production and aided by a crowd that had come expecting a loss, the Marlins bore down on defense, eradicating careless throws and ill-timed pitches. Their pitcher, upcoming prospect José Fernández, was a mere 19 years old and pitching only his seventh major league start. He was younger even than us, we who considered ourselves gratuitously young. Allowing only six hits and two earned runs over seven innings, he left the mound standing to notch a win if his team could hold on to the lead. It was a task easier said than done against the Cardinals, who proceeded to tally a run in the sixth and again in the eighth.

Our all-but-certain blowout had managed to blossom into a fiercely fought 5–4 battle. There was nothing more dangerous than an inspired and energized team already out of the playoff hunt a month before the All-Star break.

With Marlins fans finding themselves on their feet—a phenomenon that tended to only occur in the outfield nightclub—closer Steve Cishek retired the side and earned the good guys a W.

"I didn't see that coming," Ben said. "I was ready to get in, get out, put the GoPro on the hood of the car and get driving. This was supposed to be one of our short games."

Eric stopped in his tracks.

"When we left the parking lot—did you put the GoPro in the car?"

"I thought you did."

"I thought you did."

Phil shook his head. "Not a chance that thing's still there."

We jogged back to the parking lot and had his theory confirmed. The mount had been ripped off the car's hood, the camera stolen with it. Nothing but a circular imprint remained, documenting where our prized documentarian had once been.

"Well then."

"Yep."

"Oops."

"Yep."

"Did you download the pictures?"

"Nope."

"Oops."

"Yep."

A loud explosion echoed through the parking lot, sending us both jumping in unison.

"What was that?"

"Gunshot?"

Another *boom*.

"Two gunshots?"

With our cherished GoPro stolen right out from under us, Miami was instantly transformed into a dangerous city where nowhere was safe and nothing was certain. It didn't matter that we had idiotically left $250 of electrical equipment on top of a car in a public lot for three and a half hours. For the rest of our lives, we would never feel good about putting hundreds of dollars' worth of goods on top of a car and walking away ever again.

"Three gunshots. *Four*."

"This is a lazy gunfight."

Then, around a parking lot pillar, we identified the source. Friday Fireworks.

"America."

"America!"

"Gotta love America."

Game Fourteen:
Tampa Bay Rays

The ride from Miami to Tampa Bay was a short four hours, and it could not have been short enough. When the clock struck midnight, we'd officially hit the trip's halfway point as far as Eric was concerned. Ben was quick to point out that given time zone changes, the Day Zero Paradigm and the way fractions worked, we were still technically a day and a half away from being halfway home.

However much we had left, we both could look forward to Tampa Bay. Awaiting us there would be the most efficient, pragmatic and understanding force on earth: a mother. Eric's mother, Geri, had been taken by work to Orlando, a city close enough to Tampa to merit a visit. Confident that we would be bumbling disheveled messes, she'd booked us a Hotel With an H to reboot and recuperate. Because the Tampa game was not until 4 PM, its proximity to Miami meant we would have a full 12 hours to spend outside of both stadium and car.

The hotel was a gesture for which we were extremely grateful, though through trial and error we had quickly determined that we could have slept on two slabs of rocks in the wilderness and still gotten a good eight hours. So we staggered into the swanky resort at 4 AM with not the slightest capacity to appreciate the intricate pottery and sculptures lining the hotel's walls. The concierge received us with caution, doing little to hide her opinion that respectable patrons of the establishment would have gone to bed hours ago. Not in the mood to justify our existence, we wheeled our suitcases straight to a first-floor room featuring *two* beds with *two* sinks for the two of us. Geri had gone so far as to get Phil his own room so we wouldn't be woken in the morning when she arrived.

When she did show up at noon the next afternoon, she gave Eric the sort of hug usually reserved for those surviving harrowing tragedies, not baseball road trips. She gave him a hard look, confirmed he was alive and frowned disapprovingly.

"All right," she said. "Enough small talk. Where are your clothes?"

Eric waved a hand at where he guessed he dropped his suitcase the night before during his instantaneous collapse on the bed.

"When's the last time you washed them?"

"We packed heavy," he assured her.

"You haven't washed *anything*?"

We were each a day away from running out of underwear and socks, a reality we fully intended to confront in around a day's time.

"Shower and change into whatever you have that's clean. Your loving parents will take everything to the laundry room. And you must be Ben," she concluded.

Ben nodded sheepishly.

"You and I will talk later," she informed him.

She took hold of Ben's suitcase and walked out.

Ben glanced back at Eric, terrified.

"I told you," Eric warned. "She can mother like it's nobody's business."

We did as we were told, freshening up and doing our best to appear suitable for witnessing in a public setting. Eric shaved for the first time in a week, scraping off enough five o'clock shadow to turn a moon half full. Ben was not so privileged, having declared at the trip's inception that he would be growing a road trip beard. The rules of the road trip beard were simple: it began on Day One and ended on Day Thirty. The more Ben resembled a homeless baby grizzly bear, the farther we had gone. He'd been talking about the beard for months before the trip, touting its efficiency by virtue of all the extra sleep minutes he would acquire from not having to shave. On the first few days of the trip his jaw-dropping good looks appeared like they might even be salvageable. Then the hairs finally started growing in. By the end of two weeks he'd reached the dreaded stage of a beard's life when it always felt like there was something on your chin. He took to stroking it maniacally, a motion that became so engrained in his daily experience that Eric once caught him stroking it in his sleep. Baseball teams often grew collective playoff beards, vowing to keep their facial hair sprouting until they could raise a trophy above their cloaked chins. A road trip beard therefore appeared to Ben as squarely in the spirit of the trip, a belief that wavered perilously as he watched Eric trim his sideburns.

"You know," Eric offered, "I have an extra razor. There's no shame in failing."

Ben saw that slippery-slope logic from 18,000 miles away. "There's no failing on this trip," he said.

"Did I tell you that you look good with a beard?"

"No."

Eric nodded. "I wonder why."

Ben had given his word to his face. There was nothing to be done. It was staying stuck to his skin.

Eric's phone rang and he picked up to the sound of his mother's voice muffled by a churning washing machine.

"We have a Royal family for you," she said.

"What?"

"A Royal family."

"What royal family?"

"A Royal baseball family."

Ben gave Eric a questioning look. Eric shrugged and put the phone to his chest. "I think there's a royal family in the laundry room. They play baseball. Oh."

He returned to the phone.

"From Kansas City?"

"The right fielder. Your dad's talking to him down here right now."

We went in search of the laundry room.

There, in the basement below the parking garage, standing between a quarters dispenser and a dryer, was

Denny Lough, father of David Lough, Kansas City Royals starting right fielder as of one week ago.

"So you're the road trippers," he said.

Eric shook his hand. "And you're the Royal family."

He had no qualms with that title. Casual and soft-spoken, he conceded a smile borne of hard-earned pride.

"I was just telling your father," he said. "I'm a father too."

Fathers had a way of finding each other.

And it turned out the laundry room's fathers had a fair amount in common. In addition to currently washing and drying their sons' underwear, both were on baseball road trips with those sons, road trips that happened to be occurring over Father's Day weekend. Though we'd skillfully managed to sleep through any chance of running into the team, the whole Royals roster had spent the night at our hotel, driving over to the Rays' stadium only an hour prior for the game we'd be seeing later that afternoon. And they weren't alone — in celebration of Father's Day, the Royals franchise had chartered a bus for all the players' fathers to travel with the team for a four-game stretch.

This was where the similarities came to an end. While Phil's son was galloping around the country visiting games, Denny's son was actually playing in them. At the age of 27, after years of bouncing around the minors, he'd gotten The Call a week ago. Royals outfielder Jarrod Dyson had sustained an ankle injury and been placed on the 15-day disabled list. After a lifetime of waiting, David Lough was finally given his chance to prove himself day in and day out. Three days earlier he had hit his first home run, adding to a good first impression for the Kansas City fans.

The move to the big time sent his father from reading minor league box scores to traveling in a corporate jet with major leaguers in the span of a week. One out of 32,000 fathers' sons got a swing at the plate or a toss from the mound. Just like that, his son was the one.

"You've got to be a little bit ecstatic," Eric said.

"Just enjoying it while it lasts." Denny laughed, a little bit ecstatic. "He gets fifteen days to show them what he's got. Then their starter comes back and someone on the roster has to go back down. And you know how it goes. He who comes up . . ."

He checked on his son's laundry.

"He made a great snag the other day, though. Crazy catch. Announcer said he'd never seen anything like it before."

"You said he plays right?" asked Eric.

"Every inch of it."

"The catch over his back?"

"You saw it?"

"We were there. In Kansas City on Monday? We were there."

"That was the one. What a catch."

"What a catch," Eric said.

He returned to the present. "Well, one way or another, I get to see him for a few more days as a big leaguer. We play here today and tomorrow than head up to Cleveland Monday."

"We'll be there too, in Cleveland on Monday. We'll have seen your son almost as many times as you have."

"You guys travel like big leaguers," Denny said.

"If only we got paid like them."

"Put in the years and who knows."

"Well, if nothing else, you can rest assured your son will have a few fans cheering him on all over the country the next couple days."

"God bless you. Hopefully you'll be able to cheer him on a little longer."

We left him to his business. He had underwear to fold.

Ben found driving a thousand miles a day surreal. Eric found it tedious. Ben considered showing up at a different stadium every evening surreal. Eric considered it tedious. Ben viewed going to the Tampa Bay Rays game with Eric's mother as a classic case of a family night at the ballpark. Eric viewed it as the most surreal thing he had ever experienced.

Seeing his mother at a ballpark felt as unnatural as seeing her rock out at a concert. It didn't happen. She went to little league games when he was young, but that was because there was always a reckless ten-year-old throwing wild pitches at her eldest child's face. She had no stake in an MLB game and therefore no reason to attend. Eric would have had to do something incredibly stupid like go on a 30-day road trip during which he could be visited only at a ballpark for her to show up.

So he sat down behind the Rays' first baseline flanked by his mother on one side and his father on the other. It was the first family trip to a ballpark in the history of his family, and barring another act of incredible stupidity, it would without question be the last.

"The stadium's pretty ugly," Geri decided.

We couldn't argue. The domed arena was dominated by a tired gray hue, making it a more natural fit for a traveling circus than an MLB team.

"Normally they're more attractive," Ben promised her.

"So," she said, turning his way, "this trip was your idea, I hear."

Ben immediately regretted engaging her. He shrunk into the safety of his seat, hiding behind Eric and Phil.

"If you think you're not getting much sleep," she told him, "imagine how your mother and I are doing. Every time I turn on the news, there's another hurricane colliding with a tornado and I don't even know what state you're in."

"Our tornado didn't have a hurricane," Ben assured her. It quickly became evident that she hadn't been told of "our" tornado.

"We're still alive," Ben added, doing little to help his case.

Eric leaned back so Ben couldn't hide.

"I begged him to not go on the trip," she said. "I told him this wasn't worth the risk, that he was only asking for trouble. I had a bad feeling from the start about this whole endeavor. He doesn't even like baseball. He's never liked baseball. I couldn't even understand why he wanted to go."

Ben was running out of seat to shrink into. Then Eric realized where this was going and commenced the shrinking process as well.

"So I demanded that he explain to me why he should go. Why it made any sense at all to go. And you know what he said? He said he couldn't let you down. He said this trip was all you wanted and he didn't want to let you down."

We looked anywhere but at each other.

"And I told him it was still irrational and a terrible idea, but at least it was a terrible idea with good intentions. So what was I to do?"

We clutched our armrests so as not to fall out of our seats. She had done what mothers do best, embarrassing their children in frustratingly productive ways, saying what their children could not say for themselves.

In high-fiving, fist-bumping 21st-century America, it was not easy for two young men to have a genuine heart-to-heart. Feelings were flatly considered a dangerous weakness, vulnerabilities that might be used as ammo. It was understood that emotions went unspoken, carefully designed to be inferred through a sideways glance or a one-time nod of the head.

Eric's mother had blown open what Ben considered the biggest mystery of the trip—namely, why the hell Eric was on it. "To see America" was a quaint reason that could have applied to any road trip and been far more effectively accomplished with a coffee-table book. "To see baseball" was obviously not the answer, and "To complain about baseball" was reason enough to languish through one game, but not 30. When Eric had told Ben he was going on the trip to see the country, Ben was angered that the reason did not include baseball. He never paused to consider other potential motives. He had looked past the variable that would be more constant on the trip than any other for Eric: Ben himself. He was so enamored with the stadium hopping and mathematical wizardry that he never considered the possibility that Eric had agreed to the trip simply because the trip would not have been possible without him.

Eric, for his part, had misdirected his real reason for that very reason—it would have forced a real moment between us, one that would have necessitated mutual self-awareness and knocked down our facades. He probably would have dropped out of the trip had he not made that commitment to Ben months ago over a mediocre lunch.

Ben had spent too much time thinking of strangers' WHIPs and OPSs and not enough thinking of his friend who knew not what a WHIP or an OPS even was.

Ben flipped through the game program studying the players' bios, or so he wanted it to appear. He couldn't focus on the field.

In the meantime, David Lough came up to the plate in what we could only assume to be clean underwear. He'd grounded out in the second inning on his first trip to the plate and now found himself back in the batter's box an inning later after the Royals tallied two runs. This time he notched a single into right field, sending us all to our feet. Somewhere hidden in the crowd of 18,500 was another father cheering with us.

Eric's mother left at the end of the fourth inning, needing to make the drive back to Orlando and prepare for the coming workweek. Sufficiently convinced that half of the worst was behind us, she gave Eric a hug and both of us one last piece of advice.

"If you're going to be stupid, at least be smart about it."

We nodded, agreeing it made complete sense.

Phil walked her back to her car outside the stadium, leaving the two of us alone together for the first time in over a week.

"So."

"So."

"I'm going to go get my hot dog."

"I'll go look for something more edible."

We went our separate ways.

A few minutes later Eric emerged from a corridor with a plate of skimpy BBQ chicken. Rays pitcher Alex Cobb let loose a slider; Royals first baseman E.J. Hosmer slammed one directly up the middle; Rays pitcher Alex Cobb toppled to the ground. The crowd went dead quiet, Eric forgot how to chew, and some ten minutes later Cobb was carted off the field.

And as his bloodied body disappeared behind an in-field wall, all Eric could think about was Cobb's father, who would leave the game in unthinkable horror, and Lough's father, who would leave the game with giddy pride, and his own father, who had already left the game to escort his mother to her car. Sons hit and sons pitched and sons watched from afar, but nothing could keep them from being sons.

Game Fifteen:
Cincinnati Reds

The Rays pulled away to win 5–3, even if none of us noticed. We loaded into the car and drove toward Cincinnati, a 13-hour trip, giving us two hours of leeway to reach the upcoming 1 PM game. Radio reports informed us that Cobb had remained conscious throughout, and despite a debilitating concussion, fielded visits from coaches and players—the Royals' Hosmer included. The worst had been overcome.

Ben took the midnight shift of the drive, leaving father and son asleep in the car as the calendar flipped to Father's Day.

"Happy Father's Day," Eric said as he awoke to the fluorescent lights of a gas station at 4 AM.

His father only laughed.

Eric presented him a long-sleeve T-shirt he'd picked up in Milwaukee, featuring the phrase "Brew Crew" repeated over and over on the front.

"I know it's a little small, but it was the only size they had."

As was always the case with a hopelessly unusable gift, it was hopefully the thought that counted.

We made good time to Cincinnati, breaking at the Ohio-Kentucky border where we would drop Phil off at the Cincinnati airport. In the spirit of our trip, it was only appropriate that he was leaving us exactly an hour *before* the Father's Day game.

"Father's Day's supposed to be every day, anyway," he reasoned. "It is at the ballpark, at least."

We ate our last supper together, which was a 9 AM breakfast, and said our good-byes beneath the howl of jet planes.

"Eat, sleep and play ball," he ordained. He disappeared into the terminal.

We showed up at Cincinnati and quietly took our seats. Maybe it was a midtrip crisis, or maybe just the residue of days of high-octane travel. But something had changed, for both of us, and both of us could feel it. We sat in our seats with increasing discomfort, fidgeting through each and every pitch, glancing uneasily at the scoreboard as the game proceeded at the devilish pace of one inning at a time. It wasn't just Eric. Ben was no longer watching for spectacular plays; now, instead, he scanned for a swift and unspectacular end. We were back to the two of us, deprived of a buoyant intermediary, left to our own devices to watch and endure and watch and endure. It could have been the aftereffects of the Cobb debacle, or the nausea invoked by a glance at the coming days' schedule. It might have been the Cincinnati heat, or the seats halfway up to the clouds, or the drunken fans too drunk too early. What was certain was that this game was overpoweringly *not* fun. It was a painful exercise for both of us. And there were a lot of viable excuses.

And only one real reason, which we both knew. Eric's cover was blown.

Ben had devoted half the trip to criticizing his every action. He brushed his teeth too slowly, he took too long to get out of bed, he only drove three hours when Ben had driven four. His knowledge of baseball was archaic, his attitude toward the game unforgiving, his daily patience shorter by the day. There'd been stretches of entire days when Eric could do nothing that would not frustrate Ben. He was a constant threat to each day's efficiency, tacking on minutes where they needn't be added, always content to stay where he was in favor of getting a head start toward the next destination. This was a trip about *going*, and Eric was too busy *being*. In Ben's eyes, Eric had come to embody the antithesis of the spirit of the trip.

Except that there would be no trip without him. Had Eric done the sensible thing and elected not to come, Ben would have attended zero games over the course of the 30 days. Eric hated every day of it, the 15-hour drives past the Grand Canyon that couldn't afford a single hour *at* the Grand Canyon, the logic of a little league field being more worthy than his family heritage, the mad dashes to witness a first pitch while not caring in the least who was pitching it and who it was being pitched at. Eric hated the trip's fundamental premise, the quantity over any semblance of quality, the snapshot we-were-here mentality that left no time to read the inscriptions on the monuments with which we posed. But he was here. Every day he was here. When it was his turn behind the wheel he got behind the wheel. Ben had known all along that he needed Eric, but he never quite processed the fact that Eric knew it as well. In the midst of endless stretches as co-drivers, it was easy to forget that we'd once been co-friends, that two guys drinking warm, sour beers and lobbing up far-fetched fantasies was how the whole mess had started.

Eric *was* the trip.

"I'm sorry," Ben said.

Eric rubbed his eyes and looked away from the field below. "No. I made the choice to come."

"I know, but, you know."

Eric waved it off with a limp hand. "I got your back, man."

"I know."

The Reds beat the Brewers 5–1.

Since we were already in Ohio, and the next game was in Ohio as well, the only logical thing to do was to head for Kentucky.

It was one pit stop we could both agree on. For Ben, the Louisville Slugger Museum & Factory offered a rare look into how the game was literally made. For Eric, it offered Louisville, a city whose sports scene was overwhelmingly dominated by horse racing and also contained a building where they made some bats. When he'd last been in town for the Kentucky Derby, the two-minute race shut down the city as the bourbon poured out and plunged locals and pilgrims alike into the depths of a weeklong party. When horses loomed so large over a community that even the decorations at the local airport were racing themed, Eric was never going to complain about visiting. Except, of course, to remind Ben endlessly that our foray into Louisville sans a Churchill Downs stop was sacrilege.

Guarded by a 120-foot bat weighing 68,000 pounds at its entrance, the factory was home to every step of the bat-making process, producing 3,000 wooden sticks on-site every day. A large portion was souvenir bats, designated for the altars of adoring fans across the country. Most of the rest were one of 300 popular models destined to see show time in the big leagues.

The bat-making industry had advanced considerably since the early days of the game, when crafting a bat was a delicate combination of a man, a toolbox and some wood. Now there were machines to work the process from start to finish, replacing the artistry of the craft with an exacting precision. A major leaguer went through some 120 bats a year; the factory could make each of them feel identical, perfectly rendered to the player's specifications.

Ben stroked the display bats in awe, imagining the gallant hands that had held them in gallant situations. Eric roamed the exhibits restlessly, knowing full well there was a horse-racing museum some 15 minutes away.

But just when he thought he'd find nothing worth getting excited about, he came upon the most magnificent invention he'd ever seen: the boring machine.

The boring machine was not just any machine. This was the machine that bored, and it was the only machine in existence that was up to the task. It was an exhilarating display of machination. First you went to northern Pennsylvania, where you cut down a tree until it became a log. Then you put the log on the ground and measured it. Then if it was long enough, you put it in the pile of logs that were batworthy. Then you drove that pile of logs to Louisville. Then you graded the logs to bat quality. Then you sawed them into 40-inch blocks. And that's when things got really crazy. You put them into the boring machine, where a precision laser cut the blocks into three-inch wide cylinders called billets. Then the billets were dried in kilns and about 45 steps later became bats. But it was clear the real thrill came right there between the moments you cut the logs into 40-inch blocks and dried the billets in the kilns. There's nothing quite like seeing a horizontal wood boring machine in action, because that's when the wood lays down on its side like a pinup model and makes all the trees blush.

"Let's get in on this tour that's about to start," Ben said.

"No way. This boring machine is amazing. It's what this trip is about."

"We need to get there right now or the group will leave."

"What's more important in the boring bat-cupping process — speed or accuracy? How much boring can occur in an hour? What about per month? Can it bore thirty times in a month?"

"Eric. We need to go."

"Is getting bored completely necessary? Could the sport possibly function without any boring occurring? If there was no getting bored, would baseball descend into chaos?"

"*Now.*"

"Just think what we would do with ourselves without the boring. Nothing. We'd do nothing. We'd be so . . ." He paused and looked up. "I'm sorry — what were you saying?"

Ben scratched his beard. "Are you done staining a perfectly good afternoon at the bat factory with your sarcasm?"

Eric shook his head. "The staining vat exhibit is over there."

Game Sixteen:
Cleveland Indians

With a stark white exterior flanked by intricate steel beams and multitiered decks rising from its expansive base, Cleveland's Progressive Field was the closest a ballpark would ever come to resembling a wedding cake.

There was nothing romantic about the sandwiches we ate instead. Committed to locating cheap food outside the stadiums so we didn't go broke inside, we found a Quiznos sandwich shop within walking distance of the park. Eric's leisurely approach to existence applied to sandwich eating as well, leaving Ben to wait impatiently as he savored his sub and the minutes ticked away.

After staring at Eric eating for five silent minutes, he couldn't take it anymore.

"We're going to be late. We need to go now."

"I'll meet you there."

"What do you mean, you'll meet me there?"

"I mean I'll see you inside when I'm finished."

"You're going to miss the first pitch for a sandwich?"

Eric took a tiny bite. "I'm not going to miss the first pitch."

So Ben left Eric to enjoy his sandwich. He was not going to let two slices of bread bring down the entire trip.

He reached the stadium, one of the first to enter the gates. Ten minutes later, Eric entered the stadium as one of the last. We were simultaneously some of the first and last people to show up, one perk of being some of the only people to show up. The final official attendance for the game was 12,803, just barely shy of the stadium's capacity of 43,345. Unfortunately for the Indians organization, this number only factored in people. It was Puppypalooza in Cleveland — our second Dog Day of Summer on the trip — and canines were not counted toward the official attendance.

As Eric entered the stadium alone, and with fifteen minutes to spare as he'd expected, he noticed a series of large banners draped above the field commemorating Indians players of yore. He'd never heard of any of them, but the banner above home plate featured a slugger by the name of "Averill." He and Ben had a mutual friend named Averill, and the name was uncommon enough to warrant a second look. He knew there was no relation, but he didn't know if Ben knew this.

"Would you look at that," Eric said, finding his seat next to Ben. "The game hasn't started."

"You take on too much risk," Ben muttered.

We were sitting directly across from the Averill banner in our outfield seats, but Eric took a chance on Ben's obliviousness.

"We should have asked Allison's dad for better seats," he said offhandedly.

"Why? Does he know someone here?"

"He was a player back in the day."

"Really? For the Indians? She never told me that."

"Yeah. She mentioned it once when she was telling me about her family. I think she said he played in Cleveland."

"Weird," Ben said, surprised.

Eric left it at that. The seed was adequately planted.

The Indians were playing the Royals, a team we'd seen two days prior, 1,000 miles away. We would watch David Lough, our new rooting interest, tally two hits against Cleveland, resulting in crazed applause for the rookie. Two fans were more than enough in Cleveland to merit crazed applause.

Unexpectedly, most of the game's entertainment turned out to come from next to us instead of in front of us. Our seats were on the foul line in the right field outfield, just a few feet away from the visiting team's bullpen.

In the third inning Royals pitcher Bruce Chen emerged to warm up. He was a reliever of Chinese heritage, raised in Panama, who had played for eleven different major league teams. A well-traveled man in his 16th year in the big leagues, he was clearly copying our idea and attempting to play for all 30 teams in 30 years.

A young woman a few rows below took an interest in him, bored of watching her sluggish home team play for a lackluster crowd and a horde of puppies.

"Hey," she yelled into the bullpen. "Can I have some of your dip?"

Chen moseyed over to the dividing fence.

"How old are you?" Chen asked flirtatiously. "In the state of Ohio, citizens must be eighteen years old to consume tobacco products," he added even more flirtatiously.

"I'm twenty-one!"

He mulled it over. The entire section was now watching the affair in the bullpen instead of the game on the field.

"I'm going to need to see some ID."

The girl winked and went to her wallet. She handed him an ID card through the fence.

"This is a college ID," Chen said. It was obvious he'd been around the block and been propositioned by women in bullpens before. "I'm going to need to see two forms of identification."

She handed over her driver's license.

He held it up to the sun, the most fail-proof method to confirm authenticity. He turned to the security guard manning the bullpen.

"Officer? What do you think?"

He handed the two IDs over to the tune of a few boos from the crowd. He raised his arms defensively.

"I'm just respecting the law, folks. Just respecting the law."

The guard, trying not to crack a smile, nodded at Chen and gave him the thumbs up.

"All right, it looks like you're over eighteen . . . Julie. Here's your IDs and here's your Copenhagen dip."

The girl yelled an amorous "Thank you!" before sitting down and realizing she was now forced to consume the dip she had jokingly begged for.

A middle-aged woman in the row behind us grunted disapprovingly. "What a dumb girl. Smoke-free isn't cancer-free."

And to think there was a major league game going on all the while.

We returned to watching the scoreless match on the field. And that's when Ben's eyes drifted above home plate, landing on the giant banner billing "Averill."

"Oh my god," Ben said, sitting up in his seat. "Look at that banner!"

"Holy smokes," Eric said in disbelief. "Do you think her dad was a big deal?"

"He had to be—he's front and center above home plate!"

Ben did a quick Google search. "You won't believe this. Earl Averill—Cleveland Indians Hall of Fame."

"Her dad must be a legend here."

"I can't believe we didn't try to have her hook us up here. I bet he could've gotten us the VIP treatment."

"Maybe it's not too late," Eric wondered. It was time to enter Phase Two. "I'll text Allison and tell her we're here. Who knows."

Eric took out his phone and did as promised. *Allison*, he wrote, *remember that baseball trip Ben's been rambling about for months? Well, we're currently in Cleveland and I've convinced him a Cleveland hall of famer named Averill is your dad. Up for helping out with a little prank?*

He soon received a response in the affirmative. Anyone who'd been around Ben for more than half a second in the last few months had heard him drone on about the trip. Ben was himself an avid prankster and had gotten Eric well a time or two. And after the weeks of nagging and complaining that Ben had lobbed at Eric for his easygoing approach to the trip, it was time to get back at The Man.

I'm going to start a thread with you and Ben, Eric wrote her. *Respond that you're family friends with the Indians announcer and that you can get us into the announcer's booth.*

He then sent another message, this time to Allison and Ben both, informing Allison we'd spotted her father's banner.

A few minutes later, Allison replied: *Looks like you guys know the family secret! Hope the trip's going well. Did the game already start? We're family friends with the announcer if you wanted to go up to the booth.*

Our phones buzzed simultaneously with her text. Ben's jaw dropped. "That'd be unbelievable." He looked longingly upon the announcer's booth, right under the hulking "Averill" banner.

He replied to the group text: *That would be amazing. We'd absolutely love that.*

Eric discreetly searched "Cleveland Indians announcer" on his phone and determined the man's name to be Tom Hamilton.

He fed another line to Allison, who promptly texted it back to the group thread: *Great. I'll do what I can to get you up. I'll text Tom right now and let you know how it goes!*

Ben couldn't believe his luck. He'd always wanted to sit in an announcer's booth and the opportunity had just fallen in his lap. He googled "Cleveland Indians announcer" on his phone and found the same page about Tom Hamilton that Eric had landed on only minutes before.

"Look at this," Ben said, showing Eric the page. "'Tom Hamilton, Voice of the Indians.' She's on texting terms with their announcer. This is actually happening."

Another 20 minutes of nervous anticipation passed. Then both our phones buzzed again.

He says it's a go—just head to the press box and they'll have your names. He said one of you could maybe even call a play!

Ben stared at the text, astonished. This was Christmas come six months early in the middle of Cleveland.

" 'One of you could maybe even call a play,' " Ben said aloud.

Eric gave him a pat on the back. "It should be you. If one of us gets to do it, it should be you. You've earned it."

Ben gave him a satisfied look. He agreed with Eric. He had earned it.

We set off to find the announcer's booth with Ben leading the way. The press box was always directly above home plate, usually situated on the second or third levels. We jogged up a series of staircases in the vicinity of home plate and soon came upon a fancy glass-plated entrance, roped off and guarded by security. We'd found the treasure.

"We're going to the announcer's booth," Ben informed the guard.

"Who are you visiting?"

"Tom Hamilton, Voice of the Indians."

"The announcer?"

"Correct."

"The man announcing the game right now."

Ben nodded. "You should have our names."

"I don't have your names," the guard assured him.

"Don't worry," Ben assured him in return. "This happened when we visited Theo Epstein at the Cubs game. Can you call the booth?"

The guard studied him suspiciously. "I'm not allowed to call them. They can only call me."

"I'll text Allison," Eric said.

He whipped out his phone and sent a text to the group thread: *They're claiming they don't have our names? Do you mind checking with Tom?*

He then sent one to Allison alone: *Say that you will, then wait thirty minutes and reply again asking what section we're in.*

A minute later she responded to the group thread that she'd check in with Tom.

"I guess we better wait here," Ben said.

"Here" was a concrete concourse three stories high, facing a darkening Cleveland skyline away from the stadium. The baseball field was completely out of view, as were the stands below. There was nothing to captivate us but the dark and a few slabs of concrete.

We idled in the concourse for 30 uneventful minutes. The guard watched with growing distrust as we paced back and forth. It was very possibly the most boring activity achievable at a ballpark, even for those who found the game of baseball an endurance exercise. But if Eric had to suffer through the boredom of a game a day, it was only fair that Ben learned how it felt to be interminably bored and trapped within the confines of a ballpark. Now Ben could endure a baseball game from Eric's perspective, a perspective that was not unlike the feeling of staring at a concrete slab when a city of unexplored intrigue was always within arm's reach.

At last Allison replied again to the group thread, startling Ben from his stupor: *What section are you in?*

Section C, Ben replied.

Tell us we want Section E, Eric wrote her.

You have to go to Section E, she wrote to the group thread. *Someone is coming out now to let you in.*

Ben rocketed to his feet. "Hurry!"

He barreled down the sets of stairs. Eric followed in close pursuit, tailing Ben as he tore through the wandering crowd in search of Section E. Locating it, we climbed the stairs two at a time to our new destination.

It was another concrete concourse, identical to that of Section C. Another guard stared us down uncertainly. There was no one else around.

"Did someone come out for us?" Ben asked breathlessly.

The security guard shrugged.

Eric quietly texted Allison: *Tell us that Tom said he sent someone to get us a few minutes ago.*

A few moments later, the sentiment appeared on the group text: *Tom said he sent someone to get you a few minutes ago. Did you get in okay?*

We got here too late, I think, Ben wrote back in despair.

Tell us that Tom has to go announce right now, but he'll try to get us at the end of the next inning, Eric wrote to only her.

Tom has to go announce right now, but he'll try to get you at the end of the next inning, she wrote back to both of us.

And so we waited, again. We'd first come in search of the press box in the middle of the fourth inning. It was now the bottom of the seventh. Since we'd made it this far in the name of futility, Eric decided he'd see how long he could get Ben to put up with the torture of doing absolutely nothing.

Another half hour passed.

"You know," Ben said, "I'd make a great announcer."

"You would. You totally would," Eric agreed. "How would you call the game?"

"And he winds up," Ben said emphatically. "And it's a strike! Strike two."

"Strike two," Eric recited admiringly. "Such subtlety."

The ninth inning rolled around. Ben's anxiousness was visible even to the security guard, who had grown a little more guarded.

Eric sent Allison one more text. *Tell us that he's busy now and has to go do postgame interviews after the ninth, but if we wanted to wait around for an hour we could meet up with him.*

A minute later the information was regurgitated by Allison on the group text.

It was cruel perhaps, but Eric couldn't pass up the chance to see Ben struggle with a choice straight out of his nightmares. We had an 11-hour trip to Atlanta ahead of us that would require a drive through the night. Ben would have to decide between hanging out with a major league announcer and ensuring a timely trip to Atlanta.

He pursed his lips and gritted his teeth. The conflict felt like a physical weight, pushing him to a breaking point after already going stir-crazy staring at the concrete slabs for an hour and a half. The game had just ended. Fans from the upper levels waded down the staircases, soon to clutter the Cleveland streets with their car traffic.

Eric withheld his smile as he watched Ben squirm.

Suddenly Ben's eyes lit up. "Pull up the schedule!"

Eric did so, unsure where this was going.

"The twenty-ninth—who do the White Sox play?"

Eric scanned the list. "The Indians."

Ben clapped his hands. "Perfect! We'll visit Tom in the announcer's booth there in twelve days!" He sprinted down the staircase, off to go beat the traffic and hit the road.

Eric could not believe the gift he'd just been handed. An improvised one-night prank had just evolved into a two-week gambit. It was time to get to work. The fun had just begun.

Game Seventeen:
Atlanta Braves

Our day in Atlanta presented us with a rare choice of games. Thanks to a previous rainout, the Braves were playing a doubleheader against the Mets—one game at 1 PM and a second at 7 PM. The weather forecast for the evening game touted a 60% chance of rain, large enough to give us a scare after the downpour in Chicago. The first game adhered to Ben's life strategy of Better Safe Than Sorry, so we prepared ourselves for a long night of driving to reach Atlanta in time for the afternoon affair.

"We should get there with an hour or so to spare," Ben said, rechecking the travel times. "Assuming we don't stop to rest."

"I stopped assuming that a long time ago." Eric glanced in the rearview mirror. "What is this car behind me doing?"

It was unclear what the car was doing. Eric was driving in the left lane of the two-lane I-71 with a giant Mack truck taking up the right. For miles it'd been only us and the Mack truck sharing the road, cruising along at the 60 mph speed limit. Eric had been neurotically watching the speedometer ever since his first ticket in New Jersey.

The car behind us had appeared with alarming speed, and was tailing us aggressively. It could only be assumed that the car was trying to get us to let it pass. But trapped in the left lane by the 18-wheeler in the right, Eric had no choice but to zip above the speed limit to let the car by. In no mood to deal with road rage, he pressed down on the pedal and sped up past the Mack truck so he could merge right and let the car by.

He looked back into the rearview mirror to see if the car was indeed speeding past. It wasn't. It was instead merging right to take the spot behind him yet again.

"What's this guy doing?"

Then red-and-blue lights began flashing on the top of the car.

"He's a cop? Am I getting pulled over?"

Ben nodded. "That's definitely the international signal for getting pulled over."

"You've got to be kidding me."

Eric slowed to a stop on the side of the road. The officer exited his unmarked police cruiser as Eric imagined his insurance rate surpassing the speed limit and then some.

"License, registration and proof of insurance. I clocked you at seventy-seven."

"Sorry, officer. I know I was speeding, but it was a misunderstanding. I thought *you* were speeding, and wanted to get out of your way, but the only way I could get around the Mack truck was to speed myself. I swear I've been going the limit all night."

"License, registration and proof of insurance."

The truth was not working. Eric revised his plan of attack. "And not just all night, but all month. We're on a thirty-game, thirty-day road trip to every park in America and we're driving to Atlanta right now for tomorrow's game." He knew he would have to lie. "All we want to do is see some baseball."

"Oh, wow. Were you just at the Indians game? That proof of insurance is expired by the way."

"Yeah, section 112. They lost 2–1."

"Yet again. I'm going to go run your license. Don't worry about the insurance card."

The officer returned a minute later.

"All right, you're free to go. Just keep it at the limit. Safe drive to Atlanta. Who are they playing?"

"The Mets. Thanks, officer."

Turner Field, the stadium that billionaire owner Ted Turner decided to name after Ted Turner, was perfectly boring. With a symmetrically round outfield wall, a square Jumbotron aligned with center field and no other deviations from the prototypical ballpark, there was little exploring to do.

It was a blistering afternoon, so we ditched our assigned seats for two empty ones in the shade. They offered worse views of the game than the tickets we'd paid for, but also offered worse views of the sun. It was the first time we didn't even bother making a pit stop at our assigned seats, though it was not due to lack of trying. In a novel predicament we'd not yet encountered, we had absolutely no idea how to read our tickets.

Generally, tickets were printed with the section, row and seat number in one order or another. But these tickets — which we'd bought minutes ago outside the park directly from the Braves — offered only an indistinguishable jumble of numbers and letters. We attempted multiple interpretations, exhausting every possible sequencing of information the tickets might have presented. It was no use. Embarrassed by our inability to locate our own seats, we trudged up to an attendant and asked for help.

She stared at the tickets. "Left, I think," she said finally. "Left."

"Right. I think they're to the left."

Half the stadium was to the left, so we tried again with the next attendant we could find.

"Up," she said. "Probably up. How much you buy them for?"

"They were the cheapest we could get."

"Then they've got to be up, right?"

Not even the people whose job description entailed seat locating could locate the seats. Satisfied that we'd done due diligence, we settled into the first shaded seats we could find.

After a wealth of blowouts during the first few games of the trip, we'd recently encountered a stretch of tighter low-scoring affairs. At first uneventful, this game was suddenly shaping up to be uneventful in the most glamorous way possible. Through the first six innings of play, Mets phenom Matt Harvey did not surrender a single hit, laying the groundwork for a potential no-hitter.

For a game that was predicated on a degree of built-in boredom—usually defined by fans as the absence of hits and runs—a no-hitter took the ingredients for boredom and turned them into the most exciting thing that could happen on a baseball field. With a no-hitter at stake, every single at bat was a pressure-cooker situation, doused in a palpable tension that left everyone on the field and stands alike clinging to the outcome of every pitch. It was engaging in a way that baseball almost never was: a minute-by-minute thriller that grew and grew in tension, always capable of being totally shattered by a single measly hit.

The year before, in a rare moment of baseball fandom, Eric decided to bring his friend Tobi to a Mets game. Though he normally avoided the ballpark at all costs on his own time, he couldn't resist the prospect of attending a game with Tobi, a man who had grown up in England and never seen an inning of baseball in his life. They would show up for a few innings, Eric would present evidence that we've made some progress since the rebellion and then they would leave. What Eric was not expecting was to witness the most exciting game he would ever see, the masterpiece that most fans went a lifetime without witnessing. Through nine raucous innings, Mets pitcher Johan Santana allowed not a single hit, racking up the first no-hitter in Mets franchise history.

Since 1900 there had been an average of 2.4 no-hitters per year. The feat required so many more things to go right than wrong—27 things, to be exact—that they were close to impossible to predict. They were statistical flukes. They could come in any game in any season against any team. If a Mets fan had gone to every home game since the team's inception in 1962 he would have waited over 4,000 games without seeing one. But Tobi, in his very first game *ever*, was standing on the side of history. Eric never had such difficulty explaining a concept to anyone as he had trying to convince Tobi of the significance of what he'd just seen.

"So essentially, nothing is happening. Not a lot happens in a normal baseball game and that's considered boring. But when so little happens that absolutely nothing happens, it's really exciting."

"So this doesn't normally happen?" Tobi had asked.

"No," Eric understated. "No-hitters normally don't happen."

"But it's the pitcher's job to not allow hits."

"Well, yes."

"So normally they're bad at their jobs?"

"It's complicated," Eric elucidated.

Apparently, Eric was quite good at picking Mets games to attend. The no-hitter was the first he'd been to, and now he was two-thirds of the way to seeing the once-in-a-lifetime feat twice.

But as happens just about every time, especially for the Mets, it was not to be. An infield blooper in the seventh inning was misplayed by Mets first baseman Josh Satin, leaving no one to man the base. The runner reached safely, and all eyes turned to the scoreboard for the scorer's decision. The play would have been a standard out were it not for Satin's confusion. If the scorer ruled the play an error, the no-hitter would still be alive. With the quest surviving into the seventh inning, even the players were watching the scoreboard for the decision.

Then up flashed a "1" in the hit column. The scorer, an invisible official concealed in a box somewhere, had brought the no-hitter to an end. Now that something other than nothing had happened, the game was zapped of its intrigue. We turned our attention to taking catnaps in our seats.

By the bottom of the ninth, storm clouds were forming in the sky above. The Braves were trailing 3–4 with a runner on first and two outs. Extra innings could give the rain time to appear, which could in turn cause play to be postponed. Extra innings taking extra time would be a double whammy of inconvenience, as a bad enough storm could wash out the second half of the doubleheader as well. We bucked the home crowd and poured our hearts out to the Mets.

Braves slugger B.J. Upton came to the plate for his shot at heroism, just as rain began to fall in the outfield stands, creeping its way onto the field of play. Then, *BAM!* A clap of thunder echoed throughout the stadium. Four seconds later, *BAM!* The ball pounded against Upton's bat. It didn't leave the infield. The game was over. Taking the long route out of the stadium to avoid the rain, we headed back toward our car.

Right as we walked out the exit gates, Eric stopped in his tracks. "I forgot the foam finger. I'll be right back."

While sitting in our seats at the very first game of the trip, we realized it'd be sacrilege to visit every park and not come away with a memento from each one. We made sure to take a picture at every park, and surely the memories would last Ben till the end of his life and Eric till he purged them from his brain. But we needed something more, something tangible. After browsing the Yankee Stadium gift shop, we decided on a foam finger, as it was the only item other than magnets or pens that could be found at every stadium and cost just ten dollars. "Just ten dollars" was high praise for a piece of foam, but we took what we could get. Since then, we'd picked up a foam finger at every stadium we visited. We were now the #1 fans of 17 professional baseball teams, with an 18th pending if Eric could get back into Turner Field.

This was easier said than done. Exiting a ballpark was a one-way journey. There was no going back. The moment you exited the stadium's gates, you were not permitted to turn around, a rule invariably enforced by an army line of encroaching park attendants.

The nearest security guard spotted Eric's 180-degree turn instantly, stepping forward and spreading out two forbidding arms.

"No returns."

"I just need to get a foam finger."

"No returns."

"Please," Eric begged, opting for a white lie. "I left my foam finger under my seat."

The guard frowned. "Where's your seat?"

Eric threw up his hands. "Can you read the tickets around here?"

This seemed to touch upon a soft spot in the guard's heart. Seat-finding struggles were apparently a well-known Atlanta epidemic. "Make it quick."

Eric sprinted off toward the team store, encouraged to sprint less by the "quick" directive and more by the strengthening rain. Yet upon reaching the team store he discovered it to be closed. He was incredulous. They were always open long after the game ended, more than happy to milk the wallets of every last straggling fan. The game had ended not more than three minutes ago and this one had already chained down its doors.

He picked a direction and made his way around the ballpark, running to each rain-drenched stand only to find it too was closed. Everything in the park had instantly shuttered. He stopped a worker locking up a shop.

"Any chance I could I could slip in?"

"Sorry, whole park's closed to prepare for the doubleheader."

He continued on through the corridors, desperate for someone to cut him a break. He needed this foam finger. He didn't know why, but he knew it had to happen. They were ugly and overpriced, and clumsy to hold and uncomfortable to touch. There was not a single thing that was desirable about them. But we had 17 of them, so failure was no longer an option. Not now. Not after making it this far.

He caught sight of an open door carved out beneath a staircase, the sort of secret storage space that a passerby only noticed when unconcealed. He poked in his head and looked to the left. There before him was a towering stack of foam fingers, the largest supply of worthless precious foam he had ever seen. He looked to the right. There before him was a park employee, sitting in a swivel chair watching over them.

"What do you want? This is private property."

"I really, really need to buy one of those foam fingers."

"Sorry, buddy. They're not for sale."

"They're absolutely for sale. The only reason they exist is so that you can sell them."

"Not right now, they aren't."

"How much are they, ten dollars? I'll give you twenty."

"Get out!"

Eric slunk back out of the hole in the wall. He returned to his search for someone who understood capitalism.

Almost all the way around the stadium, he laid eyes on one last glimmer of hope. A team photographer was dismantling a fan photo exhibit made up of Braves pictures and memorabilia. One of the props was a raggedy foam finger, torn at the edges and stained from years of use by little kids posing for posterity.

Eric wiped the rain from his face. "I'll give you twenty for that finger."

The photographer looked at him like he was crazy. "That? That's just a prop."

"A prop that's not worth a dollar. Please. Right now that foam finger is all that matters to me in life. And I wish I could explain why to you, but let it suffice to say that I'm extremely sleep-deprived and I don't know if I even understand it myself."

"I can't give you this one," he said. "But if you exit the stadium two gates down, you'll see a highway overpass to your left. Go under that overpass and you might find a souvenir stand on the other side. They usually set up there for most games."

With no other choice, Eric once again exited the stadium. The rain had now reached Chicago proportions, falling with such force that it stung the top of his head as he ran. Wearing only a T-shirt and shorts, he could have been wearing a half-dozen layers and still been soaked to the skin.

He was receiving a shower a minute, an inconvenience far more cleansing than a game a day.

He spotted the overpass and crossed under it, coming out the other side back into the rain. The streets were completely empty. His dream of collecting 30 foam fingers in 30 days was over.

With no souvenir stand in sight, he headed for a low-hanging blue tarp to duck under and catch his breath. He collided with a man decked out in Braves gear.

"How can I help you?"

Eric dried his brow with his wet forearms and glanced around. He was standing in a souvenir tent.

"One foam finger, please."

"That'll be ten dollars."

With foam finger in hand, he darted back into the open fire. The overpass was on the opposite side of the stadium from where we'd parked, leaving him a pleasant half-mile stroll to the car.

He arrived soaked from head to toe, finger included. But it was his, all his, a piece of red-dyed foam that cost cents to produce and represented all he despised. There was no denying his status as the #1 fan of "#1 fan" foam fingers, even if the title induced nothing but self-loathing. He threw it in the trunk next to the other 17 foam fingers. It looked like a virus had taken over the trunk and overflowed into the backseat. They were taking up more space than either of our suitcases and provided no value other than a reminder of buyer's remorse. Ben put on the wipers and tossed Eric a towel. We departed for St. Louis.

Game Eighteen:
St. Louis Cardinals

In a welcomed break from wire-to-wire driving, we'd have 16 free hours to kill before the Cardinals game the next night. This provided us time for more typical road trip antics, like making an hour-long detour into Alabama for dinner simply because neither of us had been there before. Pulling into the first town we could locate across the border, we drove through a quiet set of hills before arriving at a four-way stop. In synchronized procession, three other cars joined from each direction at the stop, and from the looks on the locals' faces behind their windshields, we had just made town history.

The next afternoon we stopped for lunch at a mid-sized town by the name of Cape Girardeau, Missouri, and though it was home to nothing particularly noteworthy, it still boasted a full-time visitors' center staffed with five employees. From what we could discern at the visitors' center, there were two matters of concern of which anyone passing through the Cape should be made aware. The first was the Bill Emerson Memorial Bridge, a bridge that likely had a religious significance to the locals based on the frequency of its depiction. A close second was a line of T-shirts with Rush Limbaugh's face emblazoned across them. "Cape Girardeau — Home of Rush Limbaugh," they declared.

As we lay in our motel beds that night in an unpronounceable part of Kentucky, we found ourselves ill at ease, albeit for different reasons. Over the last several hours, Eric had developed an allergic reaction, and was having trouble identifying the culprit. His most embattled body part was his scalp, which on the one hand narrowed down the possible causes but on the other hand was his scalp. He recounted every minute of the past day, struggling to identify the break from his usual routine. If he were allergic to baseball, he'd have likely fallen apart days ago. As much as he would have liked to receive a doctor's note exempting him from the daily grind of games, the sport could be given a rare stamp of innocence on this occasion. Was it the hat he bought in Cape Girardeau? Motel shampoo? The Sonic chicken sandwich that was dinner? His car blanket that he'd just used to nap? No, that blanket would never let him down. It had to be the shampoo.

Ben, though physically flawless as always, had another pressing issue to confront. The issue was a woman, and he'd never met her. Tomorrow in St. Louis he'd be going on a blind date.

Ben never had a long-term girlfriend. He loved baseball, math and any way to combine the two. Women tended to get left out from that combination. Eric, embracing his role as Ben's monthlong wingman, took it upon himself to give his friend a push in the right direction. When Ben was asleep during a leg of the 15-hour trip from Milwaukee to Denver, he and Ben 2 took initiative in the name of love and made Ben an online dating account.

The plan was simple. We'd create a profile based in a random city we'd be passing through, be forthcoming about Ben's geographically wandering ways and score him a date to a ballgame. Ben would be in his comfort zone, able to fall back on the crutch of his one true love in case the potential of human love started to flounder.

Though combative at first, Ben reluctantly consented, comforted by the fact that one date in a city we'd never be back in would save him from the threat of a second. However, he refused to play any part in the online search himself. He wanted his fingerprints nowhere near the world of online dating, and demanded that while we could have full control of the profile, we had to delete it if he wanted us to do so. In exchange, he would go on the date if we could find him one. We agreed to these terms and settled on St. Louis as the romantic getaway, which at the time was over a week away.

And so Eric and Ben 2 set off to write Ben's dating bio with zero oversight.

Hey! My name is Ben, finder of facts, dreamer of dreams, wanderer of our great nation. I've always been one for adventure, and I like to take my adventures one day at a time. Right now I'm currently on a 30-day adventure, visiting all 30 MLB ballparks. I like baseball. Who am I kidding? I love baseball. That's right—I have the capacity to love. But that's probably also a little misleading because I'm not sure if I'm ready for a committed relationship at the moment (because you never know if the next moment will take you to Iowa!). But if you like adventures and baseball and statistically improbable love, then I'll be at the Cardinals game in St. Louis on June 19 with two tickets and only one of me. If you're looking for a good quality conversation and a good quantity of at-bats, let me know and maybe someone at the game will hit a home run!

Shockingly, it elicited no immediate requests. This led Eric to a more proactive approach: messaging girls "hey" or "heyy" or "heyyy" and checking for a positive response. It was much easier to message a girl at will when it wasn't your own ego on the line. He eventually got smart with it, targeting girls who listed the Cardinals or baseball as one of their interests, and landed Ben a date to the game within two days. Before asking Ben for final go-ahead, he took the ask-for-forgiveness approach and messaged her back assuring her that he, Benjamin, would love to take her to the game.

Eric conceded that the lucky winner might not have been Ben's match made in heaven. She liked baseball, which would please Ben. She worked at a university, which would please Ben. She liked Renaissance fairs, attended them regularly and devoted a large portion of her profile to that pursuit, which would probably not please Ben.

Outside Busch Stadium, we took our photo proving we were there and said our good-byes. We were each on our own tonight. It was the first game we wouldn't experience together. Ben would be sitting with his paramour, while Eric would be alone several sections away, romancing his laptop. With no desire to watch the game and no Ben to hound him about disgracing the American pastime, he figured the game would be the perfect chance to get a little work done.

Ben met up with his date, who we'll call Anna, by an outfield gate. They walked side by side into the stadium.

"So I take it you're a pretty big Cardinals fan?" Ben asked; he always liked to start his dates off with a witty romantic opener.

"Yeah. Huge fan. If I wasn't at the game with you, I'd be home watching the game alone."

Ben could respect that.

They found their seats on the third deck of Busch, which offered a wonderful view of St. Louis' Gateway Arch and a terrible view of the game. They chatted about baseball and Ben's road trip. On any other date, Ben would have been able to discuss other interesting topics, like football or basketball, but Anna was giving Ben's baseball wonkiness a run for its money. Every time a batter came to the plate she would recite his career statistics. *My god, is that what I sound like on a date when spouting out statistics to a girl?* Ben thought. *I must sound pretty smart and knowledgeable.*

Bringing a blind date to a baseball game was a risky proposition. Far before he could tell that the Cardinals were a lock to beat the Cubs, he could calculate that the date was going nowhere. While Ben was excited by her encyclopedic knowledge of numbers, the chemistry was lacking. She was indeed a very big proponent of Renaissance fairs, as Eric had conveniently failed to inform him, and although Ben showed some interest, he could not survive hearing about how many booths she had visited at the Texas Renaissance Festival. Going to as many fair booths in one weekend as possible was way too nerdy, while visiting as many stadiums in 30 days as possible was the definition of America. She was clearly older than the 23 years of age advertised on her profile, as she had been "selling insurance for a few years out of college and was at her new job for a couple." The last straw for Ben—whose vanity was miraculously unaffected by a ruinous beard and a month of consuming little other than hot dogs—was watching his date devour an entire plate of cheesy nachos in just a couple minutes in the bottom of the third inning. After this, he knew it was over. He wished there was a mercy rule for dates. There were still six more innings left to play.

Ben missed Eric. He wished he were sitting with him. He missed his underhanded complaints, his snarky remarks, his grumbling and lovable presence. He missed the good old days, every one of the last 19. He had taken Eric for granted.

Strangely enough, Eric felt the same way. He'd come into the game more excited than he'd been for perhaps any other. He assumed it'd be a refreshing to get a dose of solitary confinement. With his laptop and Wi-Fi device in tow, he treated section 440 as if it were a coffee shop. He got through some emails, caught up on the news and even did some writing.

Then a group of drunken twentysomething males sat down in the row in front of him.

"Look at this guy with a computer. What a dweeb."

"All alone. What a creep."

"What a dweeb creep."

Eric had been called much worse than a dweeb creep in his time, and wasn't inclined to take much notice until one of them stood over him with an overflowing cup of beer and threatened to pour it out on his laptop if he didn't "stop being a dweeb creep and enjoy the game."

That was his cue to go for a walk.

Unfortunately, the Cardinals were one of the best teams in the league and claimed a rabid fan base, resulting in a sold-out game. World Series champions in 2011, the fans still partied like they'd won in 2012. Without a free seat to steal and set up shop in, Eric was left to wander aimlessly around the park.

Five innings of aimless wandering does a lot to a man. Trapped in the park without a seat to call home and nothing to serve as a distraction, Eric did what he previously thought to be the impossible. He became lonely.

At first he tried finding company. He snuck into an employees' back room brimming with vendors refilling their trays of food and drink. He chatted up a few, getting the dirt on the job that was the dream of every five-year-old. *They pay you to be at the game?!*

"A lot of stairs," said a lemonade salesman. "A lot of stairs to climb." His manager spotted him talking to Eric and promptly interrupted.

"Who's this?"

"A potential customer," the vendor said.

"Is he buying a lemonade?"

"Just researching the market at the moment," Eric explained.

"Then get out of here, buddy." He kicked Eric out and shut the door behind him.

Next Eric wandered up to the party suites, slipping by the on-duty attendant who was chatting up a few high school girls. The suites were all named after former Cardinals players, so he found the Mark McGwire suite and walked inside.

He went straight to the food table, pretending to be right at home.

A gruff man came up to him suspiciously. The suite was largely populated by middle-aged men in business casual attire.

"Who you with?" the man barked.

"I'm with Rick," Eric said. From his years playing little league and attending games on the side, he knew that you could always find a Rick at the ballpark.

"Oh," the man said. "He'll be back in a few."

That worked better than Eric expected. He lingered for a few minutes, catching a few pitches from the suite view, eating a few free buffalo wings. He slipped out at the inning break, careful not to outstay his welcome and run into Rick.

There was nowhere left to go. He wandered back to the ground level, settling down at a bench in the "Family Zone," where he watched families play together to the sound of laughter and, every now and then, crying when someone fell down and scraped a knee.

At some point between the moment when an overweight ten-year-old scraped his left knee and when he scraped his right knee, it occurred to Eric that Ben was the closest thing he had to family on this trip. Not counting when his parents were with us, which was also pretty close to family. As much as Ben's idiosyncrasies made him go insane, he was all that Eric had to lean on. We were there to look out for each other, and of course to complain to each other about looking out for each other. Despite himself, he missed Ben. He had to acknowledge that the games were more enjoyable with him than without him. Two dweeb creeps were better than one.

We met up again in the bottom of the ninth. Ben's date had left a half inning early to beat the traffic, a great relief to Ben and most likely his date.

"How'd your date go?"

"Eh, it went all right. Probably won't meet up with her again."

"That's okay. We'll be a thousand miles away from St. Louis in twenty-four hours. That's a solid excuse."

"Did you miss me?"

"Not even for a second."

Part V

Take Me Out to the Ballgame, Unless I'm Already There

Game Nineteen:
Texas Rangers

The next afternoon we were in Texas. The all-night ten-hour drive had allotted us each an hour of sleep. We were greeted with temperatures hovering near 100 degrees. We were miserable.

We walked into the Rangers ballpark in Arlington, helpfully named the Rangers Ballpark in Arlington, and were overwhelmed by the heat and humidity. All we wanted to do was find our seats and relax, until we did find our seats and realized they were in an exposed section on the fourth deck.

We migrated yet again, hoping to find replacements with shade in the outfield. We walked down a ramp that offered a view out of the stadium.

"Are you kidding me?" Eric said as we descended our seventh consecutive ramp. "Is that a water park over there? Why are we not there? Don't answer that," he concluded.

We found our way to the lower right field level, one of the few sections heroically shielded by the inanimate concrete section above it. It was filled end to end with heat refugees, with the exception of a small vertical sequence two seats wide. We nabbed the first two we could reach and immediately learned why they were empty: a giant pole obstructed the view of home plate and the pitcher's mound. You could only see action on the field if the ball was hit down a foul line. Even the Jumbotron was obscured above, leaving no means to watch the game or keep track of the score. But shade was shade. We took the ten-degree drop in temperature and projected our imaginations onto the pole.

It was one of our more memorable games. One of the teams won by a score of something to something.

Game Twenty:
Los Angeles Angels

It was 21 hours to Los Angeles, or as Ben reassuringly phrased it, just six consecutive baseball games. That made it the longest leg we'd tackle in the entire trip, and by far the longest we'd have to tackle alone. There was a 26-hour window to get it done, a tight squeeze that afforded two or three hour-long naps on the side of the road. The route would cut straight across Texas, dip us through New Mexico, traverse all of Arizona and come to an end at the Pacific coast. It was hours of driving empty desert roads bookended by hours of driving other empty desert roads.

For once, to Ben's relief, Eric had immediate incentive to drive. At the end of the rainbow, just a long ball away from Angel Stadium, was his hometown. In 30 or so hours, he would get to sleep in his own bed. It was a prospect more thrilling than a walk-off grand slam at this juncture, and he chose not to harp on the fact that the nap would last three hours and be immediately followed by a drive straight up California to San Francisco.

We made good time and no wrong turns through the first several hours of the haul, and then according to our phones we entered Mexico.

"Ben, the GPS stopped." Eric checked his wireless. "Ben, I'm getting hit with international charges."

"I don't think we're in Kansas anymore."

"We haven't been in Kansas in at least a week."

We pulled over. Logically, we knew there was no way we entered Mexico, as America was currently in an all-out battle over immigration laws and everyone would need to back up a few steps if crossing the border was so easy you could accomplish it accidentally. But the complete lack of signage for miles on end did little to dispel our confusion, and the handful of billboards we could find offered both English and Spanish translations. And then there was the matter of every electronic device in the car unanimously deciding that we were definitely in Mexico.

"We're not in Mexico."

"Close your eyes."

Ben closed his eyes.

"Open them. Where are we?"

Ben shrugged. "Probably Mexico."

Eric put the car back into drive.

"Where are you going?"

"Forward. It's either that or I make a U-turn on an interstate."

"It's not an interstate if we're in Mexico."

We continued on through somewhere in North America. Ten minutes later, every device we had switched back to the United States.

"We're home!"

"We're home in fifteen hours."

A few miles later, squarely in the U.S.A., we reached a border patrol station. Eric pulled up to the patrol officer and rolled down his window.

"This is the United States border patrol immigration checkpoint," he stated, tipping his two-gallon hat. "Are you citizens of the United States?"

"Yep," Eric said.

"Thank you. Have a good night."

He waved us along.

"That was it?"

"I thought I looked worldly with this beard. No one checks my ID for anything anymore."

"Sorry, buddy."

Ben's emerging identity crisis was only worsened by the sudden onslaught of New Mexico's existentially troubled signs. We'd barely escaped the immigration checkpoint when one ominous highway notice mused that "Dust storms may exist." It was the uncertainty that we found so disconcerting, being forced to live one's life never quite knowing if dust storms were a real and destructive phenomenon or an even more destructive figment of the imagination. If dust storms didn't exist, then at the end of the day, what did?

Just as we were in the throes of this ethereal quandary, New Mexico did its best to quell our fears. The next sign declared "Zero Visibility Possible." It was a revelation for us there, riding with no end in sight on the open road. Hard as we look, the answers may never be seen.

Our lives failed to acquire an ounce more of purpose over the next thousand miles, and we found ourselves pulling into Long Beach, California, weighed down by both the universe and our eyelids.

Eric's house was a jarring sight because it was a house. Rolling into the driveway, it occurred to us we had seen almost no homes over the course of the month. With the rare exception of ultrarural highway connectors that were lined with the occasional backwoods abode, it was somehow possible to notch thousands of miles across America's vast landscape without encountering almost any American domiciles. Much of this was the product of sticking to streamlined interstates and the urban outlets where ballparks were to be found, but this was still a nation of 300 million. Or as we knew it, three runs in the first inning and then goose eggs for the next eight. We could say that people lived in the plains and the forests and the deserts and the mountains, which we could deduce from the easy logic of there being gas stations in the plains and the forests and the deserts and the mountains, and those gas stations had attendants. Those attendants had to live somewhere.

But aside from the daily dose of 40,000 people with whom we occupied a concrete playhouse, it was gas station attendants from here to infinity with little else to greet us along the way. We were seeing America, but we weren't seeing Americans—at least not in any manner that could be

considered anywhere close to a natural setting. At the ballpark, they were to us what we were to them: some people at
a ballpark. If baseball was an American emblem, this should
have counted for something, but it was the only emblem we
had to go on. It was a sterilized, stigmatized kaleidoscope
of red shirts and blue hats and burps and yawns and smiles.
We were encountering an American stereotype, day in and
day out, a first-world Utopia built of free time, free speech
and expensive beer.

With few exceptions these Americans never became
real to us. We showed up and they were there. They played
their part and then we left. They never went home. We just
drove away.

So when we collapsed at the doorstep of Eric's home,
we felt as though we'd arrived at some rare foreign wonder,
a prop house in a neighborhood exhibit built to show you
how an American *lived*. And if all Americans were like Eric,
then everyone realized after a 21-day drive home that they'd
forgotten to bring their house key.

He rang his own doorbell.

His father opened the door.

We threw down our belongings and took two quick
showers. We'd have to head for Anaheim within a half hour
to catch the Angels play the Pirates. Even so, it was enough
time for Eric to meet his home's newest resident.

"Hi, Grandpa."

His grandpa stood slowly, using the armrests of his
chair for needed leverage. The living room had been re-
modeled since Eric's last visit home, reconfigured into a
bedroom to accommodate his grandfather, Walter. He was

85 going on 86. It was the first time Eric had seen him with an oxygen tank.

"Your mother says you've seen some baseball."

"She would know. You enjoying your new pad?"

He flipped down his hand. "Just living out my life."

"At least you're not living it out at a ballpark. There's a bright side to everything."

He pointed a finger at the TV, his lifeline to the world. "You're going to the Angels tonight?"

"Game Twenty. Go Pirates?"

"Go Pirates."

"I won't tell anyone."

It was time to go.

After an obligatory stint sitting stalled in traffic, we reached Angel Stadium and its gigantic haloed "A" that beckoned cars in from the freeway, even if those cars could not advance three inches without causing a collision. The Angels franchise was no better at locating a home than we were, having changed its name over the decades from the California Angels to the Anaheim Angeles, and then most recently to the Los Angeles Angels of Anaheim. Apart from hurting the feelings of Anaheim, which was itself home to The Happiest Place on Earth, the name change served to contest the Dodgers' longstanding claim to local supremacy. It had been some 25 years since the Dodgers contested anyone for anything, so yawned sportswriters across the county.

We settled into our seats, preparing ourselves for a game that would feel longer than most. On top of coming off the trip's longest endurance drive, we had the disadvantage of having each already been to Angel Stadium. Ben had passed through once years ago on a family trip to California, and Eric had been at least a half-dozen times over the years for birthday parties and class trips. It had become something of a ritual for us to do a walkabout around each stadium after a game's first three innings, but this time our walkabout offered nothing new to see. A three-run second inning for the Pirates put enough distance between the teams to subdue the Angels fan base, unaided by the Angels offense failing to hit the scoreboard through six.

The best moment of the game easily came in the form of a fourth-inning deep fly ball slugged by Pirates left fielder Starling Marte. It was a long ball, the kind that brought a crowd to its feet, only to return everyone to their seats as the outfielder jogged under it and made the easy out. Everything was going as planned: Marte hit high and long to center, the crowd took interest, Angels center fielder Peter Bourjos jogged under it and held up his glove, the crowd promptly lost interest. Then one little thing went wrong: the ball landed twenty feet behind Bourjos, bouncing to the wall.

It wasn't a classic case of a slightly misplaced glove. It was a rare and beautiful case of a glove slightly misplaced by a margin of 20 feet. It was always a strange sight to watch a professional make a mistake. In a game a couple kids with sticks and balls could play on dirt lots, "professional" was often taken to mean "perfect." You did not make it to the major leagues by letting balls roll through your legs. When it happened, it was booed by fans with a fierceness unrivaled by almost any other instance in the game. If it happened in an important game, it was held against you for decades. You could fail seven times out of ten in the batter's box and be a hero, but on the field, you were either good or bad, and good meant perfect while bad meant anything else. Mistakes happened, of course, and no fielder was ever perfect over the course of a whole season or career, though players could reasonably expect to make it through any single game without an error. And there was often a good amount happening on the field at any one time. With a half-dozen players in two different uniforms running around a short infield on a moment's notice, it was not difficult to imagine how a ball could now and then get away.

But an outfielder letting a ball fall 20 feet behind him was a different story altogether. It was not a matter of being mistimed or disoriented. It was a matter of being wrong. He'd jogged under the ball, came to a deliberate stop and held up his glove. The ball didn't catch a bad bounce. The ball caught an extra half of the outfield. It was a little league play through and through, and it made everyone feel a little bit wonderful, because we were all good enough to be little leaguers.

The seventh-inning stretch arrived and we engaged in our once-a-day exercise, shaking out our legs and mumbling along to the seminal "Take Me Out to the Ballgame." It was a pleasant enough song in isolation, but no song was too pleasant after being heard 21 days in a row. And much like the question mark on the national anthem, we'd come to notice a divisive discrepancy in the song's beloved lyrics. While every ballpark agreed on the first three lines—"Take me out to the ballgame/Take me out with the crowd/Buy me some peanuts and Cracker Jack"—there were two schools of thought on the language of the fourth. While 13 of the parks we'd visited displayed it as "I don't care if I ever get back," 10 had broadcasted "I don't care if I *never* get back."

It was a point of intense contention between the two of us, as it seemed preposterous that the two lines could have the same meaning. Neither of us were crazy enough to claim that English was anything close to a completely logical language, but when you had nothing else in life to harp on, it seemed poignantly insane that *ever* and *never* could mean the exact same thing.

"I don't care if I never get back" definitely meant something. We just couldn't agree on what.

"It's saying you don't care if you never go back home," Ben declared. "Because you love baseball so much."

"Home? We're at a ballpark," Eric said. "We're singing it at a ballgame. It has nothing to do with home."

"What's the first line?"

"'Take me out to the ballgame.'"

"Why would you say 'take me out to the ballgame' if you were already at the ballpark?" Ben asked. "This is obvious."

"But we *are* already at the ballgame."

"Well, it's a home song."

"What do you mean, a home song?"

"It's a song you sing at home."

"So you're claiming that the song's narrator is currently at home, saying he wants to go to the ballgame, and once he gets there he doesn't care if he never goes back home."

"Exactly."

"But we're already at the ballgame."

"You can sing a song about something without physically being where the song takes place."

"But you wouldn't make that song an anthem sung only at the place where it says you aren't."

"But they did. It does."

"Who did? Baseball? The narrator?"

"What do you mean, *who*?"

"Who's on first?"

"What?"

"What's on second."

We finished stretching.

"All I'm saying," Eric said, "is 'I don't care if I never get back,' and I'm saying that at the ballpark."

"Well I'm saying it at home."

"But you're at the ballpark."

"Then I'll say it when we get home."

"Fine."

"Fine."

"Want to go home?" Eric asked.

"When the game ends."

Game Twenty-One: San Francisco Giants

Eric's grandfather was asleep when we returned to his home. When he woke the next morning he would have to rely on the sports section to inform him of the 5–2 Pirates' victory. After a three-hour nap, we were already back on the road by 2 AM, northbound for San Francisco.

"We should take the coastal highway when the sun rises," Eric said. "The scenic route's about as scenic as it can get here."

Ben laughed for the first time in several days.

"What's so funny?"

"We're not taking the scenic route."

We didn't.

"I forgot to tell you," Ben told Eric at a gas station somewhere in California's Central Valley. "I landed us some great tickets for the game today. Friend of a friend."

"Friends of friends are the best friends you can have. I thought you already bought tickets for today though."

"And they were pricey. Thirty-eight apiece was the cheapest I could find online. I put them up for resell the other day but nobody bought them."

"You still have them?"

"Yeah, I got the printouts."

"Sounds like somebody just became a scalper."

If peanuts and Cracker Jack were ballpark treasures, then scalpers were ballpark treasures who took your money. Never there when you needed them and always there when you didn't want them, they were a mainstay at every park, innocently loitering at parking lots and on street corners, forever ready to give you a great deal — the best deal you'll get around here, just ask around if you don't believe me. The legality of their dealings was murky, bolstered by disparate state laws that were headaches to parse even if you went out of your way to check them. What was undisputed was their status as full-fledged economies, supplying spontaneous demand with prices that fluctuated in live time. Most were staffed with multiple employees reporting back to a lead investor, creating a park-wide network of scalpers who could maintain a thick profit margin through coordinated price fixing. It was a wildly elastic business, built around a product whose value plummeted toward nothing once the game began. At low-attendance parks, scalpers made their bread and butter selling fancy low-level tickets bought for cheap at marked-down prices. At sold-out parks, the windfall came from anything that let you walk into the ballpark. A standing-room ticket could go for five times its face value on a good day.

The San Francisco Giants happened to play at one of the latter stadiums. AT&T Park boasted a streak of over 202 consecutive sellouts, raising ticket price floors to dizzying heights. It was one of many perks of being home to a team that had won two of the last three World Series.

A parking lot ticket was just as expensive as a game ticket, and Ben dropped another $30 to an overeager attendant who claimed to know where to find the best spot in the lot. How he kept it secret from the hundred cars that had entered before us, we'll never know.

"You have the tickets?" Eric asked, a sentence he spoke once daily. Ben was in charge of the all the games' tickets, possessing a folder full of them that traveled in the backseat at all times.

"We need to pick the good ones up at will call."

We embarked on the five-minute walk to the park.

We'd made it two blocks when a man in a T-shirt three sizes too big approached us with the three words that made the turnstiles turn.

"Buying or selling?"

"We can sell," Ben said, amazed at how easy this was turning out to be.

The man nodded toward a tree a little ways off the street. We followed him behind it.

"What do you got?"

"Two tickets."

"Good stuff?"

"They're the highest," Ben said in his salesman voice.

The man's eyes lit up. "Price level?"

"Literally the highest. The highest up."

"Jesus. That all you got?"

"You want them or not?"

The man frowned and looked around the tree. "Let me see them."

Ben reached into his pocket and came up with nothing. "I forgot them in the car."

Eric stifled his laugh.

The man stared Ben down. "You wasting my time?"

"I parked right over there."

"Then go get them."

Ben nodded nervously. He did his best to not appear nervous. He appeared very nervous.

We walked back toward the parking lot. He followed right behind. Eric stopped at a bench and waited with the man as Ben hurried to the car. He returned a minute later with the tickets. Because we'd purchased most of our tickets on StubHub, the vast majority were printouts with bar codes instead of glossy idyllic stubs.

The man waved them in the wind.

"This is two pieces of paper."

"We bought them online."

"These seats are terrible."

"You can see the whole field from up there, probably."

"Why aren't you using them?"

"We landed some other tickets."

"But you don't have those tickets."

"We're just selling these ones."

"I don't know," the man said. "I don't know. How do I know you're not playing me?"

The question caught Ben off guard, as it was inherent in the scalper-fan relationship that it was the fan who was always played. "They're real. I just bought them online, is all. That's why they look like that."

The man turned to Eric, who had not yet said a word. He'd been standing a few feet away, watching for anyone who might have been watching us. He'd only heard bits and pieces of the conversation.

"These legit?"

"I have no idea," Eric shrugged, thinking that "legit" was being used to mean "good" or "desirable," as in "Those seats at the Yankees game were *legit*!" He had no idea the man was questioning the literal legitimacy of the tickets. He'd done little to help.

The man stared at Ben. Ben stared at Eric. Eric stared at the tickets.

"You playing me?" he said again.

"I'm not playing you," Ben said emphatically.

The man took a long, distrusting breath. "All right. I'll give you twenty."

"I paid more than seventy-five for them both."

"Twenty or walk."

Ben nodded. The man gave him a $20 bill.

We rerouted back to the ballpark. The man waded into the parking lot to flip the tickets for a profit.

Ben wiped the sweat off his brow. "Thanks for backing me up on those legit tickets, man."

"At least it's twenty more than you would have had otherwise."

We located will call and Ben picked up the envelope in his name. Inside we found two tickets for seats smack dab in the center of the section behind home plate. They were glossy and idyllic.

"He would have liked those ones," Eric said.

Ben sighed and let it go, relieved to be done with ticketing for the day. His phone buzzed. He opened the new email.

"Oh no. No, no, no. No."

"What happened?"

"The tickets just sold." He paced back and forth.

"What do you mean?"

"On StubHub. They just resold. Just a few minutes ago."

"The tickets you just sold to the scalper?"

Ben looked around manically.

"You *double-sold* the tickets? You said they didn't sell online!"

"They didn't!"

"But they were still up for sale?"

"No one had bought them in three days—the game starts in thirty minutes!"

"You sold him bum tickets." Eric shook his head. "The tickets weren't legit."

"What do we do?"

"You!" a familiar voice screamed from behind us.

Ben leapt a foot in the air. The man stormed up to him in a raging fury.

"You played me. You think you can play me?"

"I was just going to find you—"

The man waved the two printout tickets in his face. "You give me your word, you give me your word they're legit, so I sell them to a guy, and he goes to enter the park, but they don't scan. They don't scan because they're fakes. The guy went and found a cop, and told the cop I sold him fakes. They just tried to arrest me. They just tried to put me in *handcuffs*. You know why I sold him fakes? I sold him fakes because *you* sold *me* fakes. You think you can play me?"

"I didn't know—"

"What you gonna do about it? How you gonna make this right?"

Ben fumbled for his wallet and fished out the man's twenty.

The man snatched it back. "What else?"

Ben glanced into his wallet. There were only two singles remaining. He handed them to the man.

"What's this?"

"For your troubles."

"Two dollars?"

"It was a misunderstanding."

"The cop taking out handcuffs was a misunderstanding? Me getting arrested because you played me was a misunderstanding?"

"I'm sorry."

The man threw the two dollars on the ground. "What else you gonna do?"

"I—it's just that—I have to go see the first pitch," Ben said, and ran for cover into a crowd of lined up fans and security guards.

"Like I said, I didn't know," Eric sympathized.

"You tell your friend he better be careful." He walked away.

Eric found Ben lurking in the crowd. "Here's your two dollars."

Ben inhaled, then exhaled, then swallowed hard.

"So there might be a bounty on your head," Eric admitted. "But on the bright side, I think it might be Bobblehead Day."

To Eric's great relief, it was. We collected our Ryan Vogelsong bobbleheads and proceeded into the park with our own heads bouncing over our shoulders.

We took our seats in the section behind home plate, but even in the relative security within the ballpark, Ben could not get comfortable. He scanned the crowd anxiously, unsure if scalpers ever actually attended games. They certainly had the tickets necessary to do so.

AT&T Park was a beauty, cast in glamorous sunshine against the San Francisco Bay. Long balls hit over the right field stands would plunge into the water, reeled in by makeshift fisherman who hadn't come for the fish. During the days of the Barry Bonds home run chase, the bay more closely resembled a game of bumper boats, filled to the brim with opportunists looking to make a quick $100,000.

It was a unique ballpark, but then again, it was just another ballpark.

"It's just another ballpark," said the woman behind us. This caught Eric's attention. He was always on the lookout for allies.

As the game progressed, we listened in on her conversation with the spectators in the seats beside her, chiefly comprised of complaints about how baseball was so long and so widespread. She liked Wrigley, was so-so on the

Coliseum and had not yet been to Target Field. She was well traveled for the casual fan.

The Marlins had scored on Ed Lucas' first career home run in the top of the first, and it was quiet on the Western front till a Giants ground rule double knotted the score in the fifth. The 1–1 tie held up through the next four innings, sending the game into extras.

Neither of us had any desire for the upcoming 12-hour drive to Seattle to be any more painful than it would already be, so we reverted to our now standard extra-innings practice of rooting for either team to score. Naturally, this was an uncommon rooting interest, as the overwhelming majority of people present were here for the Giants — and, if not the home team, then the Marlins. But the well-traveled woman behind us shouted a call to arms we hadn't heard once at any other ballpark: "Make the right call!"

She'd belted the declaration out a few times during regulation, but the mantra grew heavy on her lips once extra innings commenced. When the Marlins mounted a rally in the top of the tenth that put runners on first and second, she jumped to her feet.

"Be accurate!"

We thought we'd heard it all by now, but "Be accurate" was a new one.

She settled back into her seat unhappily. "Laz better not blow this," she said.

We looked at the Jumbotron. Giants pitcher Sandy Rosario was on the mound, throwing at Ed Lucas at the plate. Plácido Polanco and Greg Dobbs were standing on first and second. There was no one named Laz to be found.

Eric grabbed a program off the floor and flipped to the officiating section. "Laz Díaz. Second Base."

Ben shook his head. "Marco Scutaro plays second base."

"The other second baseman."

Eric showed him the program. Laz Díaz was the second base ump.

Ed Lucas struck out swinging to bring the half inning to a close.

"That solves that problem," said the woman behind us. "You can't blow a call if you don't have a call to make."

She was the umpire's wife.

"I think she and I would get along," Eric speculated. "We're both stuck traveling around the country visiting ballparks for the sake of game-crazed men."

"She seems to be enjoying herself," Ben countered.

"Well, her man is making money at it. The guy I'm stuck with can't even make twenty dollars."

Ben glanced around instinctively. He sunk a little in his seat.

When Giants pinch hitter Héctor Sánchez lined a walk-off single into left field to send the crowd into jubilant chaos in the bottom of the eleventh, Ben tipped down the bill of his cap, shielded his head with his bobblehead and ran as fast as he could to the car.

Game Twenty-Two:
Seattle Mariners

If the trip's schedule sometimes seemed less than perfect, California was about as perfect as Ben's little league batting average. The trajectory of games in the Golden State was exhibit A for how much the trip relied on the exact particulars of the exact 30-day stretch in which the trip was attempted. With five teams in California alone, a compliant schedule would have entered on one end of the state, driven straight through and exited the other in five days' time. Three or four days could have been hypothetically possible with doubleheaders in LA or the Bay Area.

Instead, there were no possible doubleheaders in those regions in the month of June. What was more, this was the only six-day stretch in which all five California teams played at home. Even then, it was not that simple. The Angels and Giants were in town till the 23rd, the Dodgers didn't show up till the 24th, the Athletics on the 26th and the Padres had two off days dotted in between. The result was a combination of games that made it logistically impossible to see the Angels and Dodgers or Giants and Athletics play two days in a row. Even if we were forty minutes from Dodger Stadium, it would take us forty hours of driving before we could see a game there.

This was all thanks to Seattle.

When selecting cities for professional sports franchises, the formula was not complicated. Where there are a lot of people, there will be a team. It was how California wound up with five franchises while neighboring Oregon and Nevada combined for none. Big cities meant the big leagues, and it was as simple as that. With America's population geographically distributed in a distinctly uneven manner, this meant one city could have two teams while the next six states over could have none at all. When coordinating a massive road trip linking all these major cities, this distribution was often a blessing. States like New York and Florida could cross off several ballparks with minimal mileage.

And then there was Seattle. Scenic, seaside, sleepless Seattle, so sizable and saturated, and so, so, so far away from any other team. Tucked neatly into the northwest corner of the continental United States, the nearest team was a debilitating 12 hours away. It was home to the most isolated MLB franchise by a wide and very measurable margin — beating out Colorado by a breezy 200 miles — and the need to reach it in a 30-day whirlwind was the ultimate efficiency killer. At a game-a-day pace, there was no option to get there but by passing through either San Francisco or Oakland. And once you were in California, you were so isolated from everywhere that wasn't California that it was also necessary to hit the state in one fell swoop. With the majority of teams weighing down the eastern half of the United States, California was one giant thousand-mile pit stop that mandated every other leg of the trip being structured around it. Not only did the California stars have to line up, but the Space Needle had to poke its way into the mess as well.

Because of all this, though many of the games were interchangeable within small clusters of dates, the Seattle game could be on no day other than the 23rd. Only on that day did we have a San Francisco launching pad and a Los Angeles cushion. Although it would have saved us a total of fourteen hours of driving if Oakland played at home the day after Seattle, that would of course have been too easy. Instead, we had to take advantage of the Seattle game's afternoon status to drive 18 hours down to Los Angeles for a Dodgers game. Then we'd head down to San Diego, and only *then* all the way back up to Oakland. Rather than getting to make a single — dare we say pleasant — drive up the California coast, we'd be driving the coast a convoluted three times.

So we drove toward Seattle with nothing but loving thoughts in mind, rejoicing in the quaint anonymity of metropolitan area after metropolitan area that was not quite metropolitan enough.

After four hours of progress, the radio gave out and the breathtaking views snuck in. Coming around a bend somewhere nearing the top of California, the road veered away from a sweeping expanse of pristine blue water and red rock.

A light drizzle pelting at the purple sunset did little to hurt the panorama. When we both simultaneously broke an hour of complete silence to exclaim, "Where are we?" we knew we were onto something good.

The something was called Lake Shasta, a name we identified upon taking the next exit to find food. Our electronics had lost all service miles ago, and we guessed our way into a small campground just off the jutting cliffs.

The one and only food option was a small hole in a very large wall called the Klub Klondike. It was clear from the looks on the patrons' faces that they knew as well as we did what we were doing there. Each leaned into their barstools, fiftysomething, bearded and tattooed. They knew each other by nickname and they might have never known anyone else. No one new ever came and no one old ever left.

"What do you want?" the barkeep asked.

"Do you have a menu?"

She thought for a moment. "Yeah, we have a menu." She disappeared into the kitchen and returned with one for the two of us.

Our plates came almost as quickly as we ordered them. A big-screen TV at the end of the room played none other than an A's game, delighting us with a sport we'd dearly missed in our four hours of absence.

"Who d'you think'll win?" the man with the second-longest beard asked.

"Not sure," decided the bronze medalist.

It was a quiet affair until yet another bearded man entered through the club's creaking door, cupping something unidentifiable in his hands. He went up to the nearest patron at the end of the bar and displayed his possession with pride.

"Here she is," he said. "Guinness book of world records!"

We tried to sneak a peek of what he was holding to no avail. He cupped it back in his hands and jogged to the other end of the bar. "Guinness book of world records," he announced again. "Can you believe it?"

We finished our meals and left a crisp twenty on the table, the most we'd paid outside of a ballpark in days. That's what happened when you ate food that came on a plate. As we rose to head out, a new customer entered the establishment. The world record holder immediately ran up to inform him of the news. We approached to finally get our look.

The man held out his hands, revealing a tiny piece of engraved wood. "There she is," the man smiled. "Right in front of your eyes. World's smallest bear carved with a chainsaw."

We looked at each other, confident we could not have possibly heard that right.

We walked outside. Parked in the space front and center was an open-bed pickup with two-dozen carved bear statues piled up in the trunk.

We looked at each other, no longer sure if confidence in this life would ever be possible again.

We climbed back into the car and Eric twisted the key in the ignition.

"It says 'Low Tire Pressure.' Should we get it checked out?"

"We don't have time for tire problems. We got to hit the road."

"That sounds like a great way to promote long-term efficiency."

We hit the road.

Though it rained as we entered Seattle, we were once again protected by the promise of Safeco Field's retractable dome. Paradoxically, the cities with the most rain experienced the fewest rainouts, as their stadiums were built with weather patterns in mind. The one saving grace of Seattle's scheduling headache was that once it was placed on the calendar, we could rest assured that it would not be taken off.

We could also enter knowing we'd have no shortage of conversation. After yet another long spell of having no one to talk to but each other, we'd be joined by Eric's best friend from home. Trevor was a Long Beach native now studying in Seattle. He'd grown up a mile from Eric's house. They'd gone to kindergarten together, followed by middle school and high school in due time. They had a lot in common. One thing they did not have in common was baseball. Trevor was a baseball fanatic.

He had played since he could walk, rising through the ranks of little leagues, club teams and high school ball. Though he hung up his cleats in college, he retained an avid interest in the game, brought up to love the sport by his equally athletic father. And as it happened, the two were so enamored by the game that they made it their mission to visit all 30 ballparks together. Of course, visiting all 30 was no easy task, and it was an endeavor that would take them years. They'd been hitting two or three parks a year since he was ten years old, methodically taking summer road trips in unexplored quadrants of the country as they crossed each stadium off their list. They'd so far managed to visit 21 parks, a feat that left them with fond memories and a story to tell from each. It was the ultimate father-son bonding experience, a decades-long commitment to living out all the Americana the country could produce. Eric had watched them embark on their baseball trips year after year, never certain of the allure but respectful of the undertaking.

So when Ben first proposed 30 games in 30 days, all Eric could think about was Trevor and his father. Trevor had spent half his life executing this exact trip, and now we were going to knock it out in the span of a month. Trevor's attempt was marked by the romance of generations, an annual family affair that distilled the game into its most beloved associations and delivered them in digestible doses. Ben's attempt was a haphazard free-for-all that savored nothing and stomached less. Setting out to hit them all in 30 days seemed unforgivingly cheap and superficial. It was cheating the experience, marginalizing the allure. Trevor could remember Miller Park and think of the stirring and sentimental. Eric could remember Miller Park and think of the place between Illinois and Colorado. It seemed like an injustice that he could beat Trevor to the punch on his quest to reach all 30 parks.

Even after he accepted Ben's offer, Eric was too ashamed to tell Trevor about the premise of the trip. He'd only mentioned he'd be passing through Seattle and wanted to go to a Mariners game.

"How many will you have seen by then?" he had asked.
"You know?"

"You thought I wouldn't find out?"

"Did my mother tell your mother?"

"Lucky guess."

"We'll have seen twenty-one by then," Eric had told him.

"You'll have beaten me."

We picked him up at his campus and pulled into a lot across from Safeco Field.

"We're plotting out a trip for September," Trevor said, leading us to the park's side entrance. "We're thinking of starting in Denver, then driving to Kansas City and St. Louis. There's an off chance we could even hit Atlanta."

"We did all those last week," Ben said proudly.

Eric bowed his head in disgrace.

As the Mariners teed off against the Oakland A's, Trevor recited the rosters effortlessly as Eric struggled to name a single player on either team. When Raúl Ibañez hit a two-run homer for the Mariners in the bottom of the first, Eric saw a two-run homer. Trevor saw a two-run homer by an ageless 41-year-old veteran who'd been red hot as a Yankee in October the year before. When Ibañez hit another home run in the fourth inning, Eric saw another home run. Trevor saw a man outplaying Father Time.

"So, I mean, are you surviving?" Trevor asked when Ben left in pursuit of his hot dog and beer.

"Surviving," Eric affirmed.

"Are you enjoying it?"

"Surviving," Eric said encouragingly.

Trevor shrugged. "You guys are just doing it wrong, is all."

"You ever get sick of baseball?"

"I'd get sick of anything thirty times in a row."

Mariners pitcher Jeremy Bonderman threw a wild pitch past the plate. Oakland shortstop Jed Lowrie slid into home for a run.

"Strikes!" Trevor shouted at the field. "All you have to do is throw strikes!"

When the A's tied the game at three apiece in the eighth inning, we did our best to come to terms with the prospect of seeing two extra-inning games in a row. In the grand scheme of entire seasons, around one in every ten games required extras to produce a victor. When the Seattle side was retired in the bottom of the ninth without scoring a run, it became our fourth extra-inning contest in the span of 22 games, putting us at nearly double the pace of the statistic we were most hoping to undershoot. The silver lining came in the timing of the extra-inning games; as of yet, they'd only occurred on days when we had enough wiggle room in the schedule to afford an extra hour or two of play.

The same would be the case here. Though the trip back to Los Angeles would extend past 18 hours, we had 27 to complete the drive. Extras would make one of our hardest drives even harder, but—yet again—not impossible.

When the A's couldn't advance a base runner with no outs in the top of the tenth, we settled in for the long haul. So far we'd seen two 11-inning affairs and one game stretch to 13. We weren't eager to break our record.

The players felt the same way. With one out in the bottom of the tenth, Mariners catcher Mike Zunino struck out swinging. In a play usually confined to the whims of little leaguers, the ball got away from A's catcher John Jaso and Zunino received a free pass to first base. Michael Saunders followed up the gift with a single, putting runners on first and second with one out. The Mariners sent pinch hitter Kendrys Morales to the plate.

The job of pinch-hitting was a hero's calling. Reserved for late-game situations demanding a fresh bat, pinch hitters were weighed down with more pressure to perform than any other player on a team. They were inserted for the sole purpose of offensive production. If they got out, they indiscriminately failed. There was no other aspect to their job. On the flip side, when they found success, it was often rewarded with a dog pile atop home plate. With one swing of the bat they could change the course of a game or season, and sometimes one swing of the bat was all they got.

Morales was no stranger to game-winning celebrations, nor season-ending ones. After hitting a walk-off grand slam in the tenth inning of a game in 2010, Morales triumphantly jumped on home plate into the arms of his mobbing teammates, landing awkwardly on his ankle. The ankle was broken and required surgery. He missed the remainder of the season, and then the entirety of the next. Sammy Sosa was once placed on the disabled list after a violent sneeze, and John Smoltz burnt his chest while attempting to iron the shirt he was wearing. At least Morales knew how to make the comically idiotic seem glamorous.

"He's not too good at walk-offs," Trevor said.

Morales dug into the plate and received exactly one pitch. He landed it a few hundred feet away behind the center field fence. The Mariners flooded onto the field. Morales rounded the bases and headed for home with his team waiting. He very gingerly waded in and tapped home plate.

"He's gotten a lot better at them," Trevor admitted.

Baseball was a learning experience.

Game Twenty-Three: Los Angeles Dodgers

Spending every minute of every day with a person inevitably results in telepathy. You come to know them so well you can speak their thoughts for them before they have the chance to think those thoughts themselves. You know a quick glance out the car window means we need to find the nearest bathroom stop. You know a subtle squirm means it's mealtime.

Soon it's more than just thoughts that fall in sync. It's the opinions held in those thoughts as well. You know you're both thinking the truck two cars ahead is going 12 miles an hour slower than it should be. You know you both can't comprehend how a 32-ounce drink can be sold at a profit for 59 cents. You know you're both convinced that little girl three rows down will never finish that ice cream.

But every now and then, you still find time to disagree.

The drive from Seattle to Los Angeles was as straight of a shot as we'd have all month. You left Seattle, got on the I-5 South, and got off in Los Angeles. It was that simple. You drove onto the I-5 South and then a thousand miles later you were there. There was nothing else you needed to do.

Ben took the first shift behind the wheel, commencing our quest down the I-5. Quickly running out of classic rock and NPR talk shows to listen to, we'd downloaded Ken Burns' audiobook on baseball's storied history, delicately titled *Baseball*. It was an interesting listen, detailing the sport from its convoluted birth through its present-day trials and triumphs. A hodgepodge of historical fact and glamorous re-counting of the game's more memorable moments, it sought to condense over a century of history into "nine innings" of handpicked information.

Much of the program was based on portraying base-ball as a poignant metaphor on the nature of America in each era the game was played. The theory had its merits, though much of what was said could often be attributed to nearly any American sport. While many of baseball's story lines indisputably overlapped with our nation's larger narrative—the color barrier, labor disputes and capitalistic expansion were all undeniable places to begin—it begged the question of whether it was possible to wax equally poetic about sports less soaked in uncontested Americana. We could only imagine what a Ken Burns documentary on water polo might produce. People, balls, people playing with balls—just like with baseball, the potential symbol-ism was endless.

But our favorite part of the program came in the form of a throwaway paragraph on the evolution of baseball's rules:

One afternoon in 1863 Ned Cuthbert of the Philadelphia Key-stones ran from first to second without waiting for a hit to get him there. The crowd laughed at his presumption, but he pointed out to the umpire that there was no rule against what he had done. It was the first stolen base in baseball. Although purists thought stealing deceitful, the crowds loved it.

The idea of a player deciding he could run to second base at any time simply because no one had ever pointed out he couldn't was possibly the second funniest thing we'd ever heard on audio tape during a 30-day baseball trip. The idea of the umpire agreeing with him because, hey, why not, and it henceforth became holy scripture took the number one spot.

"That's ridiculous," Ben said. "Stealing clearly wasn't intended by the rules."

"So you're a spirit of the law guy?"

"Who knows what you could do if you just started doing everything and anything the rules didn't explicitly prohibit."

"That's why you should read the rules."

"But that's what I'm saying. That sort of close reading isn't reasonable."

"You have to assume the author meant exactly what he wrote and chose those precise words for a reason."

"Close reading is illegitimate. An author's word-by-word selection is very arbitrary."

Eric turned down the volume on the audiobook. He checked the GPS. It was 6 PM and we had 15 hours and 45 minutes of driving left to complete. There was time to hash this one out. "Are you trying to tell me that you don't recognize close reading as a legitimate form of criticism in literature?"

"It's not. Analyzing why an author stuck a preposition in a certain place in a sentence on a certain page in a book is completely pointless. If he went to write that sentence five minutes later, it would come out differently."

"So you're going with a reductive argument here? If the words are arbitrary, then the thoughts that put them there are arbitrary, which means everything we do is arbitrary, and everything we touch is arbitrary, and soon we're sitting here driving through an entirely arbitrary universe."

"Well, yeah," Ben said. "But I won't go there right now. All I'm saying is that close reading is a waste of time."

If close reading was a waste of time, then arguing about close reading was a very fruitful way to pass the time. Because for the first time all month, we lost track of time. The conversation traveled with us from Washington on into Oregon. It was the most heated argument we'd ever gotten into, and it was about close reading.

At a little past seven Eric glanced at the clock as Ben lectured him on why randomness was at the heart of syntax. Eric then looked at the GPS.

"Wait a minute."

"No, you don't understand. It doesn't matter if the underlying idea is the same. The holder of that idea will express it differently at all different points in time."

"Hold on."

"Why spend an extra minute thinking about why an author chose to use the same word twice in a paragraph when you could spend that minute thinking about the actual meaning."

"Ben, stop talking."

"No. You're missing the point entirely—"

"*Shut up!*"

Ben shut up.

"We're in Washington," Eric said.

"So?"

"Remember when we crossed into Oregon? *From* Washington?"

Ben looked at the sign on the upcoming overpass. "SEATTLE—LEFT TWO LANES."

"We're headed to Seattle."

"We were coming *from* Seattle."

"But we're on the I-5."

"The I-5 North."

"But we were on the I-5 South."

"Well, two hours ago we had 15 hours and 45 minutes left to drive. Now we have 15 hours and 46 minutes left to drive."

"That's not possible."

We pulled over.

"But we were going south. Is there a second, smaller Seattle in Oregon?"

Eric scrolled through the directions. "Ben."

"What?"

"You said we just stay on the I-5 for a thousand miles."

"Yes. Stay on the I-5 for a thousand and ninety-one miles."

"But that's not what the directions say. The directions say that in eighty-five miles, you stay *right* on the I-5. Did you ever leave the left lane?"

"We were arguing!"

"You didn't stay right."

"But that doesn't explain how we're going *north* on the same exact freeway."

Eric zoomed out the map. "When you stayed left, you merged onto another highway. When you stayed left on that highway, you merged onto yet another highway. When you stayed left on *that* highway, you merged back onto the I-5. The I-5 North."

"You're telling me I took a two-hour-long U-turn on a U.S. interstate?"

"That's exactly what I'm telling you."

"Well, we were arguing!" Ben argued again.

"What's that have to do with you driving in the exact opposite direction of where we were supposed to go?"

"The lady inside the GPS would've told me to stay right, but she's hooked up to the radio. You turned off the volume because you wanted to argue about close reading!"

"At least now the argument's done," Eric said.

"You're finally giving in?"

"To the contrary. If you'd close-read the directions, you'd have never gone the wrong direction."

Ben had to admit he had a point.

"And that's how you turn an eighteen-hour drive into a twenty-hour drive."

"At least the Washington-Oregon border is scenic," Ben offered.

"It *is* scenic," Eric agreed.

If Eric were ever a baseball fan, he would have been a fan of the Dodgers. They were a baseball institution, descendants of the legendary Brooklyn franchise that rose to power in the 1950s. They were dependable, a feat exemplified by their announcer Vin Scully, who had moved west with the team in 1958 and whose smooth, soothing voice had been calling their games ever since. If baseball could speak, it would sound like Vin Scully.

And the Dodgers were Eric's home team. And they were just often good enough to be aggravating. And most important, he had their bobbleheads. There was nothing not to like aside from the fact they played baseball.

We were joined at the game by two mutual friends, one named Sierra, and, for good measure, another guy unhelpfully named Eric. (For the sake of distinguishing him from both Eric and Eric 2, who we met with in Boston, we will call him "Eric 3." Though if Ben had his way, they would be marked as Eric 0, Eric 1, and Eric 2.) Both Sierra and Eric 3 had grown up in the area and always called the Dodgers their team.

"How long have you been a fan?" Eric asked Eric 3.

"I've been a lifelong fan. Straight from the womb."

"That's pretty early on."

"Vin Scully announced my birth."

"He did what?"

"When my mom went into labor, Vin Scully's granddaughter was being born in the same maternity ward. He was just wandering around the ward when he saw a screaming woman. So he came into my mom's room as I was popping out and yelled, 'It's a boy!'"

That was one neither of us had heard before. "Well then. Straight from the womb it is."

We took our seats above the foul pole in the right field corner, overlooking Chavez Ravine. Dodger Stadium was surprisingly less than flashy for a Hollywood affair, but its five decades of lore made up for its muted tones. As long as the lore kept growing, there would be no complaints.

One new addition was a player by the name of Yasiel Puig, a Cuban refugee who had never played in an MLB game as of the start of our road trip. The Dodgers held the only roster Eric was even remotely familiar with by virtue of reading the local sports pages, so when the name Puig popped up on a score update a week into the trip, he'd taken casual notice. In the span of a week, the updates evolved from "Dodger rookie Yasiel Puig" to "Yasiel Puig's Dodgers." A player Eric had never heard of had become the face of the franchise in the span of a week. Soon he was at the forefront of every highlight reel we encountered. And suddenly the Dodgers were winning.

"What's this Puig guy's deal?" Eric asked as Puig came to the plate in the first inning.

"He's a winner," explained Eric 3. "He just gets up there and wins."

Ten seconds later Puig hit a home run.

"Well, I'm convinced," Eric decided.

Puig had rejuvenated the Dodgers, who had been lacking both energy and wins throughout the first two months
of the season. For a team that had poured $200 million into
its roster, the sub-500 start to the season had thrown the city
into lavish despair. Suddenly, out of nowhere, from the most
unlikely of places, they had found unadulterated excellence.
Eric refused to admit so out loud, but it was a little exciting.

The Giants evened the score with a run in the second.
The game might have been tied at 1–1, but it was too early for
us to worry about a third straight extra-innings game. When
it was still 1–1 in the eighth inning, it was no longer too early.

But one quick glance at the upcoming Dodgers lineup
made clear our problems would undoubtedly be solved. Puig
was third up to bat.

The rest of the team figured they might as well make it
easy on Puig. Third baseman Nick Punto opened the inning
with a double. Second baseman Mark Ellis followed up by
putting a ball in play that led to a Giants throwing error,
advancing runners to first and third.

Then up came Puig, and with every Dodgers fan in the
stadium wholeheartedly certain of what would happen next,
Puig drilled a grounder through the shortstop and third base
hole for the game-winning RBI. The Dodgers went on to
win the game 3–1, adding to the long list of Puig heroics in
just his first month in the league.

Puig was a winner, and the Dodgers were winners, and
Eric hated baseball but if he was to like it, the Dodgers were
his team. At 21 years old he was almost ready to be birthed
into Dodgers fandom—he would just have to wait for Vin
Scully to announce it officially.

Game Twenty-Four:
San Diego Padres

San Diego was a blissful two-hour drive down the coast from Los Angeles, granting us twelve full hours of sleep. The closest we'd come to feeling refreshed, we drove south to the City of Good Living.

"It'd hate to live in San Diego," Ben said as we crossed over the city limit. "It seems so boring here."

"Exactly," Eric agreed. "A beautiful beachside community with beautiful views and beautiful people, a functioning city district with national businesses, professional teams, historic buildings, international culture and a nightlife in weather that's eighty degrees and sunshine every day of the year. I get bored to death just thinking about it."

We blindly bought the two cheapest tickets available and walked into PETCO Park, which was somehow not presently engaged in a Puppypalooza. Twenty feet from the entrance gates we saw an enormous grassy hill. "That looks amazing," Eric said. "Let's just lay out and watch the game from here."

Ben didn't protest. While we were 500 feet away from home plate, they were unarguably the best seats we could find. There was not only legroom, but room to lay down. There were no numbers, just squatters marking their territory. We were still part of a crowd but were not overwhelmed by the electronic noises and distractions.

It was peaceful on the knoll. Baseball games were anything but peaceful. You went to a game to hear loud noises and make loud noises and hear other people make loud noises. You came to be surrounded by people squeezed so tight it would have broken fire codes anywhere else in the city. You showed up to eat bad food and sip worse drinks and tell the tale of survival the next day at the office. For a game that was almost meditative on the field, it was anything but in the stands. The knoll was like a game away from a game. It was a reprieve.

PETCO impressed elsewhere as well. Uncharacteristically spacious, it was casually oriented and immaculately clean, not out of place for a state that was more image obsessed than most. It even featured a miniature man-made beach on the other side of the center field fence. Children played in the sand as the grown-ups played alongside them in the dirt.

After six innings of remaining sprawled out on the grass, Ben asked Eric if he wanted to at least check out the seats we'd paid for. Eric begrudgingly nodded and looked down at his ticket.

"I don't see a seat number. It just says 'Park in the Park.'"

"No, I think we're in section twenty-five."

"That's today's date. Our seats are just 'Park in the Park.'"

"Well, where's that supposed to be?"

Eric looked at him patiently. He nodded toward the ground we were sitting on.

"Wow. We found our seats without even trying. We're getting good at this."

Part VI

It Ain't Over Till It's Over 30 Times

Game Twenty-Five:
Oakland Athletics

The I-5 North took us back through Los Angeles and up to Oakland, running our tally on the highway up to 2,700 miles. It would be our last time in California, a fact neither of us was pleased with. Eric didn't want to leave home turf. Ben was acutely aware of the turf we'd be entering. After Oakland, we had five remaining games: the Colorado Rockies (attempt #2), the Houston Astros, the Chicago White Sox (attempt #2), the New York Mets, and the Toronto Blue Jays. The stretch consisted of over 4,000 miles and 60 hours of driving in four days.

It was our worst stint of driving by far. The original algorithm would have never allowed it, but with the need to revisit both Colorado and Chicago, we'd thrown convenience to the wind. Caution had blown away long ago.

On top of the revised plan requiring lengthier individual drives, the games were now more compactly scheduled as well — so compact that they probably weren't even possible. Our drive from Houston to Chicago was slated to take sixteen-and-a-half hours, almost exactly how long we had between the cities if the Astros game was the average length of two hours and fifty-eight minutes. That was not including stops for gas and any unforeseen emergencies.

This made us nervous, and it of course made Eric's mother Motherly Nervous, as the schedule had been much friendlier when she'd reluctantly given her blessing to the trip. So we returned to our increasingly dwindling list of mutual friends who might be willing to stomach a few days on the road. We quickly agreed on Tyler, who we'd crossed paths with on our first stint in Colorado, and he quickly agreed with us. In return for flying out west, we'd give him a free taxi ride back across the country. The problem was, Tyler had booked his ticket to arrive in Los Angeles.

At first we thought we'd be going from San Diego to Denver. We would pick Tyler up at LAX, drive down to the Padres game and then continue our way back east. But the drive from San Diego to Denver was an uncomfortably close call, though only in the sense that it was theoretically impossible. It was a fifteen-and-a-half hour drive in a sixteen-hour window, assuming an average-length game and no traffic. Banking on no traffic in California was unwise even by our standards, and a more scrutinizing look at the schedule revealed that we could flip the second half of the California stretch so that we finished up in Oakland. Since Oakland was an afternoon game, it would give us enough road time to safely arrive in Colorado.

This was all good and well, except for the part where we'd already booked Tyler's flight to Los Angeles. So we sucked it up and booked Tyler a second flight from LAX to Oakland, which meant he would be notching a total of two layovers and eight hours of flying before he joined us for a 60-hour drive back to where he started from. It was 99.99% of the population's travel nightmare, but for Tyler it was an *adventure*. It was an opinion that perhaps only Ben could understand.

"Do you think we should get the car checked out before the final push?" Eric asked. "We have a free hour before the game."

"I don't know. The car feels pretty fine."

"That low tire-pressure light has been on for like 2,000 miles now."

We found an auto-repair shop near the O.co Coliseum and handed the keys off to the attendant.

"Yep," he said immediately. "That's a flat tire."

The afternoon game in Oakland was another brutally hot affair, though it did little to mask the gloom hanging over the impending drives. The Oakland Athletics shared a stadium with the Oakland Raiders, the last such pair of baseball and football teams to do so. In some respects, the grouping made sense. They were both sports played out-doors, and both needed places for fans to sit.

In all other ways, it made no sense. A football field was a rectangle to baseball's diamond. With a few seating rearrangements, an engineer could make the fields fit on top of each other the way a preschooler could fit a diamond on top of a rectangle and receive a gold star for effort.

The fundamental problem was that baseball seats were naturally supposed to be positioned toward home plate, where 90% of the action occurred. In football, seats were angled toward midfield. The middle of where the football field overlapped with the baseball diamond was clearly somewhere just past second base. At least that was where all the seats were facing. We were sitting the wrong way, and as Eric would have Ben believe, watching the wrong sport.

Strangely enough, Ben had been to the O.co Coliseum for a Jaguars football game, but never for baseball. Before that game began, stat-intern Ben was stuck on one side of the field and needed to make it back to the team's headquarters in the press box before the game started. An Oakland Raiders team employee instructed him to walk along the outside of the field. If the fastest possible route entailed getting to walk the turf of a real NFL stadium, Ben was not going to complain. But just as he emerged from the team exit, a stampede of scantily clad women mobbed him. It was a dream and a nightmare come true all at once. Every single Oakland Raiders cheerleader in the history of the Raiderettes was taking the field, all returning for a 50th anniversary reunion. He became trapped in their grand entrance onto the field. Despite a good effort, he was not named the crowd's favorite Raiderette.

If we were suffering in the heat in Oakland, the opposing Cincinnati batters were struggling even worse. Athletics pitcher A.J. Griffin tossed a gem, throwing a complete nine innings and giving up only two hits, both of which had bounced off the gloves of fielders. If both of those players had been playing a step to their left or jumped a tenth of a second earlier, Griffin would have been a household name for baseball fans. Instead, it was just another hard-earned shutout. Not even Ben could remember his name a few days later when recounting the outing to a friend.

Game Twenty-Six:
Colorado Rockies

We left the ballpark and waited for Tyler to arrive from his tour of America's airports. We passed the time by playing a game of indoor mini-golf near the airport, which served as a proxy fight for superiority on the road trip. Eric won by a stroke and Ben was left to pick up the tab.

The drive to Denver was a bruiser, looking to tilt toward 20 hours with traffic. It would have been a few hours shorter to leave from Southern California as originally planned, but that would have also meant leaving five hours later, after a night game. We pulled up to the terminal when Tyler gave news of his arrival.

"All right," Ben said, pulling away the second Tyler closed the door, "we're driving back to exactly where you came from."

Tyler tossed his bag into the trunk atop the pile of foam fingers. "Can we make a stop at—"

"We only have time for one stop on the way to Denver. It's twenty hours."

"It's the only stop I want to make on the entire trip and it's right there. I want to go to In-N-Out."

"Aren't you a vegetarian?"

"I want to go to In-N-Out."

Tyler was a vegetarian, or he was 99% of the time. He reserved the right to eat meat on special occasions, which meant Thanksgiving, Christmas and In-N-Out.

He ended up eating two burgers, both double-patties. The 130-pound, six-foot-tall man had fasted all day, since he boarded a plane in Boston 15 hours earlier, just to be able to consume the greasy goodness of In-N-Out. We returned to the car. Tyler brought with him an order of fries for the road. It was our one extended pit stop on our 20-hour drive and we'd made it within the first half hour.

We drove west into Nevada. Ben did most of the shift through the desert, often pushing 100 or 105 on the speedometer as he sped his way into the darkness. It was one of the most desolate drives of the entire trip. A sign for "No Services for 37 Miles" would be followed by an exit 37 miles later and another sign announcing "No Services for 29 Miles," which was invariably followed 29 miles later by a casino.

Eric took the Utah shift, crossing for a second time the state we thought we wouldn't be crossing once, and handed the wheel over to Tyler in Wyoming. It was 7 AM, and as both of us had been up all night driving, we promptly fell asleep the moment Tyler took the wheel.

Not 20 minutes later, we were startled from our sleep when we realized the car wasn't moving.

"License and registration."

Another speeding ticket. With this one going to Tyler, Ben was now miraculously the only driver in the car without a ticket despite speeding the most out of all of us.

"Mr. Tyler Richard," the officer informed him, "I'm issuing you a citation. You have two options. First, you can go online to pay the 160-dollar fee. Second, you can return to Evanston, Wyoming, on July 30th, 2013 at 9:00 AM to contest it at the courthouse. Is that clear?"

"Yes, Officer."

Yes, Officer, it was clear that Tyler would not be able to return to the middle-of-nowhere Wyoming a month from now to contest a ticket. When the cop saw that we were driving with a New Hampshire license plate 2,200 miles away from New Hampshire, he could feel reasonably confident about landing a guilty plea. We wouldn't have a choice, even if we were innocent. Of course, we were not. Tyler had been driving about 15 miles above the limit, which seemed like child's play at this juncture. Ben could barely remember the last time he was driving less than 15 miles above the limit. Other than the In-N-Out feast, it was the second stop Tyler had forced upon the trip before we reached Denver, and it would be our last.

We reached Denver three hours early. We knew the feeling. It was exhausted déjà vu. We'd arrived in Denver three hours early 19 days prior, except then we'd parlayed it into being an hour late.

The Super 8 motel within shouting distance of Coors Field was our Achilles' heel, causing Ben to miss the Rockies and Eric to miss the Belmont. But the sleep was so good while it lasted. Not knowing what else to do with ourselves and feeling cheated out of a nap weeks earlier, we returned to the scene of the crime. We parked in the same parking spot and reserved our room from the same receptionist. Though Ben remembered her, she could not place the face of a bearded man with bags under his eyes growing wider by the day. Since leaving Denver, we'd driven 14,000 miles, been to 29 states and seen both coasts. But chances were she'd never left Denver the entire time. She still had her computer screen open to the Yahoo! homepage. Nothing had changed at the front desk of the Super 8. Life went on, no matter how many Rockies games you didn't go to.

We were given a different room this time. Eric and Tyler settled in for naps, But Ben couldn't sleep. He had PTSD if PTSD could be diagnosed for things in life that did not actually matter. He passed the time by doing what he'd failed to do before. He checked the official game time on the Rockies' website repeatedly. He checked it on the MLB's website repeatedly. He checked it on ESPN's website repeatedly. He even forced Tyler and Eric to check it when they awoke. Repeatedly.

This time there were no blunders. Tyler dropped us off at the stadium a full 30 minutes early. He'd been to a baseball game the last time we were in Denver and one baseball game in thirty days was sufficient. He found a local record store and set off to browse its selection.

Meanwhile, we were going through the motions at Coors Field. We arrived, bought the cheapest seats we could find and immediately sat down in the first empty shaded seats we saw. The Rocky Mountains had already been beautiful, a hot dog and beer had already been devoured, a foam finger had already been purchased. We were on repeat with nothing left to do or say. We sat in silence, Ben plowing through a bag of peanuts one by one, Eric sipping on water. We had become sages of the baseball experience. When in the bottom of the fourth inning, three animated baseball hats shuffled around the Jumbotron hiding a baseball, we both muttered "three" in unison the moment they stopped. The ball was under hat number three. We did not even need to wait for the answer to pop up. We'd seen the game played on the big screen for 27 consecutive days at 27 different parks, and we were fairly sure they repeated the patterns.

There was nothing we didn't know at the ballpark. We knew that the family in front of us would not make it through all nine innings. We knew the college kid on a date a few seats down would not tip the concessions man serving him beer. And we knew the Mets would hold on to win, though that knowledge seemed like a footnote to everything else we had picked up along the way.

Tyler taxied us out of Denver once we finished righting our wrongs. The drive to Houston was 16 hours, but we had 21 to get it done. By now that was just our routine daily commute, and we knew if we followed our own set of rules we would never be late for work.

Tyler wanted to stop for dinner just out of Denver. "No," we assured him, "if we stop now we'll be hungry again in around seven hours but then it will be 3:00 AM and in the desert almost everything is closed at 2:00 AM. If we hold off for a few hours and eat at 11:00 PM, we'll get hungry again at 6:00 AM, when things open for breakfast."

It was the pattern of unhealthy eating and three-hour sleep cycles we had gotten used to on the trip. It was so simple, it was practically formulaic.

In the meantime, as Ben busied himself with scrutinizing the remainder of our schedule, Eric tidied up a little planning of his own. In the days after the Cleveland game and our oh-so-close run-in with Cleveland announcer Tom Hamilton, Eric had been laying the groundwork for a plan that would take the prank to the next level. Ever since he'd nearly gotten to call a play in the announcer's booth, Ben had been endlessly blabbing about what he would say for the world to hear and how he'd be a natural at the job. Eric had generously offered to plan the logistics with our friend Allison and set up a meet with Hamilton when we saw the Indians visit the White Sox in Chicago in a few days' time.

But Allison was not the only friend of Ben's who Eric was coordinating with. Eric happened to know a Chicago resident who was also an NFL front office exec: Ben's boss, Tony. Eric had a feeling that Tony would love nothing more than to see Ben completely freak out.

Just as Eric had hoped, Tony happened to have a friend who worked for Chicago's ESPN Radio. And naturally, he was more than happy to help prank Ben. As a stat wonk and sports lover, being featured on ESPN was the holy grail of the sports industry. He loved the network and watched it daily, intimately familiar with each broadcaster and show, all the way down to the segments.

The plan was simple: Allison would tell Ben that Hamilton had again invited us up to his booth and confirmed that Ben could do a little broadcasting himself. Since it was an away game for the Indians, he would be operating through ESPN Radio in Chicago. Allison would further tell Ben that Hamilton wanted to record a teaser for his listeners that he could play the night before, telling his audience about Ben and his "awesome road trip." The next day, Ben would receive an email from Tony's friend at ESPN Radio, requesting that Ben send over a personal bio they could use for their broadcast teaser that would go on the air. Ben, now squarely in his "completely freaking out" stage, would immediately email Tony's friend his bio, which would almost certainly be comically self-promoting. Then Tony's friend would forward Ben's bio over to Eric, who would make a few select edits. It would start exactly as Ben had written it, but then perhaps it might get a little more interesting. Perhaps it would begin to read more like his dating profile. Perhaps it would explain in inexplicable detail how he waited for hours in Cleveland in a concrete concourse to hang out with an announcer who had no idea he existed. Tony's friend would record Eric's edited version of the bio with a realistic lead-in and email Ben the audio clip just as we were nearing Chicago to "meet up" with Hamilton. He would tell Ben that this was the teaser that was played on the air the night before.

Then Ben would hook his phone up to the car's audio system—how we listened to everything on the trip—and eagerly listen to his moment of glory with an adorably egomaniacal smile. Then, as the teaser went off the rails, his joy would turn to horror. Suddenly the realization would wash over him.

And finally, that smile of his would migrate on over to Eric.

That was the extravagant plan, and Eric had all the pieces in place, ready to put it in action.

"Has Allison said where to meet Hamilton?" Ben asked as we cruised along the highway.

"I'll text her right now."

"Who's Hamilton?" Tyler asked from the backseat. He was friends with Allison as well.

"The Cleveland announcer," Ben said proudly. "Allison's dad played for the Indians and they're family friends. We're meeting up with him in Chicago. I'm calling a play."

"Wait," Tyler said. "That's not true."

"What are you talking about?"

"Wait. No. That's a lie. Her dad didn't play for the Indians."

"Of course he did," Eric quickly cut in. "Earl Averill. Cleveland Hall of Famer."

"No. You don't understand. She's lying."

Eric gave Tyler a death stare. Tyler interpreted this as Eric's reluctance to have his false reality shattered by the truth.

"She's tricking you," Tyler said. "I talked to her the other day and she mentioned the whole thing. She said she fooled you guys into thinking she was related to that guy and pretended to know the announcer. She said she got you to wander around for half the game looking for him."

"Oh my god," Ben said, furious.

"Oh my god," Eric said, furious for reasons Ben would never understand.

"Yeah. Crazy. Thought I should let you guys know."

Ben shook his head in disbelief. "Wow. We totally believed her. She got us good."

At the next gas stop Ben got out to use the restroom, leaving Eric alone with Tyler.

"Tyler."

"Yeah?'

"How do you think she knew there was a player named Averill on the Indians, which day we were in Cleveland and exactly what to tell us and when to do it?"

Tyler scrutinized him, momentarily confused. Then it hit him. "Oh no. No, no, no. Oh god. I'm so sorry."

Eric sighed. "What's rule number one of pranking?"

"Think it through?"

"The other rule number one."

Tyler slouched in his seat, unsure.

"No mercy."

Game Twenty-Seven: Houston Astros

We walked into Houston's Minute Maid Park minutes before the 7:10 central start. Tyler was once again opting for a local music and coffee shop adventure. He was on a cross-country indie café tour of America in the least efficient way possible, which gave him street cred at the indie cafés.

The game in Houston was the single most important of the trip. Since Chicago we'd managed to avert another weather catastrophe. Since our first visit to Denver we'd successfully reached every ballpark in time for the opening pitch.

For the remainder of the schedule to play out as it was supposed to, it would all depend on Houston. After the Houston game we would embark on the riskiest leg of the trip, a sixteen-and-a-half-hour drive in sixteen-and-a-half hours. That was with no stops and the feeble assumption of a game of average length. For 16 hours on the road beginning with a full tank of gas, at least three gas station stops would be necessary. Based on our previous gas station stints, Ben timed the average gas stop to take eight minutes, including pulling off the highway, suffering through the payment process and getting back on the road. The three stops would add another 24 minutes to the drive.

Each time the tank filled up we could run to use the bathroom. There would be time for nothing else. Every minute counted. To prepare, we visited a grocery store on the way into Houston and stocked up on drinks and energy bars to last us the duration of the drive.

Traffic was a giant question mark. A two-lane highway under construction in the middle of Arkansas could cost us a half hour or more on the spot. Backups in the greater Chicago area could stall us with the park so tantalizingly near.

Parking could be another issue. In almost all stadiums even the closest parking lots were a five- to ten-minute walk to the ballpark. When an online mapping service spits out an ultraspecific number like "16 hours, 32 minutes," it was factoring in none of the real-world obstacles that we'd inevitably have to face.

And this was all aside from the most present threat of all—the possibility that the Houston game could go long. This was one game where extra innings would almost certainly be a death sentence.

One way or another, one thing was certain. We were going to have to make up time on the road.

Minute Maid Park, formerly and more memorably known as Enron Field, was a domed and comfortably air-conditioned park known for its deep center field. The warning track rose on an incline, creating a literal hill in the field of play. It was the only ballpark that was not uniformly flat, pitching mounds aside. In no other major sport would such a drastic deviation in the playing surface be allowed. People would have cried fraud if the Knicks' home court advantage was one hoop shorter than the other, or if the Red Wings benefited from a part of the ice that broke through to water.

But this was baseball, and aberrations in the field of play were not only accepted. They were beloved. They were what made parks unique, why a trip such as this one was not completely preposterous in the first place. No two fields were ever the same. You could go to 30 parks and see 30 different fields. It gave the sport a local flavor, a sense of tradition that outweighed the monotonous burden of regulation. In a sport grounded in the art of repetition, it was the anomalies you remembered.

We stared down the mound from our seats behind the outfield fence, willing the pitcher to throw faster than he'd ever thrown before. It seemed to be working. The first seven innings were shaping up to be a pitcher's duel, which was good news for the speed of the play. The two teams had thrown an unusually low 184 pitches through the first seven innings. The average game contained 292. The downside to a well-pitched game was that it also had to be a hard-fought one. Each team had allowed a single run, laying the perilous groundwork for extra innings. We had no time for more baseball tonight. We needed as much time as possible for more baseball tomorrow.

In the top of the eighth inning Astros reliever Paul Clemens came out to the mound to warm up, leaving us to

agonize over his unhurried pre-inning routine. The game's
pace had noticeably slowed as the innings lumbered on, a
trend that also held true over the span of years. Over the last
two decades, the average game length had increased by 15
minutes. Longer advertising breaks combined with player
micromanagement had gradually stretched out the time it
took to reach the seventh-inning stretch.

The first batter Clemens faced was Angels catcher
Hank Conger. Seven pitches and a full count later, he hit
the eighth into fair territory for a double. The next batter,
Erick Aybar, drew a walk in another seven pitches and J.B.
Shuck flew out in five. The counts didn't seem extreme in
isolation, but each at bat was a veritable eternity to our
wincing eyes. The actual motion of a pitcher winding up
and delivering a ball to home plate took only three seconds,
but it was a 22-second wait until he was ready to throw
again. When close games dragged on into the later innings,
the average at-bat length could easily increase another ten
seconds. To our relief, the time suck was not for naught.
The Angels managed to score one run to break the tie. We
stomached a glance at the clock. If the game ended in ten
minutes, we'd be scheduled to arrive in Chicago exactly on
time. But there was still an inning and a half to play.

The bottom of the eighth was no quicker. There were
25 pitches, throws to first to keep runners in check, a stolen
base and the substitution of a pinch runner. But no run.

The 2–1 game headed into the top of the ninth. Without
consulting us, Astros manager Bo Porter decided it'd be a
good time to give his bullpen some practice, putting three different pitchers on the mound. Each of the two substitutions

wiped another five minutes from our drive. Even less help-fully, each of those new pitchers immediately let a runner on base. With every foul ball and leisurely trip to the mound, the chance of our trip's success exponentially dwindled. The half inning saw three more runs and 32 pitches, more than double the norm. It lasted an insufferable 21 minutes.

At last the Astros came up in the bottom of the ninth. We moved to seats near the gates so we could make the quickest possible exit the moment the game ended. We'd already fallen 20 minutes behind schedule and it would take at least five minutes to find Tyler waiting in the car. After Angels pitcher Ernesto Frineri finally decided he was warmed up, he stepped right up to the mound and delivered an excruciating nine-pitch walk. Then he let up a double and a sacrifice fly. The Astros had improbably scored another two runs in the bottom of the ninth, bringing the inning's running total to five and tightening the score at 4–3.

Everyone dreamt of this situation: two outs in the bot-tom of the ninth, down by one, the game-tying runner on third, the game-winning run at the plate. The moment in baseball when icons were made and glory was at its most glorious. With the odds of completing the trip plummeting in front of our eyes, we needed a bang or a whimper. A home run or an out. We needed an end. A single would tie the game. A single and our 30-game quest would be officially, irrevocably dead.

As Ben watched the pitcher waste precious seconds eyeing the runner on third, he realized the monster he'd become. A month ago, he was the ultimate baseball fan, obsessed with every microscopic detail of the game, the

numbers and the players, the tales and the traditions. He
watched games for the love of the game. Nothing more,
nothing less.

The trip had changed him, gradually, steadily and so
depressingly he'd done his best to ignore the transforma-
tion. He'd become the worst kind of fan, the sort he spent
a lifetime despising. He did not care about the outcome of
the game. He did not care how the players performed, or
how the standings were affected, or how the playoff race
would change. He did not care who played the best game
of their lives, or who was getting sent to the minors, or
who had just come off the DL. He did not care where he
was or who he was watching. He did not care who won or
lost. He did not eat green eggs or ham. He cared only for
whatever combination of strikes, balls and hits would result
in the fastest possible departure from the game he claimed
to love. He rooted only for things to end. His custom-made
journey designed to make him the ultimate baseball fan had
done just the opposite. He no longer *saw* baseball. He only
waited for it to have been seen.

"Here we go," Eric said, hunkering down for the make-
or-break at bat.

"Yet again."

"Let's go, boys. *One, two, three strikes you're out.*"

Our beloved song was slightly off the mark. The players took a few liberties with the lyrics, adding in a foul, a
batter's timeout, two balls, a pitcher's conference with the
catcher, an umpire intervention and another foul. And then,
like clockwork that stopped ticking, *three strikes you're out!*
At the old goddamn ballgame.

We stormed out the gate into the Houston night. Tyler was waiting outside the park with the car in drive. He left tread marks on the road to the 69 North.

"Well?"

"Updated travel time with current traffic is seventeen hours, twenty minutes."

"And?"

"The game starts in sixteen hours."

Tyler slammed on the pedal. It was going to be a short night and a long drive.

Game Twenty-Eight:
Chicago White Sox

Despite the overwhelming time deficit, the trip was off to a cautiously promising start. Every 20 minutes or so the GPS would knock two minutes off our ETA. Then every half hour it would tack another on. It was an unpredictable game of two steps forward, one back. The initial traffic was sparse, but there was little to be done when a tag team of Mack trucks set out to divide and conquer.

Before the trip, we would have described ourselves as unequivocally cautious drivers. We stuck to the speed limit. We stayed out of the passing lane. Now the driving barely felt real. We were operating as though in a video game. If we saw we could pass a truck three cars ahead by moving right two lanes and then merging back to the leftmost lane, we did so. Though Eric and Tyler were forced by their prior tickets to keep close to the limit, Ben threw the rulebook out the window, which meant it was exiting a vehicle going at least

20 miles per hour over the limit. We'd become our parents' and insurance companies' worst nightmares. What we did have going for us was eagle-eyed precision and focus. We'd swiftly forgotten we were utterly exhausted. Being tired was not an option. Our recklessness was calculated. Our risks were measured. Our intensity was unnecessarily militaristic given the absurdity of the task at hand. The passenger in the passenger seat truly was the copilot. "That SUV in the left lane is moving slow. I would move over one lane now," Eric would tell Tyler, "and we're in a cleared straightaway with no hiding spots. We're good on cops."

Eric took over for Tyler in Lufkin, Texas, where we made our first carefully plotted NASCAR-style gas stop. The route the GPS recommended was a series of smaller highways out of Texas, avoiding the traffic of interstates. It would be the first time we'd been on a noninterstate road for more than a consecutive hour since we'd traveled Route 54 through Kansas on Day Ten. The roads were tighter, there was no median and every once in a while we came across a stop light. "The good news is we picked up twelve minutes on Tyler's drive," announced Ben. "The bad news is we just killed seven minutes getting gas."

Eric did the math out loud as he merged off the last of our Texas interstates onto an empty four-lane highway. "All right, so if we picked up five minutes in the first two hours of driving and we still have fifteen hours left to make up another hour, that means that — No. No. *No*."

He slammed his hand against the steering wheel. He pulled over, trailed by a flashing swirl of red and blue. It was his third stop this month. He'd been able to sweet-talk his way out of the ticket last time, and he'd have to do it again if he wanted to avoid being one strike away from losing his license and zero strikes away from losing the right to borrow a set of keys to his family's car.

"License, registration and proof of insurance."

Eric had already assembled the necessary materials. He knew the drill.

"I'm sorry, officer. We're on a baseball road trip, seeing all thirty major league ballparks in thirty days—"

"Do you know what the speed limit was?"

"Sixty-five. But I was only going seventy-two. I was just in a rush because we're on Day Twenty-Seven of—"

"No. It was 55. 65 was the interstate. As soon as you got off that ramp over there it was fifty-five."

"It's just that we're driving through the night to Chicago and the Astros game went—"

"Chicago? That's far. It's going to be 165 dollars, unless you want to show for a court date on July fifth in Lufkin."

There was no getting out of this ticket. Eric was indeed over the speed limit, thanks to the cop conveniently stationed right at the sign that marked the change in speed limits. He was beyond the point of grumbling. Why was he continuing to cause himself legal problems for the sake of Ben's antics?

Of course, he begrudgingly knew the answer. After 28 days, he was on equal footing with Ben. Did he enjoy the games as much as Ben? No. Did he enjoy the drives as much as Ben? No. Did he enjoy Ben as much as Ben? No. But he'd become addicted. He was hell-bent on finishing what he regretted to have begun. The sunk costs were too high to not finish. That was all it was about now. Finishing. On Day

Eight when we missed the game in Colorado and Ben threw his phone against the couch, Eric laughed at his frustration. He was happy to see Ben botch the schedule and jeopardize the trip. It took off the pressure. But in Chicago, when the odds seemed to turn against them for good, his inner competitor was riled. It was the same gut reaction he had watching the Dodgers awake from a dead midseason to make a playoff run. He didn't want to like them, but he had to like them. He couldn't *not* root for the underdog. It was human nature. The instant *we* were the underdogs, Eric had no choice. He could no longer approach the trip with careless indifference. It was in his blood. He now had a rooting interest, and it was us. When success looked promising, he yawned himself to sleep. When all looked hopeless—now *that* was fun.

So as furious as he was about the speeding ticket, he was even more furious at how long it took the officer to print out the citation. If officers accepted cash, he would have just emptied his wallet and saved the three minutes on the road. From Day One he'd wanted to finish the trip. The only difference now was that it was no longer for the sake of it ceasing to exist.

"Let me take over," Ben said. "You can't risk another ticket."

"I can keep going."

"I don't have any tickets. You've done your part. Let me do mine."

Eric reluctantly agreed, ceding the wheel for the night after a sum total of ten minutes of driving. His leg had added more time to the trip than it had erased. He felt like he'd let the team down. He finally felt like there was a team.

We soon crossed into Arkansas, one of the ten remaining states we had not yet touched. There was nothing to see but darkness on the side of the road. Ben insisted that Eric and Tyler sleep, knowing they'd need to be fresh when he tired after five straight hours of driving. They tried to rest, though no more than ten minutes ever passed without one of them stirring, opening their eyes and asking how far we were behind schedule. The deficit was in slow descent, but the minutes dropped one by one, in spite of the occasional blip. 50 minutes behind schedule. 49. 48. 49. 47!

Each was a small victory propelling us forth.

Ben drove as fast as he could. He was hitting 100 on straightaways, easing down to 90 when other cars came into view. The trouble was still the endless supply of Mack trucks. We often got stuck behind a pair for miles at a time, wasting whole sequences of minutes that needed to be spent catching up on other minutes. Halfway to Chicago, the minutes stopped ticking away. For hours on end, no matter how fast Ben drove, we were always on pace to show up to the stadium about ten minutes after the game was scheduled to begin.

It began to sink in for Ben that we probably weren't going to make it. He tried to process what he'd be losing. Bragging rights, for one, though the whole premise of the trip was admittedly his own contrived ambition. He'd still see all 30 stadiums, just not every inning of every game. But was that what the trip was really about?

Who was he kidding. That was exactly what it was about. It was why he was here to begin with. But then what was Eric doing here? Or even Tyler, sprawled unconscious in the backseat of the car? They hadn't come to see some stadiums or sit through a bevy of games. They were transparently there to help out a friend accomplish his obsessive dream. They were here in the name of friendship. For them it was a trip about friends.

And it was no small donation of time or effort. Tyler had given up a week of work and flown cross-country to pitch in. Ben 2 had done the same to help him drive around in circles. Eric had forfeited half of his summer vacation, the last he would ever have. And not content with just being there for Ben, he'd broken the law and damaged his driving record while Ben emerged unscathed. He felt like the lead of a movie marching toward victory, somehow accruing not even the smallest scrape while all around him fell to the ground. Why had he been so lucky? Not in terms of avoiding tickets, but by simply having these friends. As he was busy putting baseball in front of everything else, his friends were putting him first.

He'd come for 30 in 30 and he was still here for 30 in 30. He'd viewed his friends as driving machines. He'd come into the trip oblivious to his fellow humans and seeking nothing but success. He was going out helplessly aware of his obliviousness and finishing a failure. It didn't make him feel warm and fuzzy inside. It was depressing as hell.

Eric awakened once again. "How are we on time?"

"If we continue making up ground at the same pace we're going now . . . we'll still be eight minutes late."

Eric opened the window for some fresh air.

"You didn't drive a month of your life to miss a game by eight minutes. And neither did I."

Now Ben felt like he was letting Eric down. Going 100, he zipped past a sign that read 65. Even at this rate, we weren't going to cut down on their arrival time fast enough. He looked over at Eric. His copilot had drifted back asleep.

He pushed his foot down to 115 and the needle crept up.

We raced up America. We came upon Illinois. We came upon it alone.

"Where are all the cars?"

"It's a Saturday, isn't it?"

"What happened to the traffic?"

We stared at the GPS device, our eyes glued to the screen.

"It's recalculating."

"Fifteen minutes behind pace."

"Ten minutes."

"Five."

"How far out are we?"

"Hour and a half."

"Get there," Eric said, matter-of-factly.

Ben weaved around the interspersed cars. The bumper-to-bumper traffic of our metropolitan nightmares was nowhere to be found. The sea was parting and the baseball gods were letting us sneak through.

"Thirty minutes out."

"Where's that put us?"

Ben ran the numbers. "We're on pace to get there five minutes—" He reran the numbers, refusing to believe the results. "Five minutes early."

It was the first time we cheered on the way to a stadium instead of in one.

We pulled into the U.S. Cellular Field parking lot 13 minutes early. At any other stadium on any other day, this would have evoked a panic attack. Today, 13 minutes felt like all the time in the world.

We walked into the gates with a lazy three minutes to spare.

Eric inspected the field from our seats in the uppermost deck, opposite an otherwise quiet neighborhood on the south side of Chicago. It looked like a ballpark. Exactly like a ballpark.

"We got there," he said.

Ben nodded and took a deep breath. "We got here."

The game was a blur. We sat upright in our seats, prostrate, silent, unable to move, unable to think without wincing. The game was nothing but an afterthought compared to the trip *to* the game. The Indians defeated the White Sox in a swift three hours and again we were off, taking to the road for our penultimate haul.

"You know what," Ben said as we returned to the car, "We should go back to Williamsport on the way to the Mets game."

"The Little League World Series park? We already went completely out of the way once and you refused to run the bases."

"I keep telling you, there was a man on a lawn mower. But it doesn't matter. Even if there's a man on a lawn mower, I'm running those bases."

"What if there are eighteen twelve-year-olds on the field?"

"I'm running those bases."

❆   ❆   ❆

The sun was rising as we entered Williamsport. Ben turned off the GPS. We'd only been there once, and 27 days ago, but it was enough to have the town's layout committed to memory.

We set out on foot from the parking lot and descended the hill toward the field. The grass was still blotted with morning dew, untouched by man-made blades. The field was empty. There was nothing for Ben to outrun aside from his inhibitions. It was just us and Casey at the Bat, standing over the clean-cut diamond in the still of morning.

Ben turned to Eric and Tyler. "You coming?"

"This one's all yours. Now go hop that fence and trespass your way to glory."

He jumped the divider onto the warning track. He walked the length of the field to home plate. He stood on it. What happened next was in Eric's opinion the most exciting and theatrical 30 seconds of baseball we saw the whole trip.

Ben tucked down into a sprinter's prerace pose. He held his breath and looked out at the empty stands. And Eric watched from the hill beyond the outfield wall. He gave himself his own countdown: 3, 2, 1 . . .

Then he remembered how baseball worked. No player in the history of the sport had run the bases starting from a sprinter's pose. He backed up and stood up straight. He planted his feet in the box. He bent his knees, raised his elbows, tucked his chin into his chest. He reached into his imagination and grabbed his 31-inch bat. He cocked his hands, shifted his weight, hung the barrel above his head. He swung. He made imaginary contact.

He put down his head and rounded first, and rounded second, and swung around third, arms flailing, waving himself home. He screeched to a stop, retraced his steps and made sure he touched third. He sprinted home.

Safe. The invisible outfielders still hadn't even found where he'd hit the imaginary ball.

He'd driven 19,500 miles since the first stop in Williamsport to come full circle around a 90-foot square. There were few distinct moments in a man's life that he could look back on and identify as the moments manhood arrived. There had been Ben's Bar Mitzvah, and now there was this. His little league life was complete. He was not longer a batboy. He was a batman.

"I did it," Ben exhaled. "I actually did it."

"It was foul."

"What?"

"I think it was a foul ball," Eric said. "You stepped in early and pulled it."

He shook Ben's hand. Ben took off his invisible batter's glove.

We headed for New York, off to come full circle around our other circle that was very deformed and suspiciously resembled the United States of America.

Game Twenty-Nine:
New York Mets

It was June 30; we were in New York and it was supposed to be the day that Ben could die in peace and Eric could get back to living in peace. Instead it was the day before the day. With the Day Zero Paradigm thrown into the mix, we still had to make one final push to Toronto tomorrow.

We reached the city 90 minutes before the Mets were scheduled to begin, and after surviving the drive to Chicago, didn't think twice about the possibility of showing up late. The hard part was over. All we had to do now was show up and punch our tickets. We were in the clear.

We stopped in at our friend Emily's apartment in Manhattan. She'd landed great seats fifteen rows shy of the batter's box and was taking us to the game. We seemed to be good at getting good seats in New York, even if we weren't much good at much of anything anywhere else.

Advised that the subway would be the quickest way to Citi Field, we set out to head underground. We turned a corner. We walked into a parade.

"Is this a parade?" Ben asked, staring at the parade. "Is that the subway station on the other side?"

"This is definitely a parade, that's definitely the subway station and it's definitely inaccessible."

It turned out Ben's distorted version of the American dream was being stymied by a procession of those who'd just come a little closer to achieving their own. A gay pride parade was marching down Fifth Avenue, toting signs and banners commemorating the Supreme Court's decision on the Defense of Marriage Act a few days before.

"Did it get struck down?" Ben asked. "Is that what we're celebrating?"

Eric sighed, disappointed in Ben. "Where have you been all week?" He watched the revelers march on. "I'd say we should join the party, but then we wouldn't have time to fall asleep watching a heteronormative battle for the upper hand in 19th-century masculinity."

Officers guarding partitions barricaded the intersections, preventing pedestrians from crossing to the other side of the street. Our clock was ticking. What had been an easygoing commute suddenly became a race against time. According to Emily, our city expert, the subway would take 50 minutes. We only had 70 remaining. We'd already ditched our car blocks away in a parking lot and with the advent of the parade, escape by taxi was not an option. Ben was fairly certain that simply walking into the street and tipping his Red Sox cap to a crowd of New Yorkers would not do the trick either.

Then, for the first time in our lives, a traffic collision came to our aid. A horse-drawn carriage butted up against a fire truck, causing a break in formation. The momentary delay of festivities was enough to convince a cop to let us pass.

"I thought we were going to have to march in the parade for a bit to get to the subway," Ben said as we descended into the station. "Inadvertently marching in a gay pride parade on the way to a baseball game would have been the cornerstone of our American experience."

The train was in no hurry to arrive, and in no hurry to speed once it did. We stopped every few minutes, picking up the next gaggle of Mets fans and exhausted parade walkers. The game had a 1:10 start time, and it was days like this when the 10 could make all the difference. Most games never started right on the hour, but it remained to us a mystery how the exact time was chosen. Some launched at five past the hour, others seven. This was a good day to be taking ten. We were expected to reach our stop at 1:02, giving us eight minutes to find the field and get through the gates.

For once it was entirely out of our hands. There was no traffic maneuver or short cut that could save us. The train went as fast as it went and stopped when it stopped. We were going to get there when we were going to get there.

"How did we let it come to this?" Ben couldn't believe he'd let it happen. He'd spent the month sweating out every second, and with one day left he'd let down his guard, convinced there was nothing left to go wrong. "After all the close calls. We're going to lose it because of this."

"Eh," Eric shrugged. "Who cares."

"Who cares? After everything, *who cares*?"

"What's a minute to a month? We both know we could have just as well have shown up here an hour early. Skip the nap in Jersey, skip the field in Pennsylvania, skip the meal in Illinois. You wanted to do 30 in 30. Hit or miss, we'll always know that we *could*."

"But still."

"Oh, don't worry. You also know we'll run."

The train pulled into the Mets-Willets Point stop at 1:03.

"See you at the game?" Emily guessed.

"See you there."

We sprinted off the train the instant the doors opened. We hurdled our way through the station. We had no idea where we were going but we were going there fast. Ben pointed to a sign for Citi Field. "Follow the Mets hats!" We veered right and up the stairs to a plaza right in front of the park. We'd made it to outside the stadium. In four minutes they'd throw the first pitch.

The security lines were long and meandering. A dozen of them stretched unevenly across the front entrance.

"You take that line and I'll go left," Eric commanded as we hedged our bets. He disappeared into the throngs of people, off to find the shortest line and bargain his way to the front.

Ben stood in his own, a line shorter than most but inexplicably slow moving. He checked his phone. It was 1:07. He checked it again. Still 1:07. He checked it again. His phone was dead.

Ten lines over, behind an insurmountable wall of people, Eric wiggled his way to the turnstiles. He would get through in time, with a minute or so to spare. He called Ben to have him join him in line and slip through. The call went straight to voice mail. He stood on his toes, struggling to look over the heads of the hundreds gathered. Ben was too short to be found.

Getting no taller and only more panicked, Ben weighed his options at the other end of the gates. His line was still not moving. It had to be 1:08 by now, maybe 1:09. No line would get him through in a minute now. It was too late to switch. He stepped out of his place to catch a glimpse at the holdup in the front of his own.

An old couple occupied the turnstile, tapping the ticket scanner in total confusion, waving their tickets at the bar code scanner to no avail.

"Excuse me," the man called out to a security guard fifteen feet away. "Do you check our tickets?"

Never before had Ben been so inspired to be a Good Samaritan. "Here, let me help," he said, snatching the pair of tickets from the man's hands and slipping his own in at the bottom. He fed all three through the scanner and darted through the turnstile behind the octogenarian lovebirds.

Eric awaited him at the base of the stairs.

"Time?"

"1:10 exactly."

We darted up the staircase, again following the people in Mets hats. It was a dubious strategy inside the stadium, but it led us to a patch of green, which soon brought into sight an adjacent patch of dirt. The pitcher's mound came into view. A batter cocked his bat. Ben whipped out his camera and snapped a photo. He'd done so at the start of every game to prove — mostly to himself — that he'd been to 30 complete games. The pitcher entered his wind up and hurled the ball home.

"Was that the first pitch?"

"Where's the scoreboard?"

We looked around wildly. Ben's heart sunk. He had picked the wrong line to the stadium. He had picked the wrong day to walk into the middle of a gay pride parade. He had picked the wrong age to outgrow little league and become a short, short man.

"Right there," Eric said. "No balls. One strike. We made it."

We caught our breaths. We found our seats.

The Mets were not as lucky. Dropping five runs by the third, fans headed for the exits early in the afternoon gloom. Storm clouds were building overhead, threatening to rain down on the exposed field and intermingle with the tears of Mets fans citywide. The clouds finally let loose in the eighth, sending hordes of spectators for cover. The rain was just light enough to warrant continued play, avoiding a delay of game that we had no patience for. With the vast majority of the stands comically empty and the Nationals just barely clinging to an 11–0 lead, the game felt more like a scrimmage.

And that was before Mets catcher Anthony Recker trotted out to the mound at the top of the ninth. Instead of holding a conference with the pitcher, he simply talked to himself. He *was* the pitcher. In the last inning with the game a lost cause, the Mets were pitching a catcher.

It was a rarity usually reserved for 17-inning games when teams emptied out their bullpens, and the novelty electrified the crowd. Recker commenced his first major league inning of pitching with a walk to Nationals right fielder Jayson Werth, surprising no one. He followed it up with a home run to shortstop Ian Desmond, still meeting expectations. With no outs recorded and two earned runs, he had an ERA of infinity.

Then he got into the groove of things, or at least the Nationals hitters started slugging balls 315 feet away instead of 320. All three of the next batters flied out to deep left field, dropping Recker's ERA to 54, then 27, and finally a hard-earned 18. He gave a nod to the raucous, rejuvenated crowd. The pitcher catcher returned to the dugout.

The Mets were not done wowing the few thousand fans who braved out the weather and the drubbing. In possibly the least pressure-packed two-outs-in-the-bottom-of-the-ninth situation baseball could ever know, John Buck—the Mets catcher who was playing catcher—blasted a two-run homer to stave off the shutout and send everyone home feeling better about losing. The 13–2 final score was the most uncompetitive match we'd witnessed and, in true baseball fashion, one of the most entertaining.

"And then there was one," Ben said. Three seconds later he tripped on a beer can and tumbled to the bottom of a flight of stairs.

Eric pretended not to know him for the sake of his New York reputation. "As you once said, what could possibly go wrong?"

Game Thirty:
Toronto Blue Jays

We bade farewell to Tyler, our valiant semivegetarian knight in shining armor who'd driven 5,000 miles to sit in a coffee shop and told us in parting that he'd locked himself out of the car in Houston when we were at the game and had to call a locksmith to get back in. We thanked him for not telling us when it happened.

We set off for Toronto at midnight. It was our final drive. We'd hit 22,000 miles by morning. The earth was 25,000 miles around the equator.

"I know you'll never admit it to me," Ben said, "but I know you had a good time. You got to see every ballpark. See almost the whole country. You liked it, didn't you?"

"You just told me I would never admit it to you."

"I'll take that as a yes."

Eric had signed up to witness the country he'd lived his life in and help a friend out with a very first-world need.

By the time he realized what he'd signed up for, he was in Kansas, and then it was only a few hours before he wasn't in Kansas anymore. And he had no qualms about giving Ben a hard time about the trip, his way of saying, "Hey, I'm doing this for you. You should be thankful, and let me sleep another ten minutes because of it." At times he felt like little more than a disgruntled shepherd, there to get Ben from Point A to Point B and then make sure he didn't choke on a hot dog at Point B.

But Ben had done one thing for Eric. He'd tricked him into doing something he would never think to do. He'd seen more in a month than most saw in a lifetime. And between the unending stretches of hours spent staring out at deserted deserts and mountains and fields, there were moments he would never forget, nor ever want to. He thought of the time in Wisconsin when Ben bought a Popsicle at 3 AM and the icy exterior became so stuck to his tongue that it took him a full five minutes to pry away. And in Tennessee, when a giant moth invaded the car on the highway and almost caused a three-vehicle collision. And in Texas, when on the 28th consecutive day at a baseball game, Ben looked into the outfield thoughtfully and said, "The thing is, they can really hit it far."

And there were the people of all colors and stripes, and the places that were by the people and for the people. And sights beautiful beyond his wildest imagination, like the sign to the Grand Canyon, or the sign to the Everglades, or the sign to his roots in West Virginia.

And of course there was Ben. If Ben could chart out the trip by geographical region, then Eric could divvy it up by relational feelings toward Ben. What started with suspicion traveled to frustration, dipped into resentment and looped around to apathy before coming to a stop at respect. Ben had begun the trip like a caricature, a diminutive number-crunching nerd programmed to shut down at the thought of opening up. A trite month later and he was still unequivocally a diminutive number-crunching nerd, though now undeniably also human. Eric had watched him grow bolder and braver in live time, building up the courage to interact with the world around him, allowing it to complement the world inside his head. Eric was even confident that had there indeed been a grumbling gardener in middle-of-nowhere Pennsylvania, Ben would have made it around the bases and been called safe at home.

Worst of all, against his most strident wishes, Eric found himself checking the Dodgers score at the end of each night. Just in case they won again. Just out of curiosity.

"And you? Was it all worth it?"

Ben raised his hands off the wheel and into the air, gesturing that the question didn't merit a response.

"Put your hands back on the wheel. And it had to be 30 in 30? Not 30 in 40, or 30 in a decade, or one today and who knows tomorrow?"

"It had to be 30 in 30."

But even as he said it, he knew it wasn't true. He lived for the purpose of efficiency. His life was one giant scheme to find the shortest this, the simplest that, the swiftest these and those. It was how he designed the trip, *why* he designed the trip. He never needed to be the greatest or grandest. Just the most efficient. He wanted it to be pure. He wanted two drivers. Then Ben 2 showed up and that went out the window. He wanted mathematical optimization. As soon as he slept through the game in Denver, that claim too was undone. He wanted temporal poetry. But when Chicago got rained out, we could no longer contain ourselves to the 30-day month of June. It was still 30 in 30, but it was with five drivers, and 22,000 miles, and 716 hours spanning 31 calendar days. And yet, there was no difference. He was the only one keeping score. He busied himself every day with worrying about the next. It was never Here Now, always There Next. He'd never learned how to savor. He only knew how to chew.

Now he was at the finish line, worn to the bone, barely able to move, and — of all things — sick of baseball. Two years ago he'd sat down at his computer, opened up his favorite statistical software and plugged away on a theoretical exercise for fun. He'd spent the bulk of his life toiling away at equations, none of which ever left the page. He'd solved problems that fired rockets to the moon. He did so knowing he wouldn't be leaving the atmosphere. He'd assumed this trip would be no different. It was an abstract mathematical construction, meant to be solved for the sake of solving, nothing more. To go from the safety of his desk in Boston to the deserts of Arizona and the beaches of San Diego and the back hills of Georgia in the span of hours was not supposed to happen. How it actually did was still as confounding to him as any numerical anomaly would ever be. He'd asked "What if?" one too many times, and then suddenly it was. That wasn't supposed to happen to theoretical mathematicians.

He was done caring about the trip. Other people had been to every park. Players, announcers and umpires made the rounds every year. Teams of megafans had concocted their own 30-game blitzes with different rules and regulations. But only he got to do it with Eric, a friend so loyal he didn't even like baseball. His algorithm had concocted the best possible baseball journey, because it had unknowingly stumbled onto the best possible friend.

We pulled up to the Canadian border at 6:00 AM on the first of July, ready for the perfect end to our all-American experience.

"Passports please. How long are you two going to be in Canada for?"

"About twelve hours."

"Then why do you have so many suitcases and living items in the back?"

"You know. Road trip."

The guard let us pass. There were only so many malicious things you could do with 29 foam fingers.

We parked the car in an empty lot at Niagara Falls and set an alarm for 8 AM. We'd wake up, see the falls, grab some breakfast and head to Toronto. We passed out immediately.

Ben awoke in a sweat. The temperature inside the car was 95 degrees. The air conditioner had shut off. He leaned up in his seat and checked his phone. An animation of an old-fashioned alarm clock bounced back and forth on the screen in total silence. It was supposed to be making rampant noise.

He checked the time. 10:15. The alarm had been going off for hours.

"We got to go! We're going to be late!"

Eric yawned and rubbed his eyes, forcing himself awake. "You drive us back to the desert? Get some air in here."

Ben turned the key to the ignition. Nothing. He tried again. Nothing still.

"Can't."

"What's the problem?"

"The battery's dead."

We stared at each other, impressed at our own knack for horrendous timing. We leapt out of the car.

Ben popped the hood and stared at the engine. He had no idea what he was looking at. He had no idea how to jump-start a car.

He reached for his AAA card in his wallet. *Does AAA even work in Canada? Do I need to get membership in the CAA? Does the CAA even exist?*

He went to look it up on his phone. It didn't matter if the CAA existed. His phone didn't get service in Canada. Neither did Eric's.

We found jumper cables stored under the trunk, which Ben could use to electrocute himself if he missed the final game. We ran out to the main road and tried to wave down a car.

An SUV with New York license plates approached hesitantly, saw Ben's beard and darted off. Finally a Canadian Corolla rolled to a stop. A French-speaking man stepped out of the car.

"I help?"

Ben handed the man the cables, not bothering to pretend he had a clue what happened next.

The man took charge, hooking the cables up between the cars and starting his engine. Ben heard his own rev up in turn.

Tears welled in his eyes. "Thank you, thank you! You have no idea—we're on this 30-day baseball trip and this is the last game and we would have missed it and thank you."

"I help?" the man asked heroically.

We carried on to Toronto like cats who'd lost count of how many lives they had to spare. Upon reaching Rogers Centre with less than an hour till game time, it became clear we would need one more.

"Are you kidding me?"

Thousands upon thousands of people buzzed around the park. It was a 1 PM game on a Monday. Attendance should have been at a season low.

"Is there a gay pride parade in Toronto too?"

We waited at a red light as a 100-strong group of face-painted banner carriers crossed the intersection before us.

Eric shook his head. "Not unless the movement adopted the maple leaf as their new symbol. And only wear red and white."

"Oh, god. It's July first."

"So?"

"It's Canada Day. We're in Canada on Canada Day."

"What's Canada Day? I didn't even know there *was* a Canada Day."

"Me too. That's why I can't believe it's today."

We pulled into the first parking lot we found, having burned fifteen minutes to navigate two blocks of traffic. We ran to the ticket booth, dodging men on red-and-white stilts and scantily clad women handing out miniature Canadian flags. We had thirty minutes to spare.

"Two tickets please. Cheapest available."

"We're all sold out!"

"On a Monday afternoon?"

"On a national holiday!"

"Perfect."

"Have fun!"

Though we'd purchased tickets for the original Toronto game we were scheduled to attend, we hadn't bothered buying seats for this one, as we were 100% certain it wouldn't be an issue because it was a Monday afternoon.

We had no choice but to buy scalped tickets, a part of the game that we'd struggled with in the past. We emptied our wallets. We had a combined forty dollars between us.

We found a scalper lurking behind a trash can near a street corner, muttering "Got tickets, need tickets" to no one in particular.

"Two tickets please. Cheapest available."

"That'll be a hundred dollars each."

We laughed. He shrugged and walked off. We stopped laughing.

We located another scalper.

"Two tickets."

"Ninety dollars apiece."

"They can't be worth ten dollars."

"When the game's sold out, they're worth what I say they're worth. This is the most expensive day all year."

We tested a few other sellers in the market. No one went lower than $80.

We ran three blocks until we found an intersection with banks on three of the four corners. We pulled at the first bank's doors, but all were locked, preventing access to even the ATM machines imprisoned on the other side of the paned glass.

"Since when is an ATM closed?"

"Since Canada Day."

The two other banks were no more fruitful. Another block led us to a convenience store with a broken ATM. The clerk pointed us down one more block where he promised the money would flow.

It was a Royal Bank of Canada, and it must have been violating the national law that gave robotic ATM machines Canada Day off. Ben withdrew $200, Canadian. There were 15 minutes to game time. We sprinted back to the army of scalpers.

We located the man offering $160 for two and handed over our wad of cash. He slipped the two stubs into Ben's hand and marched away.

Ben glanced down at the tickets. Their face value was $14.

"Since Canada Day," Eric said before Ben could ask.

We walked through the gates to the tune of "O Canada," a song that was definitely a statement and not a question. It was 1:02. First pitch was at 1:07.

As long as we managed to not leave the stadium by accident and the game lasted no longer than five hours, we would have done it.

We watched the first six innings from our fifth-story seats. The Blue Jays took a commanding 8–2 lead over the Tigers, on the way to proving once and for all that a group of American and Latin American athletes employed by a Canadian conglomeration could beat another group of American and Latin American athletes at their own game. Like always, Ben got his hot dog and beer. Like always, Eric bought his foam finger. Like always, we were semiconscious. Like always, we were there.

We retreated to a balcony off the main concourse overlooking the Toronto skyline. Although completely removed from the field of play, it offered fresh air, legroom and quiet. It was our holy trinity.

"So let me get this straight," Eric said. "The only reason thirty in thirty is possible is because of this 1 PM Monday game."

"Correct."

"If there wasn't a 1 PM game today, it wouldn't have been doable."

"Correct."

"Ben, in the thousands of game times you've seen, had you *ever* seen a game scheduled for a Monday afternoon?"

"Well, they're pretty rare. This is the only weekday afternoon game the Blue Jays have scheduled all this month or the next."

"But there just happens to be one scheduled on the exact day we needed it."

"Well, yes."

"And that didn't seem odd to you?"

"Seemed like low odds to me. But that's how odds work. Sometimes you can run all the numbers the world could know, and sometimes you just need to get lucky."

A boozing woman stumbled up to us, covered in shimmering red beads. She slapped a maple leaf sticker onto Eric's chest and headed back in toward the field.

"Ben, you realize that the *only* reason this game exists at 1 PM on a Monday is because it is Canada Day."

He nodded.

"Which means the only reason our American extravaganza is possible is *because* of Canada. No other reason. Were it not for Canadian patriotism, your quest for America's pastime would be dead."

"You could put it that way."

"Is there any other way to put it?"

Ben sighed. Then laughed. He shook his head.

"Happy Canada Day."

"Happy Canada Day."

We sat in exhausted silence, staring off into a foreign city with familiar tastes. Eric put his head down on the table to rest. Ben finished his second celebratory beer.

"All right, it's the top of the eighth now. Let's go up for the end of the game."

Eric didn't move, still facedown on the metal table under the shade of an umbrella emblazoned with maple leaves.

"You awake?"

Ben took his nonresponse as a no. He was getting better at picking up social cues.

He studied his unconscious friend, torn by the dilemma of whether to let him get his cherished rest or wake him up for the trip's final pitch. But Eric had done so much for him already. It was our last chance to watch a pitch together, but he was done depriving Eric of sleep.

He stood and went to leave. He stopped and thought better of it. He slid the foam finger off Eric's hand and slid it under his head for a makeshift pillow.

He returned to his seat alone.

At 3:37 PM, exactly 29 days, 20 hours and 22 minutes after the first pitch in Yankee Stadium, Blue Jays reliever Aaron Loup wound up for the 1–2 pitch with two outs in the ninth. It was the 8,913rd pitch we'd seen.

Ben stood and cheered along with the rest of the 45,755 drunk and patriotic Canadians. He looked over at the empty seat to his right.

"Go Jays!" the man behind him yelled. "Strike him out!" He outstretched his arm to all around him for high fives. Ben slapped his hand and then reached into his pocket for his cell phone.

"Are you all right, sir?"

Eric opened his eyes.

"Sir, do you need help?"

He squinted into the sun. Two stadium employees loomed over him.

"Do you need a doctor?"

"What happened?"

"You weren't waking up."

"I was sleepy."

The attendants stared at him.

"Thirty days," he explained, yawning. He got his bearings. He was still sprawled out on the table, the only remaining spectator on the balcony.

"We're closing up here. Sure you're okay?"

"All good. Best I've been in a while."

The attendants glanced at each other, satisfied. Eric rose from the table and staggered back into the concourse.

He found Ben approaching from the other direction.

"You weren't answering your phone."

Eric waved his arms about him. "Since Canada Day."

"How you feeling?"

"Ready to spectate. Let's go watch the end of the game."

Ben gave in and smiled.

"What? What happened?"

"It's over."

"It's over?"

"It's all over. We're done."

Eric processed the steady stream of people filing toward the exits. Ben stepped into the flow of the crowd, back to the streets, back to the car, back to America. Back home.

"Well, then," Eric said. He slipped on his foam finger. "I hope baseball won."

ACKNOWLEDGMENTS

This trip would not have been possible without the love and support of Willy Hess, Jonny Reindollar, Paul and Liz Brewster, Emily Hughes, the Williamsport Groundskeeper, Eric Macomber, Renee Rober, the United States Government, Tony Kahn, Zena and Mrs. Mengesha, Tyler and Mr. Richard, Ben Silva, Mountain Standard Time, the Harvard Banjo Club, JJ Shpall, Jimmy John's Sandwich and Sub Shop, the Arizona Diamondbacks, Runza, Ari Rubin, Theo Epstein, Philip, Geri and Mackenzie Brewster, Faith Minard, Stephen and Zach Blatt, Hail and Rain, Daniel and Jonathan Adler, the Jacksonville Jaguars, Mike Perkins, Nathan Kaplan, Arjun Modi, the Miami Police Department, Allison Averill, Tom Hamilton, the Atlanta Braves Security Team, Stacy of Cape Girardeau, Anna of St. Louis, Scalper Mike, Trevor Kellogg, the Washington University Chapter

of Beta Theta Pi, Eric and Mrs. Arzoian, Sierra Katow, the
Mt. Laurel, Lufkin, and Evanston Highway Patrols, Natalie
Li, the United States Supreme Court, Taylor Hughes, the
French Jump-starter, the Booth Fellowship, the Harvard
Sports Analysis Collective, Jackie Ko, Jamison Stoltz, and
the nation of Canada. And America.